"In Western secular thought it has been axiomatic that Christianity, like other monotheistic religions, leads to destructive conflict and war. Meic Pearse, in this wide-ranging, well-researched and clearly argued book, enables Christians to come to terms with the violence in their history. Pearse goes further, inviting Christianity's critics to examine the immense violence perpetrated by irreligion and secularist ideologies. This book challenges all positions and provokes all parties—salutarily! I have greatly enjoyed the book."

ALAN KREIDER, ASSOCIATE PROFESSOR OF CHURCH HISTORY AND MISSION, ASSOCIATED MENNONITE BIBLICAL SEMINARY, AND AUTHOR OF *A CULTURE OF PEACE*

"This is an excellent book! The topic is an enigma as old as Western civilization, but the approach is fresh and filled with poignant facts and incisive insights. I am excited about its publication."

WINFRIED CORDUAN, PROFESSOR OF PHILOSOPHY AND RELIGION, TAYLOR UNIVERSITY, AND AUTHOR OF *NEIGHBORING FAITHS*

"*The Gods of War* is a quick but perceptive march through the political, military and religious history of the past two millennia. Displaying a remarkable command of that history, Pearse disentangles the many reasons nations go to war—from economic to geographic to egotistical to religious. While acknowledging that complete separation of these causes is somewhat artificial, the exercise uncovers remarkable insights that prove the worth of the project. The compelling argument—and it is compelling—tends to rehabilitate Christianity's core and defend it from distortion, both by its two greatest contemporary enemies—secular individualistic materialism and radical militant Islam—and by its supposed friends in other parts of the Western world."

DOUGLAS L. KOOPMAN, PROFESSOR OF POLITICAL SCIENCE, CALVIN COLLEGE

"An informed and fascinating set of reflections on the causes of war, not just today but throughout history. Those who accept the modern canard that religion is the primary cause of war will be challenged by this responsible, honest analysis. With the care and detail of the historian, M [illegible] sal and complex, and are motivated by all ide [illegible] Without in any way trying to excuse the sins [illegible] rrective to modern, and often secularist-moti [illegible] view."

BRENDAN SWEETMAN, PROFESSOR OF [illegible] AND AUTHOR OF *WHY POLITICS NEEDS* [illegible]

"Professor Meic Pearse has done an admirable and fascinating job of answering the atheistic and agnostic critics who blame Christianity and other faiths for the wars of humankind. He has a breadth of historical, scriptural and sociological knowledge that makes his work fascinating to read. Evangelical scholarship now has a new and formidable proponent to deal with the forces of secular Western thought and Islamic radicalism. The author is never imperialistic in defending his faith and I believe he has understood the spirit of our Lord who is identified in Scripture as the Prince of Peace."

ROBERT G. CLOUSE, RESEARCH PROFESSOR OF HISTORY, INDIANA STATE UNIVERSITY, AND EDITOR OF *WAR: FOUR CHRISTIAN VIEWS*

Praise for *Why the Rest Hates the West*

"Meic Pearse specializes in asking difficult questions about the most significant issues facing us today—about religions, about politics, and about how cultures and societies come into conflict. . . . This is a challenging, provocative book, with a broad social and historical vision."

PHILIP JENKINS, DISTINGUISHED PROFESSOR OF HISTORY AND RELIGIOUS STUDIES, PENNSYLVANIA STATE UNIVERSITY, AND AUTHOR OF *THE NEXT CHRISTENDOM*

"This is . . . possibly the best, most intelligent, most humane brief argument that the West, rather than the Rest, needs reform."

BOOKLIST (STARRED REVIEW)

The GODS of WAR

Is Religion the Primary Cause of Violent Conflict?

Meic Pearse

An imprint of InterVarsity Press
Downers Grove, Illinois

Inter-Varsity Press
Nottingham, England

InterVarsity Press, USA
P.O. Box 1400, Downers Grove, IL 60515-1426, USA
World Wide Web: www.ivpress.com
Email: email@ivpress.com

Inter-Varsity Press, England
Norton Street, Nottingham NG7 3HR, England
Website: www.ivpbooks.com
Email: ivp@ivpbooks.com

InterVarsity Press®, USA, is the book-publishing division of InterVarsity Christian Fellowship/USA®, a student movement active on campus at hundreds of universities, colleges and schools of nursing in the United States of America, and a member movement of the International Fellowship of Evangelical Students. For information about local and regional activities, write Public Relations Dept., InterVarsity Christian Fellowship/USA, 6400 Schroeder Rd., P.O. Box 7895, Madison, WI 53707-7895, or visit the IVCF website at <www.intervarsity.org>.

Inter-Varsity Press, England, is closely linked with the Universities and Colleges Christian Fellowship, a student movement connecting Christian Unions in universities and colleges throughout Great Britain, and a member movement of the International Fellowship of Evangelical Students. Website: www.uccf.org.uk.

Design: Cindy Kiple
Images: Paul Chesley/Getty Images

USA ISBN 978-0-8308-3490-7
UK ISBN 978-1-84474-226-4

Printed in the United States of America ∞

Library of Congress Cataloging-in-Publication Data

Pearse, Meic.
The gods of war: is religion the primary cause of violent conflict?
/ Meic Pearse.
p. cm.
Includes bibliographical references.
ISBN-13: 978-0-8308-3490-7 (pbk.: alk. paper)
1. War—Religious aspects. I. Title.
BL 65.W2P432007
201'.7273—dc22

2007026755

British Library Cataloguing in Publication Data
A catalogue record for this book is available from the British Library.

P 19 18 17 16 15 14 13 12 11 10 9 8 7 6 5 4 3 2 1
Y 23 22 21 20 19 18 17 16 15 14 13 12 11 10 09 08 07

S ljubavlju za

Nenu, Darka, Kostu i Nadu

CONTENTS

PREFACE

I was excited, in the fall of 2004, to be invited by Andy Le Peau and Al Hsu of InterVarsity Press to begin work on a new volume addressing the frequent accusation that religion is the principal cause of war. The invitation came in the wake of the remarkable response to my earlier book, *Why the Rest Hates the West,* published by InterVarsity earlier the same year. In that volume, I argued that the amorality and repudiation of religion and traditional culture by the West made it despised and feared by non-Western societies and that a combination of Westerners' incomprehension of the things they had abandoned—but that still mattered to everybody else—and the aggressive export of the resultant anticulture were fueling anti-Westernism around the world. If this view is correct—and all I have encountered in the interim has tended to confirm that analysis—then this would cast a new light on the awkward fact that Islamic radicalism has emerged as the principal, and easily the most violent, new actor on the world stage since the end of the Cold War. During that interim, I have been asked to discuss these themes on countless radio programs, in journals, at colleges, universities and conferences, and even in an address to the U.S. Congressional leadership on their retreat at The Greenbrier, West Virginia. I have no idea whether any of my audiences learned much from anything that I had to say. But for me, the experience was a steep learning curve as ideas were tested against their alternatives, and thereby nuanced and the implications for different problems further teased out.

This present volume is, in an important sense, part of that ongoing project. But whereas the former work was essentially a critique of the contemporary West from a Christian standpoint, this latest book considers religious, and principally Christian, history in respect of its complicity in warfare and asks how far that complicity is culpable and how far it is merely inevitable. As will become apparent, the answers are seldom straightforward.

My debts, as ever, are numerous. My wife and children have mopped up after me, plied me with cakes, picked up the domestic slack and generally lived through the growing pains of this latest project as uncomplainingly as they have its predecessors. A number of colleagues at Houghton College read through several draft sections of this book or helped me run to earth the odd escaping footnote, though they are absolved, of course, from responsibility for remaining errors and contentious claims. InterVarsity's Al Hsu was a great help and source of guidance when it came to final preparations of the manuscript. The London School of Theology kindly allowed me to use its extensive library facilities. And, over many years, innumerable conversations with a wide range of friends and acquaintances in the Balkans have illuminated and given a personal face to various facets of the realities of warfare—from participation as combatants, to suffering as victims, to the motivations and consequences entailed in the tragedy of violent conflict. Many of them, and others much further afield (perhaps the furthest, the dearest), have become my friends for life. To all of them, I remain forever profoundly grateful.

INTRODUCTION

"Somebody's nation, somebody's cause,

somebody's d--- religion has just declared war on us."

The senior U.S. naval officer's comment, as he surveyed the appalling carnage at the Pentagon following the 9/11 attacks, made it into many of the following morning's papers. He was, understandably, an angry man—and the angry are prone to use strong language. They do not, however, generally resort to "damn" in respect of somebody or something (in this case, religion) that they had previously approved. It is not his choice of words, then, so much as the target for them that, even in the terrible stress of 9/11, marks him out as secular or as a skeptic rather than a devout person.[1]

And about this, at least, the naval officer was right. Even before the main inquiries had begun—even on the day itself—the minds of most people, religious and secular alike, jumped to the same conclusion. And they, too, were right. The terrorists were motivated by religion. For its planners, protagonists and executioners, the al-Qaeda campaign is a religious *jihad* against the infidel West. The reward of the suicide bombers is not a hoped-for Western exodus from the Middle East that the bombers will not, by definition, live to see, but the enjoyment of seventy virgins in paradise. Israel/Palestine, Chechnya, Kashmir, central Asia: for the internationally recruited *mujaheddin* and their supporters, none is the real casus belli; all are mere battles in a wider war for Islam. On at least one side of the struggle, then, the war against terrorism is essentially a conflict about religion.

Indeed, religious conflict seems to be all around us. At the time of putting the finishing touches to this book (it is the spring of 2007), I am unsure whether, before it ever gets to the bookstores, the world will have entered on a renewed use of nuclear weapons—not, as my generation grew up to imagine, between champions of differing economic and political systems but between the protagonists of a Shia Islamist state and the infidels who fear it.

Speaking in 1968, Marshall McLuhan predicted that "we're heading into a profoundly religious age."[2] Even then, as the heyday of modernist rationalism was just beginning to come unstuck with the rise of the hippie generation and the political *soixante-huitaires,*[3] few took his forecast too seriously. But the decades since have proven him correct. With the sole exception of the indigenous populations of western Europe, religion is everywhere more prominent and more politicized than it was in the 1960s. We have witnessed what Gilles Kepel has called "the revenge of God": until the 1970s, there was an "irresistible trend towards secularization" around the world, which prompted attempts by the religious to modernize in order to hold on to their following. But from the 1970s onward "this whole process went into reverse" as Pope John Paul II reaffirmed the traditional teachings of the Roman Catholic Church, tacitly downplaying the *aggiornamento*[4] of the Second Vatican Council; as biblicist evangelicalism became easily the most important force within Protestantism; as the Hindu nationalist BJP emerged as a major political force in India; as Zionist parties became key political players in Israel; and as attempts to "modernize Islam" were abandoned in favor of trying to "Islamize modernity."[5] In each case, traditional religion, or rather, new forms of religion that see themselves as defenders of ancient orthodoxies, have gained a wide following in support of religious and cultural retrenchment.

What have we seen as a result of this great reversal? War, that's what. The Balkan wars of the 1990s were fought between Roman Catholic Croats and Eastern Orthodox Serbs, between Serbian Orthodox and Muslim Bosnians or Muslim Albanians, and occasionally between Muslims and Catholics. All of them deliberately attacked one another's churches, mosques and monasteries as priority targets; in all of the conflicts, ordinary individuals were gang raped, starved in concentration camps or killed out of hand on the basis of their religion, whether actual or supposed, in the name of another. The conflict in Northern Ireland was a struggle for supremacy between Protestants and Catholics. Hardline Judaism continues to fuel intransigence in the Israeli-Palestinian dispute and was responsible for the assassination of Yitzhak Rabin, who threatened to make a settlement with the Palestinians; on the Palestinian side, it is the Islamists who bomb the situation back to conflict every time there is any danger of peace breaking out. The BJP strength in India intimidates non-Hindus in that country, does nothing to dampen intercommunal conflict with Muslims and makes compromise in the dispute over Kashmir ever harder to attain.

And as for hardline Islam, there are few conflicts around the world in which it does not play a leading role—from Chechnya to Bosnia and from Iraq and Afghanistan to Palestine; in attacks by Hezbollah (the "party of God") on Israel and the consequent destabilization of Lebanon; in the guerrilla movements in the Philippines and Thailand; in bombings in Turkey, Kenya, Bali, Madrid, London and New York; in intercommunal violence in Indonesia, Nigeria, Sudan and Pakistan; and in violent threats to the régimes of Egypt, the Yemen, Saudi Arabia and Algeria. Muslim-Christian violence in West Africa, Sudan and Indonesia has become deeply entrenched in the politics of those regions.

Religion, it seems, is responsible for most of the conflicts around the world. As Lucretius, the Epicurean Roman poet of the first century B.C., put it, *Tantum religio potuit suadere malorum* ("Religion can incite so much evil."). After two centuries of Enlightenment rationalism and unprecedented material progress and political democratization, have the tribal gods come back to haunt us? Is religion something we are better off without? Surely, as the Balkan conflicts have recently illustrated for us once again, Christianity is no improvement on the other faiths in this matter of violence and warfare.

"IMAGINE THERE'S NO HEAVEN . . ."

In the light of all this, it is not too surprising that an opinion poll in Britain in late 2006 indicated that 82 percent of adults "see religion as a cause of division and tension between people. Only 16% disagree."[6] It is only to be expected, perhaps, that the Humanist Association of Toronto sees "the pages of history books and today's newspapers stained with the blood of innumerable atrocities committed in the name of one god or another, often with the expressed approval of the highest religious authorities."[7] But the former Conservative British government minister Michael Portillo also opines that the phenomenon of "theocrats, religious leaders or fanatics citing holy texts . . . constitutes the greatest threat to world peace today." And those are categories in which he includes George W. Bush and Tony Blair. (The evidence against the latter, apparently, is that "he told us that he had prayed to God about his decision to join the American invasion of Iraq."[8])

At the level of popular culture, many celebrities take a similarly dim view of the baleful role of faith in the modern world. It was John Lennon who had exhorted us to "imagine there's no heaven," with the promise that this would leave "nothing to kill or die for" and, far from accidentally, "no religion too." Instead, there would be just "all the people, living life in peace."[9] Much more recently, the musician Sir Elton John announced that in his equally learned opinion, religion "turns people into hateful lemmings"; religious leaders should save the world from their own followers by holding a "conclave" to save the planet, whose conflicts are "escalating to World War Three." But then, as an afterthought, he added, "I would ban religion completely."[10]

Even without Sir Elton in charge of things, that is the way things are headed in some Western countries. If the "scientists and intellectuals" surveyed by the web magazine Edge are right, however, there will be no need for an outright ban. The selected experts' predictions for the world over the next few decades are "no religion and an end to war." Richard Dawkins hoped that in the years ahead, "scientific enlightenment will deal an overdue deathblow to religion and other juvenile superstitions."[11] But Anthony Grayling, BBC radio's favorite academic philosopher, can hardly wait for that moment: "If only all the gods in whose name people currently kill one another would cremate themselves and thus liberate mankind from the bane of religion."[12]

Dawkins, writing for the Freedom from Religion Foundation in September 2001, in the immediate aftermath of the 9/11 attacks, insisted that

> the human psyche has two great sicknesses: the urge to carry vendetta across generations, and the tendency to fasten group labels on people rather than see them as individuals. Abrahamic religion gives strong sanction to both—and mixes explosively with both. Only the willfully blind could fail to implicate the divisive force of religion in most, if not all, of the violent enmities in the world today.[13]

A few days before, he had written in a prominent London newspaper that "to fill a world with religion, or religions of the Abrahamic kind, is like littering the streets with loaded guns. Do not be surprised if they are used."[14]

Notwithstanding all this bile, there is only one thing that bears a heavier responsibility than religion as a principal cause of war. And that is, of course, irreligion. Nevertheless, much of the secularist establishment—in media, education and, in Western countries apart from the United States, in government—points instead, and with some reason, at the involvement of religion in many of the conflicts of our day and in the past. I shall argue the contrary of this: that the secularist establishment's accusations against religion as the primary cause of war are simplistic and ill-motivated; they have some important superficial validity but are far from the whole truth.

As a case in point, let us take the accusation by Sam Harris, in his recent bestselling book:

> There are days when almost every headline in the morning paper attests to the social costs of religious faith, and the nightly news seems miraculously broadcast from the fourteenth century. . . . [There are] daily reports of pious massacres in Iraq. . . . For anyone with eyes to see, there can be no doubt that religious faith remains a perpetual source of human conflict.[15]

Leave aside the fact that the vast majority of those headlines refer to one faith specifically: Islam. Leave aside, too, that the faith Western secularists concentrate most of their fire on is Christianity, precisely because it does not generally threaten retaliation and, therefore, seldom comes under their strictures about religion and violence. The notion that current "pious massacres" seem "miraculously broadcast from the fourteenth century" betrays the truly fundamental misunderstanding, or rather, misrepresentation, of these secularist arguments. It indicates, of course, the a priori insistence that religion has no place in the modern world. But it is also an arrogant assertion that traditional cultures, which necessarily are inextricably bound up with religion, have no place in that world either. And that contemptuous dismissal does rather make the violent reactions of the despised parties a little easier to understand.

Harris's way of talking also assumes that the premodern world was an unending round of intercommunal and interreligious violence. On the contrary, this violence is peculiarly modern. And it is modernist secularism—and the havoc its imposition is creating in non-Western societies—that is provoking a high proportion of it. As a historian, I found myself wondering what particular orgies of religious violence disfigured the fourteenth century in particular. Crusades? No; they were earlier. Reformation wars of religion? Later. Muslim conquests? Mostly earlier—and later. I do not think Harris knows either. "Fourteenth century," it seems, is shorthand for the "old days"—which we somehow know to have been frightful, bloody, ghastly—when, without the benefit of a modern, child-centered education inculcating skepticism as the only certainty and relativism as the only absolute, everyone was a bit dim. And (what is the same thing) religious. That is an uncharitable assessment on my part, of course. But if I am wrong in attributing these sentiments to Harris, it will not be by much. For he elsewhere asserts that "our ancestors embarrass us," and, in context, he is making a generalized statement about the nature of "moral progress" rather than critiquing some specific such as, say, the slave trade.[16] Harris's campaign against religion is part of a wider tendency of Western secularism: the repudiation of the human past *tout court*. Whether the fourteenth century was or was not notable for religious violence is irrelevant to his argument. For as well as embracing geographical-cultural myopia, it would seem we need to be historical ignoramuses, too—on principle. And this is a point to which we shall have cause to return several times in what follows.

Yet principled contempt for the past will let us down, time and time again. When casting around for current examples of "pious massacres," Harris settles, understandably and justifiably enough, on the eye-catching example of Iraq. Yet the ancient empires, such as that of the Ottomans, which ruled much of western Asia for centuries, found ways of enabling people of different faiths to live together. So too did the undemocratic British mandate that followed it. And, for all its horrors, even the ghastly regime of Saddam Hussein managed that much. They did so precisely by taking religion seriously. The fourteenth century—and the fifteenth, the sixteenth and the seventeenth—were frequently all right in this region. It is the recent attempt to impose a Western-style, secular-democratic model that has rendered unstable the structures that govern ordinary people's lives and has provoked violence. What remedy does Harris have for this? Governmental atheism and principled disrespect for religion? And whose fault would be the consequent violence? The locals' for defending the structures and the metanarratives that have given meaning to their lives and kept order amid hardship? Or the rationalists' for trying to sweep those things away? Lennon told us to "imagine there's no heaven"; how much violence do we imagine it would take to get to this particular no-heaven? If it were to be attained, it would presumably have to be by inflicting more force than the religious were able to deliver. Only then could we have "all the people, living life in peace."

This has been tried several times during the last century by the atheistic totalitarian regimes. Of course, the postmodern campaigners against religion wish to distance themselves from the appalling experiments of these recent predecessors. According to the current crop of secularists, communism and fascism belong in a category not over against but along with religious belief, for their common crime of daring to pronounce on meaning.

Such arguments are understandable but misguided. The new, postmodern atheism is already showing signs of affinity with the old, modernist varieties. No society can be run without a rationale of some kind, and if it does not come from faith, tradition or historic culture, then we must presumably look to reason. (Indeed, that is where Dawkins and his ilk are insistently pointing us.) But reason can only ever speak to us of means, not of ends. And in the attempts to avoid this rather obvious truth, we immediately start drifting back toward some newfangled metanarrative that, no matter how furiously it wraps itself in the mantle of reason, is yet less truly rational and certainly less human than even the most barbarous forms of animism. As we shall see, it is the rejection of God that destroys the specialness of humanity. And it is the loss of the specialness of humanity that unleashes endless horror, not just in the recent past but also in the present, not just with old-style atheism but also with the new.

Even so, once all the accusations have been thrown around in both directions between secularists and the devout, we might pause to ask what it is, actually, that causes war. This book will seek to address that issue and, in the process, to probe a number of related questions. How important, historically, has religious faith been in the immediate promotion of conflict, as exemplified by crusade or *jihad*? Do some religious faiths have a better record than others, and why? Can we distinguish between different forms of Christianity, and, if so, on what basis? Do such observable differences and distinctions have any evidential value about religious truth claims? When has religion been a smokescreen to justify particular wars that are bound up with other, more mundane concerns? And how far is the accusation that religion is the principal culprit itself merely a smokescreen behind which the irreligious pursue their attempt to drive faith out of the public square?

For one thing, religious violence is not always being judged by the same canons as other forms of conflict. Hector Avalos claims that "if any acts of violence caused by actual scarcities are immoral, then acts of violence" that are "predicated on the acquisition or loss of nonexistent goods"—by which he means religion—"should be judged as even more immoral."[17] This is too much even for some atheists. James Wellman, who believes that religions and their gods "are a human product," nevertheless insists that "to place 'religious' experience as outside of empirical analysis by definition is non-empirical" and that "to start with this assumption (even implied) is problematic, not morally but scientifically."[18]

For another thing, it is particularly interesting to note how some wars receive much wider press coverage than others. Christian-Muslim conflicts in West Africa, Sudan and Indonesia, for example, receive relatively little news coverage in Western countries. Furthermore, much coverage of the fighting that does happen misleadingly suggests that both sides are equally to blame. This is seldom the case.[19] But the suggestion that it is so serves two secularist aims at once: it creates the appearance of lofty even-handedness and of not being anti-Islamic; and it helps, or at least refrains from undermining, the anti-Christian case in the West.

For the secularist campaign against religion is a subtext of its campaign against all traditional cultures—a campaign that itself provokes violence. Neither does this violence prove the secularist thesis that religion causes war, for secularism has obtained massive power (bureaucratic, economic, technical and, via the media that it controls, cultural) that is answerable by the (mostly) poor people against whose life meanings it is directed in the only coin available to them.

I shall argue that while religion is a significant generator of armed conflict in the past and in the present, the two principal causes of human warfare are human greed and culture. The argument is contestable because both greed and culture can clothe themselves in religion. Frequently, the greed motive comes clothed in a self-justifying ideology that may as easily be religious as secular. But wars fought over cultural issues often have a religious aspect too, for religion is frequently a defining element in culture.

Those two previous sentences are deliberately question begging. Granted that a war motivated by material greed—for territory, resources or political power—may be justified under the cloak of religion. Would the war have been impossible, because nakedly unjustifiable, without the religion to legitimize it? Obviously, different cases will involve different variables, and the answer will often be imponderable. A similar, though by no means identical, problem arises in respect to culture. Professor Samuel Huntington has popularized the "clash of civilizations" thesis in respect of contemporary conflicts around the world; in the process, he correctly has identified religion as a principal definer of culture.[20] So, would a peaceful world entail a world devoid of cultures? The Western technocratic elite (usually, and ironically, styling themselves muticulturalist) seems to think so. If traditional cultures, and especially their central religious aspects, can be emasculated and locked indoors, then, they believe, peace can be assured.

The problem with that last view is that the attempt to enforce it—whether nakedly, as in Afghanistan and Iraq, or more sneakily by soft soaping and bamboozling, as in respect of the aggressive export of modernist architecture, fast foods and sexualized clothing and entertainment—is productive of extreme violence from those whose cultures are thereby threatened. And that in turn triggers counterviolence by Western states, prosecuting their war on terror.

Clearly, the particular propensity of Islam to violence, a tendency exacerbated by these current circumstances, is another factor that we shall need to take into consideration in the following pages. In September 2006, Pope Benedict XVI, giving an academic lecture at his erstwhile University of Regensburg in Germany, sparked worldwide Muslim fury—not for making the same claim as I have in that last sentence, but merely for quoting a fourteenth-century Byzantine emperor who had said something similar. The response to that quotation—words from which the pope was careful to distance himself, even as he cited them, by introducing them as "startling brusqueness" and adding afterward that they were "forceful"—was a series of protests of a kind that put Christians in Pakistan and the Middle East in fear of precisely that: Muslim violence.[21]

As the press debated this latest spat, even an American Catholic critic of the pope's supposed lack of tact in dealing with Muslims, the Jesuit Father Thomas Reese, accidentally revealed that Benedict had understated the problem rather than overstated it: "If the Vatican says something dumb about Muslims, people will die in parts of Africa and churches will be burned in Indonesia, let alone what happens in the Middle East."[22]

Exactly. It is not that Islam is not violent: it is that we may not say so out loud—or even, if we are prominent public figures, like the pope, cite fourteenth-century emperors who did so. While we will not spend large portions of this book belaboring the point concerning Islam and violence, we shall examine the distinction between forms of religion that have been or are belligerent—and these include many forms of Christianity—and those that are not. In finding normative Christianity essentially not guilty of sponsoring warfare, I have tried hard not to make myself guilty of special pleading, dubious misreadings and the like. Above all, I have sought to avoid making the mistake of putting some favored position (in this case, Christian faith) in the clear only by the dishonest device of insisting that my interpretation of it is the real thing, while all the empirically existing manifestations that all too embarrassingly stand guilty as charged are mere distortions. Nothing is achieved by holding up some particular version of Christianity—or of Islam, Judaism, Marxism—that has been manufactured to purpose and attempting to pass it off as the sole genuine article. On the contrary, it is not merely a particular reading of the New Testament that supports the view I shall advance (for such a reading might be open to challenge) but the indisputable facts of the church's behavior during the first three centuries of its life. Furthermore, although that behavior and its concomitant body of doctrine later changed substantially as church and state slid into long-term alliance, a variety of Christian movements during the centuries since has continued to insist that the faith of Jesus is not to be advanced by violence. And now once again that proposition has become the all but universal stance in theory, if not always quite in fact, of Christians, including the pope.

For the purposes of this book, we shall use the term *religion* in its generally accepted sense of "an interconnected system of beliefs and/or practices rooted in the numinous or spiritual world that gives meaning to the lives of those who embrace them or have been reared in them." Religious faith operates in most Western countries today as a personal choice, albeit one that many adherents have received from their upbringing, which may sometimes in turn be related to ethnic origin. In most other societies, the relationship with ancestral or cultural affiliation is frequently much sharper. And in some societies, past and present, the entire population is or was expected to embrace one particular faith, with slender allowances made for dissenters. On occasion, no such allowance was made.

That last description frequently characterized Christianity during the Middle Ages and the Reformation periods. In some historically Christian countries, the characteristic has endured until even more recently. Nowadays, it is more likely that Islam or, in parts of southern Asia, Buddhism will claim exclusive purchase on particular societies. In India, Hinduism makes a similar claim while allowing a somewhat subordinate place for other faiths. In these circumstances, the potential for religious conflict will be strong wherever social, political, military or economic changes threaten the historic position of one or more of the traditional faiths or wherever the expansion of one faith or the position of its adherents threatens another. Most religions, even minority and voluntary faiths, may become belligerent where the sensitivities of believers are outraged on a daily basis or where governments, circumstances or majorities threaten to destroy their ability to perpetuate their own life.

Already, it will be plain that the relationship between religion and armed conflict is often ambiguous and complicated. Like my previous book *Why the Rest Hates the West,* this volume deals with the interface between global politics and religious faith and does so by using the long lens of history to analyze what is going on. Unlike that earlier book, however, the present work is not so much a clear trumpet blast as a minuet around a complex issue, namely, the relationship between religion and war. To be sure, where the platitudes and received wisdoms of contemporary secularism are counterevidential inversions of reality, as they nearly always are, I have not hesitated to point them out as such. But where issues are genuinely multifaceted and historical assessments must be more ambivalent, then no purpose—certainly not the promotion of Christian faith—is served by simplistic judgments that overlook or distort important or embarrassing facts. The fatuousness of secularist denunciations of religion does not justify a countervailing fatuousness by Christians. Far too much of the culture wars, perhaps especially in the United States, has been characterized by such a logic of reciprocal illogicality. And in any case, as the preceding paragraphs have made clear, the secularist accusation against religion as being a principal cause of war does present believers with a serious case that needs addressing. It remains for the reader to judge how far I have succeeded in answering that charge.

For reasons of size (book) and competence (author), no book of this kind can hope to cover the full gamut of world religions. Occasional references to the outlooks of Buddhism, Hinduism, Shinto and other faiths are necessarily, therefore, fleeting and less than fully nuanced. But the central accusations against religious faith today emanate from the West, which is deeply enmeshed in the project of cultural renunciation of its historic origins in Christendom and most frequently finds itself in conflict with Islam. For that reason, and because this volume is aimed principally at a Western audience, I have focused here principally on Christianity, with glances also at aspects of this problem as they bear on Islam.

The arguments I shall advance here are, essentially, fourfold. In the first place, irreligion has produced wars far worse and far bloodier than has religion. Second, we must distinguish between belligerent and non-belligerent religion. Third, cultures enshrine religion, and wars fought for one often appear as being fought for the other, with any attempts to extricate the two factors descending into meaninglessness since neither ingredient can be envisaged without the other. And finally, the global secularist campaign against religion and traditional cultures (as supposedly violent) is already and will continue to be productive of the most ferocious violence, in which it is by no means clear that the hedonistic secularists of the West are in possession of the moral high ground.

1

THE BLOODIEST CENTURY OF ALL

All ye who pass in quest of happy hours, behold the cost at which those hours were bought.

The large, bold inscription stands above the doorway inside the lobby of Stoke Newington Public Library in London. When I first saw it, I had merely been walking past the open entrance on the street, my mind preoccupied with quite other things than "happy hours" in the library. Yet I was so struck by the force of the words that I instantly stopped and peered within the lobby. My eyes instinctively cast about rapidly, attempting to obey the instruction. What was it that I should "behold"? And, as the engraver had doubtless anticipated, it took a mere moment before they alighted on the intended object. The entire wall to the left of the inscription was covered with hundreds of names. Stoke Newington had paid a heavier price, in terms of World War I dead, than most places of its size in Britain; this was their memorial. The civic authorities of the 1920s, with a mentality markedly different from that holding sway today, had intended that no user of its principal civic amenity—the library—should ever forget that "happy hours," relaxation and the pleasures of reading and scholarship had all been "bought" in blood.

For the secular conflicts of the twentieth century mobilized populations against one another on a scale that the monarchs of the past could never have imagined possible. The peace they supposedly fought to establish (on the victors' terms) came at an ever higher price. War became total, cutting off trade and all interactions between individuals in opposing states, so that the populace could dedicate themselves to the one, overriding objective: winning the war. When peace eventually came, entire populations owned it as never before; just as they had been unable to escape ownership of the war, so the peace that followed seemed truly to be theirs. War memorials had not been erected for the common soldiers of the seventeenth and eighteenth centuries; still less for those of the Middle Ages. Just as in Roman times, such civic honor had been the preserve of all-conquering generals, and even then the practice became common only from the eighteenth century. But the increasingly popular nature of modern, total war meant that the deaths of soldiers, sailors and airmen could no longer be seen as private tragedies for the families from which they came; they were *our* war dead. They were the appalling "cost" for the "happy hours" that we, the grateful debtors to the fallen, might enjoy in consequence of their sacrifice.

While it would be foolish to deny that religious concerns have played a prominent part in many conflicts throughout much of history, it nevertheless remains an unavoidable fact that the modern, total wars have been avowedly secular in nature. Indeed, the twentieth century must provide the litmus test for the question of whether secularism can ever do better than religion in conflict avoidance, for it is during that era, so recently ended, that the ideas of the Enlightenment fully seized hold of the levers of government in all of the world's leading powers and in many minor powers besides. Kings, together with the churches that they had upheld and that had in turn upheld them, were replaced by republics upholding no church at all.

Some of the new states became totalitarian dictatorships, while others clung to democratic forms of government. Many of the former claimed the legitimation of science, not faith, and often persecuted religion either cautiously and semi-secretly, as with the Nazis, or openly and on principle, as did the communists. Even in the democracies, there was a presumption among academics, journalists, politicians and the other leading opinion formers in society that there was a fundamental conflict between modern science and religious faith and that the latter was essentially obscurantist. Inevitably it was a view increasingly shared by the ordinary people whose outlooks were shaped by what they read, heard and, later in the century, saw in the media, and what they were taught in school. Some of the most important political forces, especially on the left, were disdainful of the role played by the churches and were at least sympathetic to Marx's dictum that religion was "the opium of the people." Libertarians, who were a small minority early in the century but formed an overwhelming majority of the Western establishment by its end, also opposed religion as restrictive of human freedoms, especially in sexual matters.

The Enlightenment principles tended to indicate that power inhered, or should inhere, not in monarchs but in the people. Politics, the economy and the law should be organized on rational principles, not on the basis of received wisdom, hereditary privilege or medieval presumptions about a society revolving around the ownership of land. How has rationalism worked out in matters relating to warfare?

During the course of the nineteenth century, the most advanced states possessed sufficiently competent bureaucracies to introduce military training for all able-bodied young men, along with the idea of holding them in permanent reserve in case of need during time of war. As John Keegan observes, this development "produced large, relatively cheap peacetime armies, while the reserve obligation promised to produce very large wartime ones."[1] The great Russian novelist Fyodor Dostoyevsky pointed to the consequences for the sheer scale of hostilities during time of war:

> Well, just take a good look round you: rivers of blood are being spilt, and in the jolliest imaginable way, like champagne. Take all our nineteenth century. . . . Look at Napoleon, the Great and the present one [Louis Napoleon]. Look at North America—the everlasting union [sundered by the Civil War]. Look, finally, at Schleswig-Holstein. . . . And what, pray, does civilization soften in us?[2]

Modernist Western rationalism was proving capable of mechanizing more than just the production of cotton cloth and pottery. It made people more efficient, not more peaceful. Modernity was making possible the era of total war.

The four bloodiest conflicts in human history have all taken place in relatively recent times. The most lethal conflict was World War II, which claimed between fifty and sixty million lives. (Precise figures are impossible, and even approximations remain disputed, though they fall generally within this range.) The second costliest, in terms of loss of life, was the T'ai-Ping rebellion in China, from 1850 to 1864, in which the dead may have numbered somewhere around twenty million.[3] World War I inflicted perhaps fifteen million dead: around eight and a half million in battle and perhaps another six and a half million civilians, though, again, estimates vary.[4] And the fourth was the Russian Civil War, which followed in the wake of the Bolshevik Revolution of 1917. Estimates of the number of casualties in that conflict continue to differ enormously, and even definitions are problematic, but around nine million seems to be the safest figure.[5] The claim, therefore, that the wars of secular modernity were bloodier because they were essentially secular seems almost irresistible. Secularism, it seems, has caused far worse conflicts than has religion.

However, there is a certain fatuousness in pointing out that the bloodiest wars have been the most recent. As technology has leaped forward, everything has been made more efficient, including the appalling business of killing people. The invention of the machine gun, of barbed wire, of tanks and of aerial bombardment all represent the early-twentieth-century application of the industrial revolution to the process of warfare—that is, of organized mass slaughter. The development of nuclear, chemical and biological warfare represents further technologization, and with it, a vast extension of the same enterprise. As Roland H. Bainton observed,

> The great change came through technology. New weapons pre-

> cluded humanitarian restraint. . . . The submarine could and did send out a wireless as to the location of a stricken vessel, but it lacked accommodation for the removal of the crew and passengers. Poisoned gas cannot be palliated. The blockade in the Middle Ages had been applied usually to cities from which noncombatants were sometimes permitted to withdraw. . . . Such permissions could not be granted when the whole of Germany was ringed around and the object was to break the war potential of the populace.[6]

The wars of secular modernity, then, were more catastrophic not because they were secular but because they were modern. Warfare would have become bloodier, it might be argued, even if secularization had never happened because, in technologically advanced societies, the means of killing people are bound to be more effective. And however lamentable that fact may be, its ideological or religious significance is limited; although social beliefs, religious or otherwise, may affect a society's ability to develop technology, the application of that technology, once it exists, to any and all of the exigencies of that society, including warfare, has a certain inevitability and is unaffected by whether the society is religious or secular, conservative or radical, open or totalitarian.

So the kind of religious objection that points to the mere fact of enormous casualties in modern conflicts, generated by secular societies and atheistic ideologies, does not demonstrate as much as it appears. If religious people wish to hang the phenomenon of mass death in modern war around the neck of secularism, then they need to do more. They must be able to point to the belligerence of secularist creeds and the societies that embrace them and perhaps to the determination, or at least to the tendency, of nonreligious combatants to inflict death and destruction on principle.

In fact, however, this is not hard to do. Keegan, perhaps the greatest living historian of war, points out that though the Greeks and Romans thought of war as being an integral part of human existence, this idea was "deprecated both by Christianity and Islam" but was revived powerfully in the nineteenth century, partly under the impact of Charles Darwin's understanding of life as a process of permanent struggle with competitors for survival.[7]

There is much to be said in favor of this understanding of how views about warfare have changed over the centuries. Heraclitus, in the fifth century B.C., expressed the then common view that "war is common to all and strife is justice . . . all things come into being and pass away through strife." Indeed, the inhabitants of the Greek city-states took warfare, either between themselves or against the looming presence of the Persian Empire, as part of the natural order of things.

The extent of Christian deprecations of this position we shall have cause to notice presently. But the classical view was revived in a new form from the late nineteenth century onward, claims Keegan, as a result of Darwin's "theory of the natural selection of the fittest" spilling over into other disciplines, such as philosophy, the social sciences and politics. (It seems that he is right: think of the proliferation of nonbiological uses of the term *evolution* from the late nineteenth century down to the present, to denote something supposedly higher and inevitable.) The Darwinian direction of thought, in which history is impersonal, people are mere products of nature, conflict is the engine of the universe and the key to understanding its complexity is held by some scientific theoretician: this had "its direst outcomes" in the totalitarian creeds of the twentieth century, "particularly the Bolshevism of Lenin and the National Socialism of Adolf Hitler."[8]

The godless and supposedly scientific creeds have proven to be far bloodier than their religious antecedents, precisely because they have no basis for any doctrine of the preciousness of each person. As Leon Trotsky, one of the Russian revolutionary leaders, put it, "We must put an end once and for all to the papist-Quaker babble about the sanctity of human life."[9] Trotsky, himself of Jewish background, had chosen his "papist-Quaker" epithet well. "Papist" was shorthand for Western, over against which Russians, who were overwhelmingly Orthodox, had long identified themselves; "Quaker" stood for foreign sectarian. But, despite the careful nationalist positioning of his chosen terminology, Trotsky's real target was the Judeo-Christian tradition itself. Later in the century, the same point was made by the Latin American Communist guerrilla leader Che Guevara (1928-1967), whose romantic image has been ceaselessly used as adolescent affectation of chic violence. In 1956, he wrote to his mother from a Mexican jail, "I am no Christ, nor a philanthropist. I am the very opposite of Christ. . . . I will fight with all the arms within reach."[10] The teaching of Jesus was inseparable from the philanthropy (the love of human beings for their own sake) to which he referred, and this was an insuperable obstacle to crushing one's enemies.

According to Trotsky, "Repression remains a necessary means of breaking the will of the opposing side" as long as class society continued to exist. "Terror can be very efficient against a reactionary class which does not want to leave the scene of operations"—and he recommended employing it; such terror could be condemned only, he contended, by complete pacifists. "You do not understand this, holy men?" he asked, mockingly.

> We shall explain to you. The terror of Tsarism was directed against the proletariat. The gendarmerie of Tsarism throttled the workers who were fighting for the Socialist order. Our Extraordinary Commissions shoot landlords, capitalists, and generals who are striving to restore the capitalist order. Do you grasp this distinction? Yes? For us Communists it is quite sufficient.[11]

Of course, there was a certain disingenuousness in the parallel he was making: even at an early stage, the Bolshevik regime was killing many times more of its enemies than the tsarist governments had ever done. And later, when the Bolsheviks were firmly in power, more prisoners were shot at just one Soviet camp, Serpentinnaya, in a single year (1938) than had been executed by the tsarist regime during the entire nineteenth century.[12] But Trotsky's central argument was that violence was right or wrong solely according to who was perpetrating it against whom.

"Who? Whom?" Lenin had coined the famous phrase before the revolution had even begun. And he agreed wholeheartedly with Trotsky's principled ruthlessness about individual human lives. "What is better?" Lenin asked in July 1919,

> to ferret out, to imprison, sometimes even to shoot hundreds of traitors from among the Kadets, nonparty people, Mensheviks and Socialist-Revolutionaries, who "come out" . . . against the Soviet power, in other words, in favor of Denikin? Or to allow matters to reach a pass enabling Kolchak and Denikin to slaughter, shoot and flog to death tens of thousands of workers and peasants? The choice is not difficult to make.[13]

Indeed, the Russian Civil War saw massive violence unleashed against all manner of opponents of the revolution and, as historians unite in pointing out, against countless thousands who were merely accused as a result of personal grudges or who belonged to the "wrong" social class. Each town and village, Lenin urged, should devise its own method of "cleansing the land of all vermin, of scoundrel fleas, the bedbug rich." According to him, the socialist state was intended to be "a system of organized violence" against the bourgeoisie.[14] In August 1918, when writing to the Bolsheviks in the district of Penza, who were putting down a peasant uprising against the Communists, he ordered that it be "*mercilessly* suppressed. . . . Hang (hang without fail, so the people see) *no fewer than one hundred* kulaks, rich men, bloodsuckers. Publish their names. Take from them *all* the grain. Designate hostages." He finished his communication with an instruction to "Telegraph receipt [of this] and *implementation*," and added, "P.S. Find some *truly hard* people."[15] Concerning the clergy who opposed the revolution, he urged that "we should now wage the most decisive and merciless war" against them and "suppress its resistance with such cruelty that they will not forget it for decades to come. . . . The more members of the reactionary bourgeoisie and clergy we manage to shoot the better."[16] Two years later, in August 1920, when the Red Army was engaged in an ultimately failed attempt to invade Poland, he sent an urgent telegram to the Polish Communist Karol Radek: "I beg you, go straight to Dzierzynski and insist that the landowners and kulaks are destroyed ruthlessly and a bit more quickly and energetically."[17]

It should be stressed that Lenin's view was neither an aberration nor a distortion of the revolutionary ideals: it was intrinsic to the atheistic creed. And the reason for that, as we saw with Trotsky, was the principled repudiation of the sanctity of human life. This may seem obvious to many readers, yet there remain those who persist in positing a "nice Lenin" in juxtaposition to a "nasty Stalin," with the latter having somehow corrupted a good and noble project or one that was, at worst, nobly misguided.[18] But this is wrong. Lenin's ruthlessness was longstanding and antedated by far the Russian Revolution. In 1891 and 1892, when the Volga region, where Lenin had been living at that time, had been gripped by famine, he was scornful of the relief efforts of liberals and even some radicals on the grounds that famine would serve to radicalize the masses: "Psychologically, this talk of feeding the starving is nothing but an expression of the saccharine-sweet sentimentality so characteristic of our intelligentsia."[19] The more people starved to death, the likelier the survivors would be to blame the government and support red revolution: that was what mattered. That is exactly the point of the Bolsheviks' maxim of the prerevolutionary period: "The worse, the better."

Human lives as such were unimportant: what counted was the grand scheme of things—the attainment of the set of abstract ideals that constituted communism. It was Lenin who insisted that

> only after we have overthrown, finally vanquished and expropriated the bourgeoisie of the whole world, and not merely of one country, will wars become impossible. And from a scientific point of view it would be utterly wrong—and utterly unrevolutionary—for us to evade or gloss over the most important thing: crushing the resis-

> tance of the bourgeoisie—the most difficult task, and one demanding the greatest amount of fighting, in the *transition* to socialism.[20]

Until that glorious future was attained, war was needed and desirable. Efraim Karsh has observed that Lenin saw "nothing immoral in war as such: what determines its moral value is the cause for which it is being fought."[21] As the anarchist A. G. Zhelezniakov had argued, "For the welfare of the Russian people even a million people could be killed."[22]

The actuality of the revolution cost far, far more lives than a million. But the principle was clear all along: actions were good or bad not in and of themselves but according to whether they served for or against the cause of worldwide socialism. Until that goal was reached, the globe would unavoidably be divided into armed camps. Real peace was a synonym for the triumph of socialism; any peace before that was a mere tactic, a stratagem for regrouping forces before a fresh bout of fighting against the capitalists.

The parallel with the Muslims' division of the world into the *dar al harb* ("realm of war") and the *dar al Islam* ("realm of Islam") is both accidental, in the sense that Lenin and the Bolsheviks would have had no reason to copy it, and far from accidental, in the sense that Islam and communism share the same teleology, or dynamic, toward universal, this-worldly rule.[23] It is this feature, and its frequent though far from unanimous adoption by Christian churches, that will form a recurring theme in this book.

Karl Marx, the intellectual mentor of all the communists, never had the power to practice violence. Even so, one modern writer, noting his violent speeches, his interminable rows, his propensity to inform the police about the activities of fellow revolutionaries with whom he had quarreled, his habit of dismissing opponents with the words "I will annihilate you," his outbursts of fury on all manner of occasions and his repeated advocacy of terrorism, concludes, "That Marx, once established in power, would have been capable of great violence and cruelty seems certain."[24] His chief collaborator, Friedrich Engels, was similarly minded. In an 1849 article in the

Neue Rheinische Zeitung, published by Marx, he wrote that only the Germans, Hungarians and Poles could be accounted bearers of progress in Central Europe: "The chief mission of all other races and peoples, large and small"—peoples he described as *Völkerabfall*, ethnic trash—"is to perish in the revolutionary holocaust." It was prescience indeed.[25]

For secular revolutions, violence and warfare are always justifiable if they serve the cause. This had been seen as far back as the French Revolution, when Robespierre had opined that for the revolutionary government, "terror is only justice prompt, severe and inflexible . . . an emanation of virtue." He was writing in 1794, the year after the notorious Terror directed against enemies of the revolution, which he sought to justify. Because the business of killing priests and royalists helped to secure the new regime in power, it was "a natural consequence of the general principle of democracy, applied to the most pressing wants of the country."[26] To be sure, governments were supposed to protect their citizens, but this hardly applied to those whom the revolutionaries were killing, since "all citizens in the republic are republicans." It followed that those who were not republicans, such as royalists, "are strangers, or rather enemies."[27]

This principle—that only those who agree with or fit into the favored categories of the government count as citizens or even as human beings—was to be used again and again during the nationalist and socialist regimes of the modern era. Mao illustrated the same tendency when he said that "the right of reactionaries to voice their opinions must be abolished and only the people are allowed to have the right of voicing their opinions." Reactionaries—that is, people who opposed the revolutionaries—were not people.[28]

The life of human beings, therefore, did not have value intrinsic to itself except in its collectivity. The abstract system of the revolutionaries, into which mold a bright and shiny (if not always willing) new humanity was to be pressed: this was the sole repository of value. Nevertheless, the French Revolution invoked liberty, equality and fraternity, ideas that were to be echoed to one degree or another by all of the mutually contradictory secularist regimes of the twentieth century. Despite this, however, the ideas were hardly given the force in real life that an outsider might have been led to expect. Partly this elusiveness was aided by the fact that liberty and equality are, in practice, mutually exclusive concepts, unless the latter is understood merely in its minimalist sense (before the law; before God; possessed of a life of equal value, etc.).

More often, though, it was the former concept, that of liberty, that was inverted into meaninglessness by the secularist creeds in the interests of a nationalist or else some supposedly egalitarian project. When Robespierre asserted, as an apologia for the French Terror, that "the government in a revolution is the despotism of liberty against tyranny," he was merely echoing the idea of Jean-Jacques Rousseau, whose book *The Social Contract* had spoken of "forcing men to be free."[29] The Bolsheviks spoke similarly of the "dictatorship of the proletariat." And all of these self-consciously paradoxical phrases were euphemisms for force, pure and simple. They initiated a convoluted duckspeak, in which words assumed a rarefied meaning somewhat distant from, perhaps even opposite to, that of their generally accepted sense.

When Rousseau had written in 1762 of "the general will," for violating which a person must be "forced to be free," he seems, in the context of his words, to have meant that the political entity to which a person belongs could constrain him or her, especially in forcing the payment of taxes for the support of essential public purposes. But by using such cloudy language to do so, he opened the door to all kinds of incantatory mumbo-jumbo. The "general will" could be divorced from the actual wills of the individuals who make up the "generality" and held to be existent on the say-so of some theoretician or ideologue. Furthermore, by arrogating to themselves the ability to define true freedom, the modernist, secular ideologues had few qualms about using force to bring people into that state. Indeed, there are strong signs that Rousseau inclined in the directions his rhetoric had made possible.

Alexander Yakovlev, once a member of the Soviet Politburo but later a supporter of democracy, lamented that the French Revolution had portended all of the horrors that were to come in the twentieth century: "the idealization of violence traces back to the very sources of the European revolutionary tradition."[30] Robert Conquest concedes that it is possible to acquit Rousseau and even Marx of "envision[ing] mass terror," but insists that the real point is that they were "propounding unattainable utopias" for which "any attempt to put them into practice" was possible "only . . . by such means." Godless revolutionaries of all stripes—fascists, communists and others—came to believe it to be "in the nature of things that dictatorship and terror are needed if the good of humanity is to be served. . . . The means are acceptable, being inevitable—that is, *if* the theory is correct."[31] The feminist writer Simone de Beauvoir recorded that she and Jean-Paul Sartre, the Marxist existentialist philosopher, both rejected the French Socialist Party "firstly on the grounds that it was infiltrated by the bourgeoisie and secondly because we were temperamentally opposed to the idea of reform: society, we felt, could change only as a result of sudden cataclysmic upheaval on a global scale."[32]

For anything to change, everything had to change: this was the central conviction of the atheistic creeds. It was Nikolai Chernyshevsky (1828-1889) who is credited—if that is the right word—with coining the phrase "the worse, the better." It was adopted, like the title of his novel, *What Is to Be Done?* and like the ascetic habits and single-minded dedication to revolution of its hero, by Lenin.[33] The worse things are for the toiling masses, the more likely they are to be interested in a violent revolution. Once again, the individual lives of the workers are not what matters; the final attainment of the idealized utopian state is what counts. Even after the fall of communism, lifetime Marxists were still prepared to defend this. When the historian Eric Hobsbawm, interviewed by Michael Ignatieff in 1994, was asked whether "the loss of fifteen, twenty million people" in the manmade famines caused by collectivization of the farms in the U.S.S.R. in the 1930s "might have been justified" if the "radiant tomorrow" that the communists envisaged had been attained as a result, he immediately responded "yes."[34]

The Italian fascist dictator, Benito Mussolini, went even further than the Marxists: he considered war to be unambiguously a good thing for its own sake. "It matters little who wins. To make a people great it is necessary to send them to battle even if you have to kick them in the pants. That is what I shall do."[35] And, as we know, he did.

Jesus had warned (Mt 24:6) of the inevitability of wars in human affairs, but this is merely gritty realism in view of human sinfulness. The aim for all followers of Jesus is to be peace, not just in eternity after the parousia but also in the here and now, however transitory that peace may prove. That is why the peacemakers are "blessed . . . sons of God" (Mt 5:9). Mussolini's skepticism about peace, however, is rooted in no Christian-style gritty realism; on the contrary, it is an idealization of violence that is the antithesis of the New Testament approach. "Fascism," he insisted, "believes neither in the possibility nor the utility of perpetual peace. . . . War alone maximizes to its highest tension all human energy and puts the stamp of nobility upon the peoples who have the courage to meet it."[36]

Pierre Drieu La Rochelle (1893-1945), the French fascist poet and intellectual, also criticized Christianity's repudiation of war and violence as "effeminate" and detrimental to "'moral' well-being."[37] The hero of his novel *Gilles* dies in battle for fascism as a sacrifice to the ideal; the hero of another opines that "there is the Devil in God and God in the Devil. I have never made a distinction between good and evil; Christ does not. . . . Christ has his elect not because they are good but because they are his elect—beyond good and evil." His is a religion of "the anger of love, the fury of preference."[38] He wrote in 1927 that "the only life that men are capable of . . . is the effusion of blood: murder and coitus. All the rest is but the end of the road, decadence."[39]

This, for fascists, was the true struggle—what Alfred Rosenberg, the Nazi theorist, called the "romanticism of steel."[40] The philosopher Ludwig Klages believed that Christianity had contributed to "the virtual extinction of the ancient Germanic nature wisdom"—a wisdom he was determined to resurrect. Christ, thought Klages and his associated Nazi-inclined academics, might be acceptable if he was seen as an expression of the mystical, cosmic spirit. Belief in the historical Jesus or in the Christianity of Paul was "Jewish" and inimical to the idealization of force: "Humanity wants what is best, the fighter accomplishes what is best."[41] Logically enough, such thinkers preferred the Protestant liberal theologians of their day, who were busily deconstructing the Gospel accounts of Christ and inserting in their place an idea of God as life-force.

The first half of the twentieth century saw the appalling carnage wrought by the competing irreligious ideologies as they fought and struggled against one another. After World War II, fascism was a spent force except in very few parts of the world. But communism had rather longer to run. However, neither communism nor fascism nor their supposedly milder variants had any real basis for the sanctity of human life. Indeed, they opposed such a doctrine as mere sentiment. "To make a socialist omelet" (to cite an oft-quoted phrase among left-wing activists), "you have to break a few capitalist eggs." To translate the metaphor: if you want to achieve the greater good of a socialist society, you have to kill capitalists and others who might stand in the way. The Soviets and, after 1948, the Chinese Maoists determined to eliminate their class enemies. And, as the historian Sheila Fitzpatrick has shown, once a person was designated a class enemy, the stigma could not be removed, even from that person's descendants.[42] In the same way, the Nazis set about killing not only German Jews, German gypsies and other "non-Aryans" but also Germans who were disabled, mentally retarded or found to be in some other way defective. Germans were supposed to be a flawless master race; the Nazi solution to the problem that this central claim flew in the face of the facts was the same as the solution of the communists. Indeed, the strategy of the Nazis and communists, faced with millions of living, breathing contradictions of their ideas, was, at heart, one and the same: to immiserate and kill them until the racists' and socialists' falsehoods were turned into truth and the demographic facts on the ground conformed themselves to the abstractions in the ideologues' heads.

It was those abstractions that mattered: the people as a theoretical construct rather than people of flesh and blood. This was understood very well by everybody involved, as the death throes of communism illustrated. On the one hand, antigovernment demonstrators in the dying days of East Germany adopted the ironic slogan "*Wir* sind das Volk!" ("*We* are the people!") For four decades, everything had supposedly been done in the name of "the people," in defiance of what they themselves would actually have chosen to do or to have done on their behalf. On the other hand, the Securitate (the security police) in communist Romania, who for decades had lived a secluded, privileged existence dedicated to fighting "the enemies of the people," knew instinctively how to act when confronted by vast, universally supported demonstrations against the hated dictator Nicolae Ceauşescu: they fired on the crowds from rooftops and other vantage points. Despite their constant refrain, the Securitate had known all along that it was *they* who were, in the literal meaning of the words, the enemies of the people, and they fought a desperate last stand to keep the people down. The rhetoric had fooled no one, not even the Securitate who deployed it. Like political correctness today, it was an enforced public discourse, the real purposes of which were to render disapproved thoughts literally unspeakable and to cow ordinary people into silence about the things that mattered.

The modernist ideologies, in both their harsher and milder forms, were built on an atheistic view of humanity and of people that rendered ordinary lives dispensable and war in the cause of the abstract social ideal a positive good. As Heinrich Himmler commented,

> Whether the other peoples live in comfort or perish of hunger interests me only in so far as we need them as slaves for our *Kultur*. Whether or not 10,000 Russian women collapse from exhaustion while digging a tank ditch interests me only in so far as the tank ditch is completed for Germany.[43]

Boris Pasternak noted the same tendency among communists. In his massive novel about the Russian Revolution and its aftermath, one of the refrains put into the mouths of his characters is that "the personal life is dead in Russia. History has taken over." The lives, deaths and suffering of countless individuals were of no account in the pursuit of creating an ideal society on the pages of "history."

We noticed, early on in this chapter, that modern wars have been bloodier than anything that came before because of their modernity and the horrifying advances in humans' ability to kill one another—and that these advances mean that not all of the blame for the carnage can be laid at the door of the secularist creeds. Nevertheless, as we have shown, those creeds took the same mechanistic view of humanity as of the machines and bureaucratic structures that were designed to enhance the process of killing. And the link between that mechanistic view and the appalling destructiveness of modern warfare is no accident. Religions have generally held human life to be sacrosanct, since pacifism is not practical as an actual policy of government, or else to have circumscribed closely the circumstances under which it may be taken away. Atheism and agnosticism, by contrast, have had no such confidence in the value of individual human beings. Neither do their modern, nontotalitarian variants show any sign of filling the void thereby created. That absence has allowed, and continues to allow, the abstract theories of ideologues to assume center stage—with catastrophic results. Irreligion has proved more lethal than religion ever was.

2

IN THE LONG RUN

Religion as a Cause of War

Though many wars in human history have been caused mostly by religious differences, many more have been caused by the things that religion, for the most part, keeps in check: greed, pride, revenge, inhuman, godless ideologies and disdain for the well-being of others. That being so, it is not clear that sweeping religious faith aside would be the gateway into a more peaceful world.

Even so, religion hardly has a clean bill of health on this matter; there is a lot of evidence, in history and in the modern world, to which secularists can point an accusing finger. In this chapter, we will look at the variety of conflicts in the human experience, noticing those in which religion is implicated as a principal cause, or at least a significant one, and those that are entirely secular in nature. Of course, the gains of such an exercise are strictly limited. We can hardly attempt to count the various conflicts, weigh one category against another and come to some conclusion as a result. That would be a foolish enterprise.

In the first place, few events, and wars least of all, are monocausal, and that makes it a difficult question how much weight to assign to religious and nonreligious causes in respect of many particular conflicts. Furthermore, even if we could make such measurements, how would we then weigh one conflict against another? How do we compare like with like? If we can all agree that the brief, localized, secular Falklands War, for example, was less appalling than the supposedly religious Thirty Years War (1618-1648), how would one compare two conflicts of broadly similar scale with one another? Do we merely add up body counts? When asking about the frequency of religion as the motivator for violence, do we simply count the numbers of wars? (Do the French Wars of Religion count as nine, because the same basic struggle kept breaking out over three decades, compared with the secular Franco-Prussian War's one?) The stupidity of even asking such questions should put us on our guard and make it clear that our goals in this chapter are necessarily modest. We can do no more than note the fact that some conflicts can be traced to causes in which religious considerations loom large, while in others they have been minimal or irrelevant.

That fact alone, however, is well worth the having. For in recounting the different kinds of conflict, we can begin to get some idea of what we mean by religion as a cause of war and can remind ourselves of the frequency of other, more mundane factors in provoking violence.

PAX ROMANA

The revolts in the classical period of the Jews against their various conquerors would probably count as religious conflict. In the third century B.C., Palestine, like most of the rest of the Middle East, fell under the control of the Greeks. The conquest was motivated by the ambition of the Greek kings and as part of their long-running battle with the Persian Empire rather than by any zeal to spread the worship of the Greek gods. But the revolt of the Jews under Judas Maccabeus against their Greek-Seleucid rulers *was* religiously motivated; Gentile rule of the land that Jews believed had been given to them by God, and the indignities that were being heaped on Jewish religious sensibilities, boiled over into violence. It is significant that Judas Maccabeus was not a prince or a man who might have calculated that a successful revolt would bring him to power; though from a priestly family, he was a relatively ordinary person whose rebellion sprang from religious zeal rather than from any hope of personal gain. Those who followed him did so on the same basis. This is a phenomenon that recurs in other contexts: military movements whose inspiration is genuinely religious tend to garner support from below and in terms of conventional military resources are frequently inferior to the infidels they choose to attack. What they lack in hardware and even in political astuteness they make up for in determination and in willingness to suffer death.

More than a century later, the pattern began to repeat itself when the Romans conquered the Holy Land in the later part of the first century B.C. In contrast to most of the other provinces of the empire, where rebellion was more likely to come from overly ambitious Roman army officers than from disaffected locals, Palestine constantly seethed with religiously motivated resentment against foreign rule. The plotting of the Jewish Zealot party; the fear or hope of a messianic leader who would free God's people from the heel of the ungodly; the detestation of collaborators such as the Herods; and the more mundane irritation of ordinary people at having to go to their home cities to be registered, or to carry the packs of Roman soldiers for a mile or to pay taxes to Caesar all form the background to the Gospel narratives. When it comes to the issue of the identity of Jesus (Is he a potential warrior-messiah? Is that what "king of the Jews" means?), the violent politics of Palestine are not mere background to the Gospels; they are the central thread of the story. In that context, it is significant for later parts of our argument that Jesus refused to validate religiously motivated violence. He would not be the military rebel leader against the Romans that so many wished for. It was the combination of outraged disappointment (by many Jews) that he was not such a leader and the nervous fear (by the Romans and their highly placed Jewish collaborators) that he might be, paradoxically, that sealed the determination of both parties to have him crucified. Zealots (the religious war party) and Romans and Herodians (the superpower and their secularist allies) wished one another dead, so they compromised by executing Jesus. If that fact is not a parallel for the present moment, then I do not know what is! Christianity is everywhere embattled today, and as often as not it is caught in the crossfire between Western secularists and Islamists or supporters of Hindutva. To the Western secularist establishment, Christians are either beneath notice, as in Iraq and the Middle East, in Sudan and the Sahel, or else to be subject to disingenuous analogies with dangerously violent Islamists, as if undifferentiated "religion" is what is threatening the peace or generating "intolerance." To Islamist (and, in India, Hindu) radicals, Christians are agents of Westernity, contaminating Iraq, Egypt, Pakistan or India.[1] Opposition to Christianity is, it seems, the only thing that these contradictory forces are agreed on—each side insisting that Christian faith is a manifestation of the other against which it is fighting.

But if, in first-century Palestine, killing Jesus enabled the Romans and the Herodian party to squeak past without a rebellion for a while, popular religious fury nevertheless erupted in full force a generation later. In 66, the first Jewish War broke out, overwhelming the local Roman forces. Eventually, however, and with grinding inevitability, the Romans brought a full-sized army to bear on the rebels, who could never replace their losses by drawing on such vast resources as the empire had available. The Romans could see quite clearly that it was religion that had motivated the revolt; that was why, when they recaptured Jerusalem in 70, the second temple was destroyed. A band of diehards continued the struggle for a further three years at the staggeringly intimidating desert fortress of Masada. Finally, the defenders chose death by mass suicide rather than surrender.

With the war over, the Romans hoped that the destruction of the temple in Jerusalem would remove the focus of Jewish religious aspirations, thereby punishing the rebels and dashing their hopes for any future revolt. The brutal calculation was rational enough and worked for two generations. But it was inadequate to squelch Jewish fervor on a permanent basis. In 132, many Zealots rebelled again under the leadership of Shimon Bar-Kokhba. Significantly, he reawakened the hopes of many—hopes that Jesus had failed to fulfill—by claiming to be the warlike messiah who would throw out the Romans and re-establish a Jewish kingdom. Militarily, however, the three-year uprising was as foredoomed and bloody as its predecessor. In 135, concluding that the mere destruction of the temple sixty-five years previously had been insufficient, Hadrian had the entirety of Jerusalem leveled and re-established as a Gentile city, with no Jew permitted to enter it.

What are we to make of these revolts? On one side, at least, it was outraged religious sensibility that had exploded into insurrection. And that fact alone meant that religion was central to each of these wars. In each case, the irreligious side, or at least the side motivated by mundane considerations, was stronger. So, was the faith of the Jews responsible for generating the conflicts? Or does responsibility lie with the scornful attitude of the Greeks and Romans toward it and their consequent refusal to take its demands seriously in their own quest for universal domination? Furthermore, if we change the names of the participants, is it not evident that precisely these questions remain pertinent today, as the West, like the Romans of old, gets embroiled with various of the societies that it dominates—most notably Islam, but also other societies with strong attachments to their traditional cultures and religions?

The Romans' annihilation of the Druids of Anglesey in North Wales, in 60, might also be considered a religiously motivated conflict. The island was the center of Celtic Druidic paganism in Britain, and though, unlike that of the Jews, the Celtic culture was not dominated and defined by religion, its priests were nevertheless the principal force in galvanizing native resistance to Roman rule. The historian Tacitus, writing almost fifty years later, records the battle on the Menai Straits:

> By the shore stood an opposing battle-line, thick with men and weapons, women running between them, like the Furies in their funereal clothes, their hair flowing, carrying torches; and Druids among them, pouring out frightful curses with their hands raised high to the heavens, our soldiers being so scared by the unfamiliar sight that their limbs were paralyzed, and they stood motionless and exposed to be wounded.[2]

Despite being somewhat unnerved, the Romans won the battle and proceeded to massacre men, women and children and to destroy their enemies' groves of sacred oaks. The decision to inflict such savagery on the defeated derived, in a sense, from religious considerations, though not because any zeal for the scarcely-believed-in Roman gods made them want to destroy the native religions of all the peoples whom they conquered. On the contrary, their empire was religiously highly pluralist. But the Romans recognized that religiously motivated enemies, such as the Druids, were implacable, and so their recourse was to extirpate them. Alas, the calculation makes a certain degree of military sense. (One might make the same judgment about *mujaheddin* today.) Who or what is to blame for the massacre? The religion of the vanquished? The aggressive, imperialist secularism of the victors? Or the impersonal, cold logic of military-political calculation?

Christians Against Christians

From the fourth century onward, when Christianity was embraced first by the kingdom of Armenia after 303, and later by the Roman Empire, the Christian churches and their leaders have played a full share in supporting or even generating violence. In the early Middle Ages, Christian faith was often invoked to support the military or political claims of the various barbarian kings. When kingdoms were Christianized, as all of Europe had been by the fourteenth century at the latest, force was an almost invariable accompaniment. Clovis the Frank, Ethelbert of Kent, the kings of Northumbria, Stephen of Hungary and Volodymyr of Kievan Rus' all made Christianity an instrument of state and, generally after they had initially hesitated about embracing the new faith, went on to exact the obedience of their subjects to it at the point of a sword.[3]

Later in the Middle Ages, however, Christendom found itself threatened from without by the new and rising power of Islam. We shall consider the principal Christian counterattack, which we have come to know as the Crusades, in the next chapter.

As well as the Crusades proper, however, religion played a similarly baleful role in other conflicts that have been labeled as Crusades. The Albigensian Crusade (1209-1229) was directed against Cathar heretics in southern France. This dualist religion had put down deep roots in the poorly governed region, where even many of the nobility had become adherents. When a papal legate was murdered there by agents of Raymond VI, count of Toulouse, the French king determined on re-establishing royal authority. He had papal backing. The Albigensian Crusade crushed Provençal civilization and saw much of the land of southern France expropriated from its hereditary owners and given to the northern French knights who had participated in the crusade. The Inquisition was established in 1233 under the new order of Dominicans for the express purpose of finally extirpating remaining Cathars. By 1250, when Rainier Sacchoni, a former Cathar turned inquisitor, produced his manual to help the Inquisitors in their work, he estimated that there were only about four thousand left.

In this religious conflict, as with the Crusades for the Holy Land, secular motives are all too apparent. Secular historians today are torn between the desire to emphasize these (for secularists are often incredulous that the people of former times genuinely could have been motivated by religious faith) and the desire to use the conflicts as a stick with which to beat religion, though the sting of such a line of attack demands that the participants be allowed to have been sincere. The latter desire is particularly strong in respect of the Albigensian Crusade, since not only were the Cathars the losers and therefore, on the scale of values of today's victim culture, ipso facto in the right and peace-loving, but also the beliefs of the heretics run close to contemporary New Age thinking and current fascination with the esoteric. The temptation to write the history as a confrontation between good Catharism and intolerant Christianity is irresistible. Indeed, a flood of books on this previously little-studied (little-studied, that is, in the English-speaking world) crusade has been published over the past decade and a half and shows no sign of abating.[4]

The Northern Crusades were another series of conflicts that, as the name suggests, were conducted as a religious campaign for forcible christianization. The field of conquest was the Baltic region of northeastern Europe during the late twelfth, thirteenth and fourteenth centuries. The pagan areas of Europe had, one by one during the early Middle Ages, formally embraced Christianity. By the twelfth century, only the eastern end of the Baltic remained outside of Christendom; the Northern Crusades were a series of brutal military campaigns of incorporation, in the name of Christian faith, conducted against the Prussians, Lithuanians and other Baltic peoples. One recent historian has commented that even there "religion *per se* was not the most significant cause of the wars between the Christians and pagans along the Vistula River"; more important were the persistence of pagan Prussian raids to capture and enslave Christians and the desire of Polish and German Christian lords to extend their territories. Once the conflicts were underway, then "religion became important later, of course, for all parties."[5]

Candidates for admission as knight-brothers to the Order of the Teutonic Knights—the vanguard of the Northern Crusades—promised "chastity, renunciation of property, and obedience, to God and to the Blessed Virgin Mary," as well as submission to the master of the order, unto death. Monastic discipline was practiced, even as each Teutonic Knight readied himself for battle. "He was expected to kill, intimidate, and govern" and "believed that he was advancing Christianity thereby." Even so, his native auxiliaries were "drawn to the same cause for purely secular reasons," such as opportunities for land grabbing, rape and plunder.[6]

While crusading made progress in northeastern Europe, it was proceeding also at the far end of the continent in the form of the *reconquista,* the gradual expulsion of the Muslim rulers, along with the forced conversion, expulsion or suppression of the Islamized sections of the population from Spain and Portugal. In 1063 and again in 1072, Pope Alexander II (1061-1073) issued indulgences—a full generation before Urban II did so for the crusades to the Holy Land—to those who undertook to fight the Muslims in Spain and Sicily.[7]

To say that the habit, in the past two centuries, of calling evangelistic campaigns "crusades" has been unfortunate is, therefore, a gross understatement of the case. The actual crusades were a bloody catastrophe and an utter distortion of genuine Christianity. They spread murder and mayhem and conflated conquest with conversion. To associate modern evangelistic preaching with them is to hang an albatross around the evangelist's neck before so much as the first Bible text has been read aloud.

THE INFERNO: PROTESTANT HERETICS AND THE CATHOLIC ANTICHRIST

The sixteenth-century Reformation ushered in a period of intra-Christian wars that did not subside until the mid-seventeenth century. Martin Luther made his initial protest in the fall of 1517 against what he perceived to be the religious, financial and moral abuses, as well as the doctrinal errors, of the Catholic church. During the mid-1520s, several German states began to embrace his ideas and to impose them on their populations. As the war of words deepened, Luther did not hesitate to insist that the pope was Antichrist—an idea that quickly became axiomatic among Protestants and remained so among at least some of them until fairly recent times.

By the late 1520s, military confrontations were taking place across the new religious divide. One leading Protestant Reformer, Huldrych Zwingli, was killed with sword in hand at the Battle of Kappel in 1531, fighting for the Reformed faith of the city of Zürich against an alliance of Catholic Swiss cantons that intended to re-Catholicize it by force of arms.

The Holy Roman Empire, that ramshackle collection of quasi-autonomous principalities, dukedoms and city-states that together made up what nevertheless amounted to Europe's most important political entity, was divided down the middle along the new confessional lines, with states rapidly forming rival alliances. The Protestant Schmalkaldic League formed first, in 1531. In 1546 and 1547, it came into military collision with the Catholic emperor, Charles V, who was determined to restore the religious unity of his realms. The emperor came off best, and the Protestants had to lick their wounds. But after a fresh bout of fighting in the 1550s, they returned to restore something closer to the previous precarious balance of power.

The Peace of Augsburg of 1555 staved off religious warfare inside the empire for sixty-three years, though there were several close calls. But Protestant-Catholic wars continued elsewhere unabated. The Dutch revolt against Spanish rule in the Netherlands was motivated, to no small degree, by religious concerns; the Reformed were the spearhead of the rebellion against the determination of Philip II of Spain to impose stern, Counter-Reformation Catholicism on his Dutch subjects. The revolt dragged on from 1566 until 1648, with a twelve-year truce from 1609 to 1621, causing immense suffering and destruction. Apart from his troubles in the Low Countries, Philip II was also engaged in fighting the Protestant heretics of England, sending an armada into the English Channel in the cause of re-Catholicizing the country. After that failed, he sent troops to help the Catholic Irish rebels against English rule.

Worst of all, during the late sixteenth century were the bitter civil wars in France that lasted sporadically from 1562 to 1598 and saw the attempt by the French Reformed to secure the elevation of a Calvinist prince to the throne, and hence the Protestantization of France. These wars were frequently savage and the occasions of massacre of one side by the other. Most notorious was the St. Bartholomew's Day Massacre of 1572, in which at least three thousand Parisian Protestants were killed by their Catholic fellow citizens, and a similar number were slain out in the provinces. A survivor, Maximilien de Béthune, Duke of Sully, recalled in old age a Catholic informant telling him that "the order was to kill every one down to babies at the breast."

But even these horrors were to be outdone by the sheer scale of killing during the first half of the following century. The Thirty Years War, from 1618 to 1648, was fought between the German states adhering to the Protestant Union and the forces of the emperor and the Catholic

League. The conflict devastated central Europe, killed a higher proportion of Germans than were to perish during World War II, and reduced the population of the Czech lands (Bohemia and Moravia) by 50 percent and those of many other districts by lesser, though still shocking, amounts. It took all the rest of the century for Germany and Central Europe to recover from the demographic effects alone. In 1631, two-thirds of the thirty thousand inhabitants of Magdeburg were slaughtered wholesale by the imperial soldiers, who did not shrink from locking and then burning down a church filled with terrified women; later that same year, the army of Gustavus Adolphus, the king of Sweden who had intervened on behalf of his Protestant co-religionists, had its revenge by inflicting similar savagery on the helpless peasantry of the Rhineland and Bavaria.

Though various outside powers became embroiled in the war on the Protestant side such that the emperor Ferdinand began to search for a peace agreement, he was warned against it by successive popes, Urban VIII (1623-1644) and Innocent X (1644-1655), who insisted that no compromise or agreement was possible with heretics.

There was the problem. The very existence of Protestant heresy, let alone its expansion, seemed to threaten the undoing of the Catholic *corpus christianum,* Western Christendom and its civilization, and to mislead millions of souls into hellfire. Far from coincidentally, it also threatened the power of the pope. This it did, obviously, by causing some monarchs to break away from the church of Rome. Less obviously, but no less surely, the existence of Protestantism left even those rulers who remained faithful to Rome in a position to do so on their own terms—in sharp contrast to the Middle Ages when, for the most part, the church had been stronger than the state and so the pope stronger than the monarchs.

On the other side of the equation, the Catholic attempt to roll back the Reformation portended the destruction of Protestant culture, including its business and commercial ethic, in those lands where it had swiftly put down strong roots (many of the German states, England, the Netherlands) and its replacement by the new brand of inquisitorial, austere, Counter-Reformation Catholicism.

Both sides, then, were desperately fearful for the future, with a tendency to view one another as evil incarnate. And although what we have described here, even seen as a quick outline of a vast subject, is not the whole picture; as we shall notice in later chapters, it nevertheless remains true to say that the traditional description of these conflicts as wars of religion is by no means a distortion—it is the ugly truth.

Religion of No Account

Finally, it is worth remembering that despite the catalog of religiously motivated conflicts we have just been reciting, most wars, even before the rise of the twentieth century's secularist creeds, owed little or nothing to religious causation. We shall do little more than note some of the more important of these here, without extensive elucidation, since that would carry us away from the central questions of this book. But the mere brevity of space those hostilities occupy in this chapter should not lull us into thinking that nonreligious wars have been a minority species in the human experience of armed conflict: quite the opposite.

The invasions conducted by the empires of antiquity against neighboring states sprang, in general, from mundane motives: booty, desire for expansion of the state, martial glory and a kind of telescoping logic whereby each fresh expansion was deemed necessary in order to safeguard the previous conquest. Alexander the Great's vast empire was conquered during the 320s B.C. largely for its own sake. At the outset, he seized on the military reversals inflicted on the Persians as an opportunity to press home the advantage. Alexander took the battle into the heart of the Persian Empire and then, when that had been overcome, he pressed on further into Asia, turning back only when he ran out of resources. In the process, perhaps two hundred thousand men were killed in battle, and a quarter of a million civilians in cities were massacred.[8] The oft-repeated saying that

Alexander wept that there were no more worlds to conquer may be a fabrication of the poet Milton, but it reflects a sound insight: the conquests were for their own sake and for the glory of the conqueror.

In the case of the Romans, the early battles, those against the Latin and Etruscan tribes for control of the Italian peninsula, were at least partly a struggle for security against rivals who, the Roman leaders believed, could never be trusted as allies. The wars of expansion beyond that point—that is, from around the mid-third century B.C. onward—were, as one historian has noted, "because of the force of events and the logic of [Rome's] own temperament"; neighboring powers, such as the Carthaginians, were "ambitious, and their neighbors were afraid: threats to Rome's allies were threats to her, and, speaking generally, she went to war to remove those threats."[9] The struggles between Rome and Carthage were, as those earlier wars between the Persians and the Greeks (or, much later, in the eighteenth century, between the British and the French), struggles for imperial ascendancy, or "sheer greed," as the historian Michael Crawford puts it.[10]

The civilizations of antiquity were legitimized by the gods whom they sponsored, or rather, as they would have insisted, who sponsored them. (In the same way, the "gods of the nations" [2 Kings 19:12; 1 Chron 16:26] were seen by the peoples of the ancient Near East as their protectors, or at least as protectors of the lands they inhabited.) But neither the Persians nor the Greeks nor the Romans fought either to protect or to advance the worship of their gods. The clashes between empires were, in that sense, entirely secular and mundane.

In the same way, the wave after wave of barbarian invasions that swept across Europe and, in the case of the Mongols, Asia and the Middle East also for three quarters of a millennium after the early fifth century, were not in any sense driven by religion. The Goths, Huns, Avars, Franks, Anglo-Saxons and Slavs invaded the Roman Empire in pursuit of land and livestock, not in any attempt to impose or to defend their gods. The centuries of virtual lawlessness that those invasions ushered in, with each king making war on his neighbors until the myriad of little kingdoms had shaken down into the smaller number of larger entities that dominated the central and late Middle Ages: these were naked plays for power by rulers whose status differed little from that of tribal chieftain.

The Viking conquests began as mere raids for booty on the settled coastlands of eastern England, Scotland, Ireland and northern France. But they turned into campaigns of conquest and, in Iceland, Greenland and "Vinland," of exploration and settlement. Although the Norsemen were motivated to ferocity by their gods, however, their motives were hardly religious.

Worst of all these invasions were those of the Mongols, who swept all before them militarily and often exacted a fearful slaughter on the populations they had overrun. The population of China may have fallen by as much as 50 percent during the early thirteenth century, in direct consequence of Genghis Khan's campaigns. It is believed that more than 1.5 million were slaughtered in the capture of Herat. In the same way, the later campaigns of Timur Leng (or Tamurlane, c. 1336-1405), during the late fourteenth century, spilled an ocean of blood, with millions killed in India alone during 1398. Further north and west, between 70,000 and 100,000 were massacred at Isfahan, while in Baghdad 70,000 people were beheaded so that towers could be built from their skulls. Although a Muslim, Timur Leng made little distinction between co-religionists and infidels in his various attacks and the cruelties that followed them.

In Europe, the wars of the late Middle Ages were generally contests over possession of feudal property. The Hundred Years War (1337-1453), fought over the French provinces that had, as a result of dynastic marriages over the previous two and a half centuries, come into the possession of the kings of England, is a major case in point. Perhaps 180,000 soldiers died, but the larger loss was among French civilians; estimates vary, but these may have run to two or three million.

The numerous wars of the eighteenth century between British, French, Spanish, Dutch and Portuguese owed nothing to religious concerns, even if propagandists on all sides were not above invoking the conflicts of the Reformation era (where the enemy was of a different religious complexion) in order to galvanize popular support. And even this leaves out of account the fighting conducted against Asian, African, American and Pacific natives in the process of establishing empires so enormous that, by 1900, they constituted the majority of the world's surface and controlled the majority of its population.

The American Revolutionary War would also have to count as a secular conflict, even if religious apologists, especially on the Revolutionary side, liked to wrap it in Christian garb. But the fact that biblical arguments were trotted out on both sides and that most denominations—even the Presbyterians to a small extent—were at least somewhat divided between patriots and loyalists illustrates all too clearly that the real causes are to be found elsewhere: in British interference and mismanagement and the public reaction these provoked; in taxation policies; and in the opportunities offered to certain business sectors in the colonies by slackening or loosening the ties with the crown.

The Napoleonic Wars (1792-1815) brought a far more fearful death toll: probably three million soldiers and a further million civilians, though some estimates are higher.[11] These conflicts may count as the first to be fought over modern, secularist ideologies, even if Napoleon's (1769-1821) hijacking of the revolution in 1799 and his creation of the empire in 1804 make it a less clear-cut case. Despite Napoleon's compromising of the original revolutionary ideals, the occupation by France of most of continental Europe during the period served to spread the creed of nationalism far and wide. This new ideology went on to dominate the politics and so, in turn, the wars of the nineteenth century.

In sum, only a small proportion of the deadliest conflicts in human history can be traced principally to religious causation. Primarily, religion was important as a cause of war during two distinct periods of time. In the Middle Ages, it was a significant factor in confrontations between Muslim and Christian powers. Even then, faith was more often invoked in support of causes that really originated in mundane matters than it was a genuine casus belli. But religion became especially prominent as a cause of war between Catholic and Protestant states during the sixteenth and the first half of the seventeenth centuries. And, for reasons we shall explore, it has again become a root cause of many conflicts quite recently. If those are the brute facts of the balance sheet, then we shall need to look a little more closely at the fine print behind those large figures.

3

ISLAM AND THE ABODE OF WAR

Although much of the history of the Christian churches is disgraceful in that their creeds have often been stained by bloodshed and spread by violence, the churches did not begin that way. For the first three centuries of its life, the faith of the Prince of Peace was spread entirely by pacific means, usually in the face of violent persecution.

The Beginnings of Islam

Islam, by contrast, was from the beginning propagated by military conquest, or *jihad*. "There can be no doubt," insist the Islam scholars Riddell and Cotterell, "that Islam was cradled in violence, and that Muhammad himself, through the twenty-six or twenty-seven raids in which he personally participated, came to serve for some Muslims as a role model for violence."[1] At the heart of that violence lay the notion of the religious duty of *jihad*. Although this term has often been interpreted by genuine Muslim moderates and by a wide range of apologists for Islam as a way of denoting a more generalized or even spiritual struggle for the true faith, Bernard Lewis, the Jewish scholar and doyen of historians of the Middle East, notes that the far more usual understanding of *jihad* by Muslims has been simply military.

> The overwhelming majority of early authorities, citing the relevant passages in the Qur'an, the commentaries, and the traditions of the Prophet, discuss jihad in military terms. . . . Jihad is thus a religious obligation. . . . For most of the fourteen recorded centuries of Muslim history, jihad was most commonly interpreted to mean armed struggle for the defense or advancement of Muslim power.[2]

Lewis points out that the sense of *jihad* being an essentially military activity was so overwhelming, historically, that there are instances "in which the word *jihad* has lost its holiness and retained only its military connotation"—such as the title given by Ali Pasha, the early nineteenth-century westernizing ruler of Egypt, to the new-style war department in his government: it was called the *Diwan al Jihaddiya,* and its minister the *Nazir al Jihaddiya.*[3]

The meteoric rise of the religion founded by Muhammad commenced with his conquest of the city of Mecca at the head of his armed followers. As one historian observes, "a primary activity" of Muhammad's community of followers during his lifetime "was raiding and warfare, as its influence (and, later, conversion to Islam itself) was extended."[4] In his final address, the Prophet told his followers that "I was ordered to fight all men until they say 'There is no God but Allah.'"[5] These are words that have been consciously echoed, in their differing contexts, by figures as varied as Saladin, Ayatollah Khomeini and Osama bin Laden. According to the *hadith* collected by Bukhari in the ninth (Christian) century, Muhammad told his followers that

> the person who participates in [holy battles] in Allah's cause and nothing compels him to do so except belief in Allah and His Apostles, will be recompensed by Allah either with a reward, or booty (if he survives) or will be admitted to Paradise (if he is killed in the battle as a martyr).[6]

Of the Four Rightly Guided Caliphs (i.e., the immediate successors, after his death in 632, to Muhammad as leaders of the *ummah,* or Muslim community), the second, third and fourth—respectively, Umar, Uthman and Ali—were murdered as a result of fighting among fellow Muslims.[7] But even while such infighting was going on, Muslim growth continued with campaigns to subdue the entire Arabian peninsula and impose the new faith on its inhabitants. It is not completely certain, however, that the earliest attacks were motivated by this religious imperative; it is possible to see them instead as being merely raiding of the kind that had always been perpetrated by Arab tribes against one another but that now, being forbidden by their new faith to make war on fellow members of the *ummah*, was directed instead at outsiders.[8] Be that as it may, the attacks were spectacularly successful; within two years of the prophet's death, the peninsula and its borderlands had been brought, by war, within the *dar al Islam*, the realm of peace. Amir 'Amr told the Byzantine emperor Constantine IV in 638: "The earth belongs to Allah; He gives it as an inheritance to those of His servants, who please Him, and it is the success of weapons which reveals His will."[9] Indeed, this was the general view of those earliest generations of Arab conquerors. As the historian Patricia Crone concludes, "Whatever Muhammad may have preached, jihad as the bulk of the Arab tribesmen understood it was Arab imperialism at God's command."[10]

Though some of the Arab Christians were given a tightly circumscribed toleration—and there is evidence that two Monophysite Christian tribes had given military help to Muhammad—polytheists were absolutely obliged to become Muslims: "There was no choice between idolatrous polytheism and Islam. Arabs must be Muslims or die. There was no middle ground, no way of evading the death penalty by payment of taxes."[11]

However, the initial conquests brought the new faith into conflict with the surrounding empires of Byzantium and Sassanid Persia. By 638, Syria, Lebanon and Palestine had been wrested from the former, with Cyprus and Egypt following during 640 and 641. In 655, the Muslims came within an ace of capturing the Byzantine emperor when his main battle fleet, which he was commanding in person, was destroyed by the Arabs. The following year, the conquest of the Persian Empire was completed by the propagators of the new faith.

THE ARAB CONQUESTS

During the remainder of the seventh century, Muslim forces conquered almost the whole of the Middle East, Persia and North Africa, bringing to all of these territories an Islamic rule that would redefine their cultures and societies and give them a character that has endured down to the present time. In 711 and 712, the Muslim Berbers swept through the Iberian peninsula, crossed the Pyrenees and were prevented from overwhelming France and the rest of northern Europe only as a result of defeat in battle at Poitiers (or Châlons) in 732 by Charles Martel. But Spain and Portugal remained under Muslim rule for centuries thereafter. As one historian notes, "The breathtaking scope and speed of early conquests generated . . . floods of European, Turkic, Indian, and African slaves."[12]

The new Muslim rulers distinguished between Arabs and non-Arabs and did not force the latter to convert at the point of a sword, although that did happen on a number of occasions. But the conquests were nevertheless motivated by a desire to convert the *dar al harb* ("sphere of war," i.e., the non-Muslim world) into the *dar al Islam* ("sphere of Islam"). Of course, this terminology can be taken in two ways. It could imply that Islam brings peace, while unbelievers are in a permanent state of war against one another or against the truth of Islam. However, given the fact that war between Muslims is hardly unknown, either in the past or the present, the second reading looks more plausible: that the *dar al harb* is an obligatory sphere of war for Muslims and is destined to be made war on by the faithful until it submits to the faith of Muhammad. The price of peace is submission to Islam.

In the territories that had been newly conquered by the Arabs, a pattern was set up that has persisted to this day: arms were the exclusive preserve of Muslims; governing positions were similarly reserved for them; legal disadvantages were imposed on non-Muslims (their testimony in court was worth less than that of a Muslim; they often had to dress differently; they had to dismount, if on horseback, when approaching a Muslim) and so on. And there were financial penalties for non-Muslims, most notably the poll tax, or *Jizya*:

> Fight those who do not believe in Allah nor the Last Day, nor hold that forbidden which hath been forbidden by Allah and His Messenger, nor acknowledge the Religion of Truth, (even if they are) of the People of the Book, until they pay the Jizya with willing submission, and feel themselves subdued.[13]

All of these, especially in combination, and especially over an extended number of generations, were designed to induce non-Muslims to convert. And conversion was a one-way street; the penalty for Muslims, however nominal or dubious their status as such, who converted away from the faith of Allah was death. Even where governments of Muslim countries today have come under outside pressure to do away with this penalty officially, they can usually rely on local action, even by families, to do the work for them.

It is this that has made Christian missions work among Muslims so incredibly difficult, and Muslim societies as a whole so resistant, relatively speaking, to cultural erosion. The Muslim world is one that can only expand; it cannot contract.

And in the first two centuries of Islam, that expansion was enormous and dramatic. The Arab conquests of the seventh and eighth centuries were undoubtedly motivated, for the most part, by religious fervor to spread the one true faith. Although the same cannot be said of every single territorial advance by a Muslim state ever since, that consideration has certainly played a role.

The great Muslim philosopher Ibn Khaldun, reflecting on this phenomenon in respect of the Berbers who conquered Spain, ventured the general hypothesis that "vast and powerful empires are founded on a religion." This, he suggested, was because military success was necessary to bring empires into existence in the first place, and success was best achieved when "men's hearts are united and coordinated, with the help of God, by participation in a common religion." It was religious fervor, he thought, that made people less competitive with one another, focused their group solidarity on apprehension of "the truth" and gave them "a desire common to all . . . for which they are prepared to die."[14]

It was an interesting theory, and highly plausible. Even so, it is far from having been universally the case that empires come into existence through religion and make their conquests motivated by it, though a number of already-existent empires have attempted to buttress themselves internally through establishing one particular form of religious belief. The Roman Empire was established centuries before it adopted Christianity as its formal religion: indeed, it battled against it for three hundred years. The Byzantine Empire was a mere continuation of the Roman. Neither were the Persian empires established on the basis of religious zeal. In respect of Ibn Khaldun's particular claims, however, the Muslim realms that had resulted from the Arab conquests of the seventh and eighth centuries would seem to bear him out. And in that more limited respect, the details as well as the overall religious linkages he suggests hold up rather well.

Jacques Ellul, one of the greatest French Christian intellectuals of the twentieth century, thought that fighting for Christianity did not begin until the time of Charlemagne and that it was a tactic borrowed from Islam. This is an appealing idea and, for Christians, it would be consoling if it were true.[15] However, kings were justifying their wars in the name of Christianity before the time of Charlemagne (late eighth century) and before the rise of Islam. It is no accident that Constantine, in the fourth century, had viewed the Christian God principally as the god who enabled him to win his battles, though that is not the same thing as saying that his claimed adherence to Christianity caused the wars he fought. Later on, the Frankish king Clovis (reigned 481-511) claimed that his wars of territorial aggrandizement, especially those against the Burgundians and Visigoths, were fought in order to spread Catholic Christianity. "It grieves me," he told his soldiers, "that these Arians should hold a part of Gaul."[16] But if Ellul overstates his case, it remains true to say that Christianity, unlike Islam, did not enshrine violence from the beginning, either in the theory of its foundational documents or in practice. For early Christianity had no equivalent of the Muslim *ummah,* the believers whose life must be expressed as a political entity. Christians saw themselves as "strangers and aliens" in the world; Islam was established with a view to turning the world into the *dar al Islam*. Until that point was reached, however, the infidels' lands were designated the *dar al harb,* the abode of war.

THE ERA OF CRUSADES

Despite what is frequently claimed for Islam in the present, whether by Muslim apologists or by Westerners who wish to damn Christianity, some medieval Muslims saw their faith as legitimizing holy violence in a sense that Christianity did not. When the thirteenth-century writer al-Qarafi criticized the Crusaders and defended Islam, he chose a line of attack that few would expect nowadays. By engaging in violence for their faith, he contended, the Christians were contradicting the central tenets of the Gospels, which prescribe peace, whereas such behavior would be more appropriate for Muslims, because the Qur'an positively encourages taking up arms against the enemies of God.[17] Few Muslims of the period were so well informed about the Christian Scriptures as to be in a position to level such criticisms. But the same applied to Christians. The French theologian Peter Comestor (c. 1100-c. 1198) rejected the patriarch of Jerusalem's pleas against holy war and implored him to "act in a manly way, be composed, and shed the blood of Christ's enemies."[18]

The Crusades, mounted by the various kingdoms of Catholic[19] Europe against the Muslim occupation of the Holy Land, are the most famous or notorious example of religiously motivated warfare. Time and again, they are trotted out as the classic example of religious bigotry and the massive bloodshed to which it leads. The study of these conflicts has an assured place in the curricula of secular schools, whose textbooks (in Europe, at least) now have to satisfy the demands of growing numbers of Muslim parents, as well as of the secularist educational establishment, both of whom share a common interest in vilifying Europe's Christian past. The recent film *Kingdom of Heaven*, which was set in the years immediately prior to the Third Crusade, portrayed every cleric as a sort of pantomime demon. But, despite the film's railing against religious fanatics and other outbursts that owed everything to postmodern sensibilities and nothing to the likely speeches of people in the twelfth century, even Hollywood recognized that the motivations for the participants in the Crusades were frequently mundane—prospects for plunder, local politics and bids for power by leading individuals—with religion as a sort of rhetorical veneer to give plausibility and justification for the otherwise unjustifiable.

All of this said, however, it is abundantly clear that the Christian record in these conflicts is bad enough. The capture of Jerusalem in 1099, during the First Crusade, was marked by a general massacre of the city's Muslim and Jewish inhabitants. One of the participants recorded that

> the horses waded in blood up to their knees, nay up to the bridle. It was a just and wonderful judgment of God that the same place should receive the blood of those whose blasphemies it had so long carried up to God. . . . O new day, new day and exultation, new and everlasting gladness. . . . That day, famed through all centuries to come, turned all our sufferings and hardships into joy and exultation; that day, the confirmation of Christianity, the annihilation of paganism, the renewal of our faith![20]

The day is indeed "famed through all centuries to come," though the evaluation of the events by the people—Muslim, secular and even Christian—of subsequent ages is not exactly what the chronicler supposed they might be. No one, it might safely be said, now looks on them with anything but revulsion. Whatever could have possessed the perpetrators to see them differently?

The Holy Land had remained accessible to Christian pilgrims even after the original Muslim invasions of the seventh century. But when it subsequently fell under the control of later Muslim invaders (an event that illustrates the frequent willingness of Muslims to fight one another, in spite of theoretical prohibitions), Palestine was closed to Christian visitors.[21] This provocation is often seen as one of the causes of the Crusades, but almost no major conflicts are monocausal, and in this case also several other factors were involved. In the first place, the Saracens were encroaching on the eastern borders of the Byzantine Empire. Bernard Lewis describes the Crusades as an "ultimately unsuccessful series of counterattacks" in the face of relentless Muslim advance into Christian space.[22] Furthermore, although the Byzantine and Roman churches had drifted into schism, at least formally, from 1054, hopes for reconciliation lingered; the pope calculated, with good reason, that rescuing the ailing Eastern empire from the infidels might facilitate a healing of the breach—on Western terms. The papacy had recently emerged from a period of internal reform and was recovering its power on the European stage; a papal call to arms would emphasize the pontiff's leadership of the Catholic world.

All of these elements are, in a sense, religious. And yet, in each case, religious zeal is eclipsed by institutional wrangling for power and leverage. So what is primary? The religion, as motivator of the various institutions involved? Or the institutions and their leaders who, by the nature of the case, wrestle eternally for power vis-à-vis one another, and for whom religion is a mere instrument in that endless conflict?

Such questions are almost unanswerable, since the political institutions and the religious beliefs of the Middle Ages, as with other periods, are, for all practical purposes, inextricable. But let us think the unthinkable: let us imagine the Catholicism of the West, the Orthodoxy of Byzantium and the Islam of the Saracens out of existence. Would West and East still have come into conflict? And the answer, obviously, is yes. Those conflicts would have been framed in somewhat different terms and have taken different forms. But the collision would have happened anyway. Conflict in the zone between modern Turkey and Iran had been perpetual since long before the time of Christ. It had been there between the Greeks and the Persians. Then, when Greece had been included in the Roman

Empire, the conflict had become one between the Roman and Persian empires. After that, when the western Roman Empire collapsed in the fifth century, the recurrent fighting had become a contest between Byzantines (that is, the eastern Roman Empire) and Persians. Then, following the collapse of the latter to Muslim invasions in the seventh century, the wars in the same zone—eastern Anatolia, northern Syria, Lebanon—were fought between the Byzantines and the Abbasids. During the crusading period, the participants shifted again. And, even centuries after it was all over and the Turks were firmly in possession of Asia Minor, the wars continued in the lands south of the Caucasus down to the Levant, but this time between Ottomans and Persians. During these conflicts, religions changed several times over. In the early phases of the Roman-Persian wars, the Persians harbored Christians, while the Romans persecuted them. Later, when the Roman Empire promoted Christianity during the fourth century, the Persians reversed themselves and began to persecute Christians as a potential fifth column for the Romans.

From all of this, it should be clear that religion was, in a certain sense, beside the point in respect of these conflicts, however loudly it was proclaimed as the casus belli by the various antagonists. Any religion or none would still leave the northern Middle East a dangerous border zone, prone to conflict between empires. As Aziz Atiya, the Arab historian, has argued, the Crusades were part of a pattern of behavior that goes "far back into antiquity. . . . The bone of contention was the undefined frontier of Europe, otherwise described as the spiritual frontiers of the West vis-à-vis Asia." Edward Said thought that this boundary "already seems bold by the time of the *Iliad*."[23] Not exactly bold, perhaps; the frontier has always been fuzzy, leaving linguistic, religious and ethnic minorities strung out along the areas contested by invading armies over millennia. But at least it was well-entrenched.

None of this exculpates religious institutions or religious people from the ghastly consequences of the Crusades. If crime levels are high in a particular neighborhood today, then that fact does not excuse the individual criminal for his actions, as if there were some inevitability about them. For actions are freely chosen by their participants; we are not automata at the mercy of blind impersonal forces, even if we like to excuse ourselves by claiming that we are. In the same way, if the northern Middle East had for long been a flashpoint between cultures to the region's east and west, that is hardly a justification for declaring war in the name of Christianity. And if mundane considerations played an important part in the minds of the Crusaders, religious zeal was nevertheless the most important motivation for many, and for some it appears to have been the only motivation. The military leaders even of the Fourth Crusade, which never reached the Holy Land but satisfied itself with sacking Constantinople, the center of Eastern Orthodoxy, claimed at the outset of their enterprise that they had "taken the sign of the cross to avenge the shame done to Jesus Christ and to reconquer Jerusalem." The pope, Innocent III (1198-1216), had already promised that "all who take the cross and serve in the host for one year, would be delivered from all the sins they had committed, and acknowledged in confession."[24] This was a lower offer (just one year's service) than that offered by his predecessor of a century before, Urban II (1088-1099), who had called for the First Crusade at the Council of Clermont in 1095: "If anyone who sets out should lose his life either on the way, by land or by sea, or in battle against the infidels, his sins shall be pardoned from that moment."[25] And how many people did lose their lives in the Crusades for the Holy Land? Estimates vary wildly, but a total of 1.5 million, on all sides, is perhaps not too far from the truth.[26]

4

WHERE RELIGION PLAYS AN AMBIGUOUS ROLE

Many wars in which religion seems to be the cause of the problem turn out, on closer inspection, to be more ambiguous in their origins. For, as we have noted, religion was and is often used as a morally convenient cloak for nationalism, human greed or other mundane motives. This, it must be said, is a cloak that religious leaders have frequently been more than willing to lend.

In 2004, for example, Fyodor Ushakov, the highly successful late-eighteenth-century admiral of the Russian fleet, was canonized as a saint by the Russian Orthodox Church. In September of the following year, Patriarch Alexei II carried a reliquary and an icon of the sainted admiral into the chapel of the Air Force's Thirty-seventh Air Army, where he was designated patron saint of the country's nuclear-armed, long-distance bombers. "I am sure he will become your intermediary as you fulfill your responsible duties to the fatherland in the long-range air force," the patriarch said. "His strong faith helped Saint Fyodor Ushakov in all his battles."[1]

If Russia ever uses this Air Army and its weapons of mass destruction, would the survivors (presumably on a Pacific island somewhere) be safe in concluding that Russian Orthodoxy and faith in Saint Fyodor had made the development thinkable? It would be an improbable conclusion. Russia's nuclear capacity and the willingness to use it date from the era of the Soviet Union. All of the fundamental realities that might make a Russian nuclear strike, however unlikely in practice, at least possible in theory are Soviet. Only the justifying rhetoric has changed since the period of the Cold War, from the proclamation of atheistic, scientific materialism and the worldwide cause of the working class to the defense of holy Mother Russia. Significantly, that rhetoric is as much nationalist as it is Orthodox Christian; it is, in every sense, *Russian* Orthodox.

In the previous chapter, we considered the clear-cut, historical cases of religiously caused warfare, or, at least, those that have the reputation of being clear-cut. The Crusades, we might say, were called by the pope because "God willed it"; the Hundred Years War was about feudal rights to land.

Here, however, we shall look at a small sample of major conflicts that do not obviously fit into either category and whose origins must be found in a mixture of causes. This will enable us to see how, in practice, religious and nonreligious factors interact in political affairs, as these relate to warfare.

THE ADVANCE AND RETREAT OF THE OTTOMAN TURKS

From the fourteenth century onward, the Ottoman Turks progressively invaded southeastern Europe until by the early sixteenth century they were within striking distance of Vienna, the heart of Christendom. They twice besieged that city: in 1529 and again in 1683. The wars between the Ottoman Empire and the states of Christian Europe are scattered over almost six centuries, down to World War I. The thing to note is that although there was an almost unavoidable religious element in that long series of confrontations, yet the struggle was partly a simple case of imperial expansion and, after about 1690, of imperial contraction.

The empire was undoubtedly Islamic. Its ruler was the sultan. Muslims held a privileged position within his realms, and they alone could bear arms. Islamic law held a higher place than the limited jurisdiction given to the patriarch and the chief rabbi. Non-Muslims had to pay a poll tax. Their places of worship had to be lower than any nearby mosque. They had to wear distinctive clothing. And so on.

Yet the Ottoman Empire did not paint its conquests of the infidels as a campaign for Muslim sovereignty. The sultan's armies often consisted in part of Christians, such as the Serbs who fought loyally for Bayezid at the battle of Ankara in 1402, where his Muslim troops deserted him. It was only with the conquest of Mameluke Egypt in 1517 that the Ottoman realms become predominantly Muslim in population.[2] In the years immediately preceding and during the Ottoman conquests, the Balkan Christian princelings had fought one another, with only occasional regard for forming a common front against the Muslims. After the battle of Kosovo Polje in 1389, in which the Serbian prince Lazar was killed, his widow, Milica, made alliance with the Turks against her domestic Christian enemies.[3] When Constantinople was finally besieged in late 1452, the Italian trading cities from whose fellow Christians the Byzantines hoped for help were "too deeply involved in Ottoman trade, too much at daggers drawn themselves" to give aid.[4] Indeed, Christians served in the Ottomans' besieging army. To paint these conflicts as a series of Muslim-Christian battles, then, is too simple; the pattern was more complex than that.

Even so, the threat posed by the incessant expansion of the Ottoman Empire into Europe was perceived in religious terms, at least on the Christian side. Calls went out frequently, even if they were seldom heeded, for Christian unity in the face of the rising Muslim tide. During the crisis of the Reformation in the sixteenth century, Protestant and Catholic pamphleteers took it as axiomatic that the likelihood of imminent invasion by the Turks was the judgment of God on Christendom for its sins, though the Protestants put the blame on the Catholic church for its corruptions, while the Catholics blamed the Protestants for the sin of schism.

Even if fighting for the Ottomans was not necessarily to fight for Islam, yet to oppose the empire was to strike a blow for Christendom. That was the construction placed on the battle of Lepanto in October 1571, when the Holy League—an alliance of Spain, Venice, the pope and the knights of Malta—destroyed the main Turkish fleet, inflicting the loss of thirty thousand men, of whom many, ironically, were Christian galley slaves on Ottoman ships.

The later decline of the Ottoman Empire, from the end of the seventeenth century onward, is equally ambiguous. It can be seen in religious terms, with Christian monarchs, most notably the Austrian emperor, liberating the Christians of the Balkans from infidel rule and then subjecting them to their own. Alternatively, the process can be viewed as normal great power behavior: taking advantage of weakness in order to expand territory by agreement with other great powers or else by coercing or outmaneuvering those others. This was the pattern of behavior that characterized events elsewhere, as in northeastern Europe: in the case of the partitioning of Poland-Lithuania in the late eighteenth century, religious considerations played a negligible part in the process. The Turkish Empire, meanwhile, came under intolerable pressure from the Austro-Hungarian Empire, Russians, British and French; its existence was prolonged until the early twentieth century more by the great powers' fears of one another than by the ability of the Turks to defend their old conquests in the new circumstances. The Austrians and Russians posed as protectors of the Ottomans' Christian subjects, though in reality each was fearful of the influence of the other. In the nineteenth century, even the British played the Christian card in supporting the Orthodox Greek and, later, Bulgarian nationalists against the supposed savage cruelty of their Muslim rulers.

The Christian inhabitants of the empire were divided among themselves over such issues, even though religion was frequently invoked to support or foment violence during the break-up, as well as to dampen violence. Thus, in April 1821, Patriarch Gregorios of Constantinople excommunicated the Greek rebel leaders who were attempting to overthrow Ottoman rule. Likening them to Herod, he declared that they had "sinned with an audacity beyond example, and have sent emissaries to seduce others, and to conduct them to the abyss of perdition."[5] Gregorios was, admittedly, acting under great duress from the authorities in order, as one historian has put it, "to save his powerless and hard-pressed population from being massacred."[6]

Many local priests took a different line. The following year Sir Thomas

Maitland, the governor of the British-held Ionian Islands, told the House of Commons in scandalized tones that

> pastors of religion . . . in defiance of the pure principles of the Holy Gospel, which inculcate universal charity and benevolence, publicly . . . offered up . . . prayers for the destruction of the Ottoman Power, thus blasphemously adding even the voice of religion, to increase an unfortunate irritation.[7]

Indeed, at Naxos, the Orthodox bishop ordered the Turkish prisoners in the town to be shot, denouncing those who demurred as *Turkolatri*, Turk worshipers. He implored a crowd to exterminate the local Latin Christians while they were about it. These had remained aloof from the rebellion; fearful of what their status might be in an Orthodox-dominated state, they flew the French flag from their churches in the hope of Western protection amid the ensuing anarchic violence. Yet, if the bishop at Naxos had behaved badly, his colleague at Athens, Dionysios, behaved well, trying, albeit unsuccessfully, to use his moral and spiritual authority to dissuade his co-religionists from murdering their Turkish captives. Others went further and disowned the rebellion; the Greeks in the early 1820s were bitterly divided among themselves.[8]

For it was the new notion of nationality, rather than religion as such, that was being contended for. The religious conflicts were symptoms of the uncertainties about the terms under which a new nation state might be set up. And yet religion was a vital determinant of what "Greece" meant and would mean. The constitution of 1822 declared in its second chapter that "all the inhabitants of Greece professing the Christian religion are Greeks," which implied that those who did not, were not. While agreeing to religious toleration (for the benign attitude of Britain and the other powers of the West was essential to the enterprise), the bishops' meeting at the Areopagus the previous year had nevertheless affirmed that "the Eastern Church of Christ and the current language only are recognized as the authorized religion and speech of Greece."[9] Religion and language were, if not entirely conflated, then at least closely juxtaposed in defining what it meant to be Greek.

What are we to conclude from this pattern of behavior, extended as it was over so many centuries? It seems safest to conclude that the wars that saw the expansion and then later the contraction to nothing of the Ottoman Empire did bear a religious aspect, but this served as a rallying cry in support of other factors. The Ottomans seldom explained themselves to themselves as embarking primarily on *jihad*. They ruled, engaged and traded with non-Muslims. Yet the Ottomans could see that infidels could never be their natural allies, nor could the *rayah* (Christians and Jews over whom the Ottomans ruled) be reliably loyal subjects. On the other side, the European powers that opposed the Ottomans did not consistently place resistance to the Turks at the top of their own agendas. But, when they did so, they tended to use the defense of Christianity—and later, the rescue of oppressed Christians from the Muslim yoke—as their rationale, though resistance to an expansionist empire needed no rationale; the rationale was a mere play for cementing likely solidarities among those who had the most to lose from further Ottoman conquests.

To dismiss religion from the equation is as ridiculous, therefore, as to insist that religion alone is responsible for the wars that attended the rise, and then fall, of the Ottoman Empire. Religion is inextricable from the cultural, social and political forces that generated the conflicts.

THE IBERIAN CONQUEST OF THE AMERICAS

Outside the Union Station in Washington, D.C., stands the Columbus Monument. Erected in 1912 by a commission that included the U.S. secretaries of State and War as well as other dignitaries, the inscription reads: "To the memory of Christopher Columbus whose high faith and indomitable courage gave to mankind a New World." It may be doubted whether the erection of a monument to European conquest over the Indians or the wording of its inscription ("high faith . . . mankind") would have commanded across-the-board support in today's politically correct climate. But is it true to say that the conquests were motivated by faith?

Certainly, the fervent Catholic Christian identity inspired by the *reconquista,* and lovingly nursed by successive Spanish rulers thereafter, accounts for much of the religious ferocity directed by the Iberians toward the natives of the New World, when Spaniards and Portuguese became the most prominent among the European explorers and settlers there from the end of the fifteenth century onward. (By a grim coincidence, the year 1492 is the date of both Columbus's first voyage across the Atlantic and of the final defeat and extinction of Granada, the last Muslim state in Spain, and the expulsion of Muslims and Jews who would not convert.) The spread of Christianity was used as a justification for the ruthless conquest and subjection of the American Indians, which had such catastrophic results for the population of the New World, even if the worst killer, imported European diseases against which the natives had no natural resistance, was accidental. The Catholicization of the territories that became Latin America was a spin-off of the crusading ideal that had been so prominent in Europe for the preceding four hundred years. It received the sanction of the papacy, which divided the New World into zones of Spanish and Portuguese influence, on the understanding that the natives would be brought into the fold of the one true church.

In the case of the conquest of Latin America, however, the extrication of religious and mundane motives is a little less complex than in the case of the conflicts between Europeans and Ottoman Turks. For one thing, the *conquistadores'* greed and desire for domination appear all too clear, their religious verbiage an all-too-transparent façade covering and justifying their real quest for wealth, especially gold and precious metals. As a Habsburg ambassador commented, looking back on the whole process from the distance of 1555,

> We seek the Indies and the Antipodes over vast fields of ocean, because there the booty and spoil is richer and can be wrung from the

> ignorant and guileless natives without the expenditure of a drop of blood. Religion is the pretext, gold the real object.[10]

This reading of the situation is not inconsistent with that of the Catholic missionaries who followed in the wake of the *conquistadores*. Although the friars' view of the surviving Americans was not always kindly and was all too often tinged with myopia, yet the Franciscans, Dominicans and, later, the Jesuits frequently expressed horror at the treatment meted out by the Spanish and Portuguese conquerors to their hapless subjects. As early as 1511, Father Antonio Montesinos had thunderously denounced in a sermon the "cruel and horrible slavery" visited on the Indians and the "detestable wars" that had "consumed infinite numbers of them with unheard-of murders and desolations." Yet the violence of Cortés, Pizarro and their soldiers was triggered or made permissible to them in their own minds by the paganism and the human sacrifices of the native Americans whom they encountered. Those who practiced such things, the Europeans were able to tell themselves, could hardly be accounted as human. (That the same judgment might, on the same grounds, have been drawn concerning the *conquistadores* does not seem to have occurred to them.)

In that sense, religion did play an important part in the conflict between Iberians and native Americans. Their different outlooks shaped the wall of incomprehension between them. Human sacrifice, polygamy and, in Brazil, nudity: these the conquerors felt a duty to uproot. We, mindful of the Iberians' wickedness, may rightly pillory them for hypocrites. Yet their sincerity on these points, so far as it went, can hardly be faulted. The truth is that even the conquerors, who were hardly specimens of the best type of Christian European, grasped instinctively at religious categories to demonize the Indians. And the latter dignified in religious terms such resistance as they were able to mount at the time of the initial assaults and for later uprisings such as that in the Andes in the 1560s. The terrible wave of deaths among the indigenous population from imported Western diseases were, the survivors came to believe, a punishment from the old gods for embracing Christianity.

Yet it is apparent to any dispassionate judgment that the conflict sprang from mundane motives on both sides—greed (the Europeans) and survival (the Indians)—and that it amounted to a clash of cultures or of civilizations. That both sides sought to justify themselves in religious terms—the universal claims of the Christian God and the jealous regard of the pagan gods—is hardly surprising. In both cases, culture and religion were inextricable. To fight about one was to fight about the other.

The English Civil War

"Religion was not the thing at first contended for," mused Oliver Cromwell, looking back over a distance of more than a decade on the outbreak of fighting in England in 1642, "but God brought it to that issue at last."

When Englishmen had drifted unwillingly, and with a certain sense of absurdity, into battle against one another in the summer of that year, few had any notion or intention of fighting about religion. In their minds, constitutional, legal and fiscal issues were at the heart of the struggle. The king had overstepped the bounds of what he was permitted by the traditional constitution to do. He had marginalized the Privy Council in the government of the realm and, the parliaments of the late 1620s having proved uncooperative, sought to dispense with calling parliaments for eleven years; he had imprisoned without trial (and by leaning on judges) those who had displeased him; he had sought to raise taxes beyond those granted to him by tradition and prerogative, yet without consulting parliament until absolutely constrained by circumstances to do so. Now he was trying to raise an army, ostensibly to put down rebels in Ireland, yet which the political classes feared he might use against themselves.

Despite all of this, as the gentry and burghers of England uncomfortably found themselves forced to make the agonizing choice between loyalty to their sovereign and loyalty to the constitution and liberties of England as they conceived them, the best predictor of their choices was the test of religion. When the sides lined up, the large majority of those who might be described as Puritan were with the Parliament; the overwhelming majority of anti-Puritans were for the king.

How could this be? To be sure, religion had been a cause of furious debate during the decades before the English Civil War, but that was not in itself what either side conceived itself to be fighting for. Not all royalists even approved of the king's high-church Arminianism; still less were they prepared to fight for it. The parliamentarians were already, even at that early stage, fully aware that they were hopelessly divided among themselves as to what kind of church settlement they wanted; given the absence of any kind of unanimity, few saw themselves as going to war over explicitly that issue.[11] And yet the differential religious coloring on either side was as striking to any observer as that between Democrats and Republicans in the United States today.

The best explanation for this curious phenomenon is that religious orientation was bound up with a host of other social and economic phenomena, such that individuals were overwhelmingly likely, when it came to the ticklish matter of fighting the civil war, to choose one side rather than the other.[12] Puritanism had for long appealed strongly to traders and commercial farmers, and these were particularly likely to support parliament.[13] To have internalized the categories of Reformed theology was to prize abstract conceptions of law, which the king was widely held to have abused. Puritanism and its somewhat more egalitarian approaches to organizing parish churches held relatively little appeal to the aristocracy or to traditional landlords and subsistence farmers, and these were most likely to support the strong, traditional hierarchy that was epitomized by monarchy. For them, personal relationship mattered more than the legal fictions that dominated modern trade and Reformed theology alike. On both sides of the divide that was tearing England apart, the thing that incarnated political, social and economic culture turned out, in the end, to be religion.[14]

So, did religion cause the English Civil War of the 1640s and early

1650s? The question evaporates into near meaninglessness, not because it is in any way frivolous or stupid but because every aspect is bound up so completely with every other that the attempt to answer it is to stare down a hall of mirrors. All one can do is what contemporary Englishmen did: to vacillate between, on the one hand, fretting and hand wringing about how they will explain themselves to their posterity for fighting and, on the other, pointing insistently at the concrete events (the illegal imprisonments; the turbulence of the parliament; the Irish rebellion; the fears about raising an army) that had caused them to take up arms. And then, that done, one can join with contemporaries in observing how remarkable it is that the large bulk of the Puritan godly are for the parliament and the overwhelming majority of the anti-Puritans for the king.

The American Civil War

If religion played an undeniable though complex part in the English Civil War, its role in the American Civil War (1861-1865) is more complex still. For the same kind of religious beliefs predominated on both sides of the conflict, and both sides constantly declared themselves justified by reference to it.

"Religion," two recent historians observe, "became the *sine qua non* for the South's defense of slavery."[15] As a Presbyterian minister of Charleston, Ferdinand Jacobs, wrote, "If the Scriptures do not justify slavery, I know not what they do justify."[16] And yet the same could be said for the abolitionists: their arguments were expressed overwhelmingly in religious terms. "Christians can no more take neutral ground on this subject," fumed the evangelist Charles Grandison Finney (1792-1875), "than they can take neutral ground on the subject of the sanctification of the Sabbath. It is a great national sin." When the war was underway, the black chaplain William Hunter claimed that the Union forces were "the armies of the Lord and of Gideon."[17] And, as the popularity of the "Battle Hymn of the Republic" made plain, many white soldiers on the Union side took the same view.

Churches had divided over the issue of slavery, in the two decades before the Civil War, between Northern and Southern states. The Baptists split along these lines in 1844; the Methodists did likewise the same year. Although the Presbyterians were divided over the same issue and eventually sundered into separate denominations over it, they had managed to quarrel over mission boards and degrees of Calvinism, in 1837, with fault lines that were similarly geographical. One may suspect that the theological issues were riding surrogate for the slavery issue, but it is also arguable that all of these issues both reflected and hastened a divergence of cultures between North and South. One modern popular work of historical analysis summarizes the matter well: "Churchmen played leading roles in the moral revolutions that swept North and South in opposite directions. For twenty years before the Civil War the churches shored up cultural positions with theological justifications."[18]

And yet it was those cultural positions, not the religious differences, that caused the conflict. Religious influences, give or take some nuances, had been broadly similar north and south of the Mason-Dixon Line; it was the growing political and cultural gap that had caused Christians on either side to drift apart and to turn the same Christian ideas into different political currents. And even then, they barely succeeded. The result was a war in which the name of God was endlessly invoked on either side, in broadly the same terms and within the same general framework of understanding. As Mark Noll observes, "Faith as such was not a cause of the conflict, but it did provide a network of influences which intensified the political, social, and cultural differences that brought on the strife."[19] Urban and cosmopolitan versus rural and hierarchical; modernist versus traditional and conventional; individualist versus familial; egalitarian versus paternalist and deferential: these were incompatibilities that led to war. The abolitionists' claims for central government over states' rights made it inevitable that the Southerners could defend their peculiar institution only by seceding and that the North would fight to reincorporate them when they did. And yet, as Noll rightly concedes, those differences were exacerbated at every turn, through the generation that led to the war, by religious legitimation of every point—on both sides and by the same religion (much though the recently sundered Methodists and divided Baptists sought to distance themselves from their co-denominationalists on the other side of the line).

As in the English Civil War, culture came clothed in a religion. Unlike that earlier struggle, the conflicting sides of the culture came clothed in the same form of religion, each claiming to be vindicated by it. The American Civil War, as much as and perhaps even more than the English, is a classic example of the interpenetration of a culture and its dominant faith, such that its ideals and its disputes are inevitably expressed in religious language—that is to say, in that culture's most highly valued moral currency. In consequence, even those who suffered so much in the conflagration of 1861 through 1865 did not dream of blaming their downfall or the deaths and injuries of their loved ones on too close an adherence to religious faith. Americans' judgment on how far Christianity was responsible for the outpouring of blood (more than six hundred thousand lives were lost) is shown clearly by the fate of the churches during the decades afterward. The churches, North and South, those among blacks and among whites, continued to grow. Neither did they drift further apart. When decline eventually came, as it did from century's end, it occurred for reasons that had little to do with blame laying for the sufferings of the 1860s.

Religion as Effect, Not Cause

As we have seen with the examples surveyed in this chapter, the tendency for many human cultures to enshrine or to be enshrined by a particular religion or form of faith means that conflicts between human societies will frequently be expressed in religious terms. That is because, by their nature, the claims of faith—in respect of morality, loyalty and meaning—trump those of any other. If I am called on to fight and to risk death, I shall want to know why. If plagued by doubts about the rightness of killing strangers, I shall want assurance. If our side appears to be facing defeat, I shall need motivation for fighting on. And if the usual motivations fail—if my loved ones do not seem to be at risk or their death has put them beyond further harm; if my fear for the homeland is not so great, because our enemies seem little different from ourselves or because my lowly position gives me little to lose—then the command of God or of the gods will supply that missing determination to fight. The culture I know and that has shaped all with which I am familiar has itself been shaped by the faith of that divinity. It is the will of that god, or those gods, that I risk death and kill. The divine presence may turn seeming defeat into victory or give meaning even to the sacrifice of overwhelming defeat. Even after the debacle of 1865, the Confederates could console themselves, at least, with this.

It is considerations such as these that make the resort to religious language irresistible not just for governments and generals but for ordinary people at times of war or of threatened war. And, as the ferocity of the conflict mounts or its duration stretches out, so the reliance on such language may become still greater, as the ever-heightening toll of sacrifice demands ever greater assurance about the meaning of the struggle and that our losses are not in vain. As the intensity of the questions (Why are we fighting? Are we justified? Is the sacrifice worth it?) deepens, so the kinds of justification and assurance that only an appeal to the transcendent can provide become ever more urgent.

That being so, conflict is as likely to intensify religious feeling as the converse. This is not merely theoretical; the English Civil War is one example of just such a phenomenon. So too are the Balkan wars of the 1990s; although Catholic and Orthodox piety were observed to become more pronounced and demonstrative during the period shortly before the break-up of Yugoslavia, this was part of the cultural struggle itself. The levels of religiosity in the late-twentieth-century Balkans became far more significant while the fighting was underway and during the period of shock, anger and grief immediately after it was over. Islam in Bosnia had been almost entirely nominal before the war of 1992-1995, and though the Muslim identity there remains primarily cultural rather than religious, Islamic belief is rather less nominal now; the numbers of pious Muslims have increased as a direct consequence of the struggle. If I am a Bosnian Muslim and people like me are in danger for being Muslims, then I am more likely to be ostentatiously Muslim, if only to make the risk and the suffering in some sense worth it.

In such cases, religious intensity is increased as a direct result of the process of conflict; it was brought in to steel conviction and provide a rationale for quarrels that were primarily related to something else. And, as we have seen, that something else is generally religion's inextricable, concomitant culture.

5

TRIBAL GODS I

The Phenomenon of Religious-National Myths and the Cases of Serbia and Russia

Most modern nationalisms have developed national myths: the projection of ideas and a sense of collective identity onto ancestors who may have experienced nothing of the sort—or at least a drastically diminished and differently nuanced version of that collective consciousness.[1] It is not simply that such collective identity in the past is mythical—though it is—but that modern nationalisms inculcate a belief in some particular specialness of the given nation. Italy is not simply the home of cheap and cheerful cars and of chaotic government; it is the fount of European culture, the inheritor of the mantle of Rome, the source of the Renaissance. Wales is not just postindustrial wasteland with rain-blasted sheep grazing attached; it is the "land of song" and of bards, with Welsh as the language of heaven. Croatia is not merely a rather impecunious part of formerly communist eastern Europe, with a legacy of wretched concrete tower-block housing to prove it; it is the bastion of Western civilization against Eastern barbarism, standing firm even when, in the sixteenth century, it was reduced to "the remains of the remains." And so on. People will fight or die for the myths; no one will be a martyr to Fiat cars, unemployment in the Valleys or evil-smelling stairwells. The myths give us a collective sense of self that is worth living for. And that is hardly to be despised, despite the danger that such myths may lead us, if not carefully channeled, into violence against others who hold countermyths of their own.

Furthermore, most national myths make some appeal to religion, but only a select few make it central to the myth: a religious-national myth. Where this happens, where a claimed religious destiny or mission is made central to the identity of the nation, then the nation has in effect been deified. For its enemies are God's enemies; its purposes are God's purposes. The capacity for self-criticism is eviscerated, since it is identified with blasphemy. External critiques are per se invalid, since they come from outside the supposedly chosen nation. Such grotesque misuses of religious faith can conceal (sometimes, barely conceal) idolatry and collective self-worship. Religious people need to beware of these myths and of the forms of religion that justify them. For, like rebellion, they are "as the sin of witchcraft" (1 Sam 15:23 KJV).

In this chapter and the next, we shall examine three such religious-national myths and allude to a couple of others, noting the ways in which they have exerted their power and contributed to violence and war. We shall look at the cases of Serbia, Russia and England. The first of these remains powerful and widely, even generally, believed in. The second is still a factor in popular consciousness. The last is no longer current but was important from the late sixteenth century until the nineteenth, a period that included Britain's rise to world power status and helped to inform and justify it.

The Heavenly Kingdom

Serbia has been a troubled country in recent years. Serbs had dominated communist Yugoslavia since World War II, notwithstanding the fact that its long-time dictator, Josip Broz Tito (1890-1980), was half-Croat, half-Slovene. Since Serbs were the largest ethnic group, this dominance was partly inevitable. But Serbs had never formed an absolute majority of the Yugoslav population; their relative power rested on more than just demography. The earlier, noncommunist Yugoslavia of the interwar period had come into existence in 1919 as a sort of greater Serbia, created by the peace treaties that redrew the map of Europe after World War I. Serbia had fought on the winning side from 1914 to 1918; it had suffered a huge loss of population due to fighting and disease, especially during 1915; it had for long coveted possession of Bosnia;[2] it had quite recently acquired Kosovo and northern Macedonia in the Balkan wars (1912-1913); Serbian diasporas were numerous in Croatia and Vojvodina, lands that had belonged to Hungary before World War I. All of these factors had contributed to the creation of the new state. The monarch of the so-called Kingdom of the Serbs, Croats and Slovenes was simply the reigning king of Serbia.

Resentment of this situation by non-Serbs contributed to the bitter fighting in Yugoslavia when that country was occupied by the Axis powers from 1941 to 1945. The coming to power of Tito's partisans in 1945 and the ensuing decades of communist rule merely acted, as elsewhere in communist Europe, as a deep freeze for previous tensions, which reemerged as socialism started to come unstuck during the 1980s and then decisively fell apart at the end of the decade.

This is no place to recount the complicated ethnic, political and military history of postcommunist Yugoslavia. Nor do we wish, as in so many simplistic Western attempts to account for those conflicts, to place all of the blame on Serbia or the Serbs. Yet it is undeniable that of all the competing nationalisms that fostered and generated the wars of the 1990s, the most potent was the Serbian national myth. And that national myth is profoundly religious in nature.

When Slobodan Milošević gave his famous speech in Kosovo in 1987 at the beginning of his rapid rise to power from relatively junior status in government, he was self-consciously striking chords with the central aspect of the religious conception of Serbia. In that conception, Kosovo is the heart of the ancient Serbian kingdom, the home of its most precious monasteries and the place where, in 1389, nearly six centuries before Milošević's speech, that kingdom fell to the power of the Turkish Muslim infidels.

In the received religiomythic account of the battle of Kosovo Polje, Prince Lazar had a vision the night before the battle. In it, he was told that he faced a choice. If he chose an earthly kingdom, he could defeat the Turks. If, however, he chose a heavenly kingdom, then he and his knights would all be slain. The saintly Lazar chose the heavenly kingdom and went down to death and defeat,[3] telling his wife, Milica, that "I go now, oh sister, to Kosovo, There to shed my blood for Christ his honor, For the faith to die there with my brothers."[4] Serbia, as every Serb will tell you (though sometimes, to the relief of outsiders, with a wry smile on the face), is "the heavenly country."

In the poetic epic account, Lazar was betrayed by his son-in-law, Vuk Branković, who switched sides at the last moment, a deed quite frequent in medieval warfare but that the myth requires to be uniquely evil. On the other side of the moral equation, Lazar's heroic ally, Miloš Obilić (or, in some versions, Kobilić), broke into the camp of the sultan, Murad II, and dispatched him personally, a deed that necessarily involved the sacrifice of his own life. In consequence of the Turkish victory, however, Serbia was subjected to alien, infidel rule for almost five centuries and, in the case of Kosovo, for rather longer than that.

And what, amid the fog of myth, are the facts? In the first place, the battle of Kosovo Polje was not the single most crucial military confrontation with the Turks. The most serious Serbian defeat at their hands had already been suffered eighteen years before, at the battle on the Marica of 1371, a battle in which Lazar had refused to help his then liege lord, Uroš Nemanjić. Indeed, it is at least arguable that the later confrontation at Kosovo Polje was a drawn battle rather than a glorious defeat. Its reputation as a Serbian defeat may have been as much a strategic consequence of attrition than a military disaster on the day itself, for the much larger Ottoman resources could replenish the losses of one-for-one killing, whereas the more lightly populated Balkan kingdoms could not. As for Branković's treachery, it may never have happened at all; Ottoman accounts of Kosovo Polje have him fighting bravely for Lazar and not retreating until the battle was over. The only damaging fact about him is that Branković did survive the battle and went on to become a political rival of Lazar's widow,

Milica, and her son, Stefan. Milica and Stefan, faced with few choices, yielded up Lazar's daughter, Olivera, to become the wife of the new sultan, Bayezid, and allied themselves with Ottoman power. Despite the compromises made by Lazar's nearest and dearest, the epic poetry about the battle of Kosovo Polje, which in all likelihood began to be composed during the years of the Lazarević-Branković rivalry, portrayed Lazar as a saint and martyr for Christianity and Vuk Branković as a Judas. That is to say, they seem to have been the product of a propaganda war between the surviving would-be princes, as the Serbian kingdom gradually became a client state of the Ottomans. As for the brave Miloš Obilić, he is known to no historical sources outside of the epic poems. All that is known is that Sultan Murad did, indeed, die in that struggle; at whose hand it was, only the Serbian epics record.

As with all nationalisms, however, the myth is more powerful than the reality. If enough people believe a thing to be true, then, for many practical purposes, it is true. And the myth insists that Serbia is a martyr nation that must avenge itself for the honor of Christianity. The oath that Lazar had supposedly imposed on his vassals included a curse on those who would not fight for the holy cause:

> Whoso is a Serb, from Serbian mother,
> Who has Serbian blood and Serbian lineage,
> And comes not to battle, to Kosovo,
> May there never to his heart be granted
> Children, neither yet a maid nor man-child.
> Underneath his hands shall nothing prosper,
> Neither vine-yards nor the silver wheat fields,
> And from him shall misery be oozing
> Till his name and race die out and perish.[5]

Lazar was quickly canonized as a saint by the Serbian Orthodox Church. The myth makes a strong parallel, replete with last suppers, temptations and Judases, between Lazar and Christ.

Nor is this all. The Balkans was occupied by the Muslim Ottomans from the late fourteenth century, before crumbling and receding during the nineteenth and early twentieth centuries. One early incident in the retreat of the Ottomans has fed into the religious myth of Serbia. In 1689, the Austrians crossed the Danube in southern Hungary and routed the Ottomans as far south as Kosovo and Macedonia. During that Austrian incursion, many of the Orthodox Slavs of Kosovo rose in support of the invaders and then, when the military tide reversed itself as quickly as it had advanced, found themselves in fear of Turkish revenge. Perhaps fifty thousand of them (though far more, if you believe the myth) trekked north, out of Kosovo, led by their patriarch, Arsenije III, in the wake of the now-retreating Austrian armies, and to the safety of Habsburg soil north of the Danube.

This is the *Velika Seoba,* or Great Exodus. In practical terms, it "explains" how Kosovo has come to be populated in more recent times principally by Albanian-speaking Muslims rather than by Orthodox Serbs.[6] In religious terms, it is even more important, for it is a parallel of the biblical exodus, with Arsenije III as a stand-in for Moses and depicted in similar fashion. It also makes yet more emphatic the religious link with Kosovo as the soul of the martyr nation.

Popular Serbian nationalist art of the late nineteenth and twentieth centuries was dominated by two images. The cheap reproductions of those images, on display today in most public buildings and literally millions of private homes, make them the common currency of popular discourse. They are of the *Kosovska Devojka,* the Serbian Maid, giving succor to a dying hero on the field of battle at Kosovo Polje in 1389, and of the *Velika Seoba,* the Great Exodus of Serbs from Kosovo, exactly three hundred years later, in 1689. The former is the crucifixion; the latter is the burial.

So when Slobodan Milošević made his speech in Kosovo in 1987, nearly three hundred years after the *Seoba,* he was touching the deepest chords of the national psyche. And he was insisting that Serbs living in

Kosovo were being mistreated by the Albanian majority there and that he would put a stop to it.

But something else had intervened since 1689 to compound the strength of the myth: there had been a resurrection. A small, independent Serbia had emerged during the nineteenth century (the Ottoman Empire, remember, was losing its grip on the territories it had ruled since the late Middle Ages) and had inculcated nationalist fervor as an instrument of state in order to help territorial expansion. Finally, in the Balkan Wars of 1912-1913, Serbia had extended itself southward to take in, among other territories, Kosovo, with its by then non–Slavic-Orthodox majority population. The conditions for the tragedy of the twentieth century were almost in place.

But the conquest was—is—seen as a resurrection of the martyr nation, vindicating Lazar's choice of the heavenly kingdom more than five centuries before. The conquest was welcomed in 1912 with ecstasy by countless thousands who had been brought up to believe in the myth and that they or their sons would be the avengers of Kosovo.

To say that this is a strange way of thinking about one's national history is perhaps an understatement, though it is not much stranger than many other national myths. Nor is it any less reliant, once we start to pick it apart, on vehement assertion and emotion rather than reason than are, say, the myths used to underpin American exceptionalism, or, equally dangerously, American universalism, or the "civilizing mission" of the British Empire, on which "the sun never sets." Like all national myths, religious or otherwise, events of the distant past are given a significance that their participants never would have recognized. And those participants are portrayed as possessing a national consequence and nationalist motivations that, in reality, would have been incomprehensible to them. Self-evidently absurd from the outside, such modern myths maintain their hold by scything down external critiques in advance. Foreigners do not—cannot—understand. (Even when they do.) Our point here, though, is that religion is the principal ingredient of the Serbian myth. And what better than religious chosenness to render external criticism illegitimate and, indeed, wicked?

Given all of this, it hardly mattered that Serbs were, in the early twentieth century, one of the least pious populations in Europe. The church nevertheless enjoyed prestige, because the national myth *was* the religion. It demanded not brokenness, prayer and exacting standards of morality but zeal and watchfulness for the cause and a readiness to sacrifice oneself or one's sons in battle.

It should be noted, however, that the religious nationalism stood in a symbiotic relationship with Serbian tendencies toward war in the modern era. Serbian expansionism and nineteenth- and twentieth-century Serbian nationalists fostered the religious myth of martyred, heavenly Serbia, and the religious myth fostered belligerence.

I have hesitated many times to recount these facts. The reason for that hesitation is that to write as I have done here implies a certain kind of judgment about proportionate guilt for the wars of the 1990s. And I make no such judgment, not because I hold to the Western, postmodern fad for nonjudgmentalism (as if insisting on false moral equivalences between perpetrators and victims somehow solved some kind of problem) but because I know otherwise: that Croats, Bosnian Muslims and Kosovar Albanians played a full share in provoking the various conflicts that tore Yugoslavia apart and, like Serb forces, perpetrated fearful crimes as and when they had opportunity to do so, though their opportunities were generally less frequent than those of the JNA-backed Serb militias. My interest here is not so much in proportionate guilt as in the special role played by certain kinds of religious ideas in causing war, that is, in the central theme of this book. And, on that scale, it has to be admitted that the most rabid Serbian nationalists are right about one thing: the Serbian idea is a rather special case. Croats may have justified themselves with reference to Catholicism and Bosnian Muslims in a rather defensive, merely cultural sort of way, with reference to Islam. But neither of them developed such religious arguments into a case for Croatian or Bosniak specialness to anything like the degree that Serbs did in respect of their own identity. And the reason for that is the unavoidable universalism of Catholicism and Islam. By contrast, Eastern Orthodoxy and Protestantism can be frighteningly content, on occasion, to be parochial.

The Third Rome and Russian Messianism

Russia is another example of a powerful religious-national myth that continues to exert a hold on large sections of the population. Perhaps significantly, the country is also predominantly Eastern Orthodox, with the consequence that the church exists, for all practical purposes, exclusively within the country and is concerned primarily with national spiritual welfare.

The late tenth century saw the formal christianization of Kievan Rus', which Russians today claim as their predecessor state. (So, too, do Ukrainians, but the arguments are meaningless, for there was no distinction then or for many centuries afterward.) The early thirteenth century saw the dissolution of the state and devastation at the hands of the invading Mongols or Tatars. From then until the fourteenth and fifteenth centuries, various small principalities under the rule of Slavic princes (I choose my words carefully) eked out an existence by paying tribute to the Tatar khans based on the Volga. Eventually, one of these principalities, Muscovy, became predominant by playing the role of the Tatars' tax collector in chief vis-à-vis the other statelets. When that point was reached, Muscovy then sought, at first unsuccessfully and then successfully, to assert its autonomy from the now-waning power of the khans.

The first such challenge was that of Muscovite prince Dmitri, at the battle of Kulikovo Pole in 1380. Like Kosovo Polje in the Balkans nine years later, the battle has come to bear a far greater significance in recent centuries than it had at the time. At Kulikovo Pole, however, the Orthodox Christians did not go down to glorious defeat; they were victorious. The Tatars' Golden Horde was smashed. It is true that the infidels returned to burn and sack Moscow two years later and forced Muscovy to continue paying tribute for another hundred years. But the real import of Kulikovo Pole was that the mystique of Tatar invincibility had been shattered.

The battle is more important, however, for the myths it created than for those it destroyed. Dmitri had gone to war against the dreaded Tatars, acting under the advice of the monk Sergius of Radonezh (now Zagorsk). Sergius had a great reputation for piety and now took the role of Old Testament prophet, assuring Dmitri that God was on his side. Indeed, God did appear to be on the side of the long-suffering Orthodox Russians and against the oppressive unbelievers. Sergius, far away from the battle in his monastery, is believed to have foreseen the victory and to have called his monks together to pray for the souls of those who were at that moment being killed. The battle, instead of being one more bid for power by a local prince against a distant liege lord—the kind of event that happened all too frequently, even where all combatants were of the same faith—was recast as a holy enterprise, with God on the side of the oppressed Orthodox Christians. This religious vision was compounded with later events to foster what would become, in time, the Russian religious-national myth.

That myth adhered first merely to the princes (later tsars) of Muscovy and only later to "the Russian people" themselves. Even in the fourteenth century, a number of monastics developed "the ideological claim that Muscovy and her Grand Dukes were chosen to represent the climax of Christian history."[7] The realization of such claims was greatly facilitated, during the fifteenth and sixteenth centuries, by the collapse of the principal centers of Eastern Orthodox political and ecclesiastical power in Byzantium to the forces of Islam, at exactly the time when Muscovy was emerging as a principality of some weight. The Eastern Orthodox and Roman Catholic churches had been in formal schism from one another since 1054, and the former had fostered an identity that was in no small part based on a repudiation of the latter. This repudiationism was fully shared by the Orthodox of the Russian lands. Yet, as the Byzantine Empire sensed the Turkish noose tightening during the early fifteenth century, it put out feelers to the West for reconciliation, in the hope that this might prompt military and other assistance from fellow Christians. The result was the Council of Florence (1438-1445), an abortive attempt to reunite the Eastern and Western churches, with the former making all of the concessions.

These concessions were so extensive as to be denounced even in Constantinople and the Orthodox lands most closely threatened by Muslim invasion. (Better to die with dignity and integrity than to be rescued with dishonor, especially when rescue seemed so unlikely in any case.) In Moscow, however, manufactured indignation at the concessions to the perfidious West enabled many to claim that the Council of Florence had triggered virtual apostasy by Byzantium. It was a claim that suited the princes of Muscovy very well. Russia alone was faithful and reliable; the fall of Constantinople a few years later, in 1453, seemed to vindicate that assessment, for it could be seen as a judgment of God.

Even so, the escalating claims made by Moscow for itself did not begin until much later. As one of the great historical theologians of our own age has put it,

> The implication of these events for the future destiny of Russian Christianity did not become evident right away; but a century or so after the fall of Constantinople, Russian leaders in church and state concluded that it was time for them to assert a greater measure of independence.[8]

This process was helped by the fact that Muscovy was now the only Eastern Orthodox state of any size that was not under infidel rule. In 1589, the Muscovites succeeded in persuading the old, established patriarchates of the East to erect a new patriarchate in Moscow; Patriarch Jeremiah of Constantinople duly traveled there to install him. "Under the sun there is [now] only one pious tsar . . . ; it is fitting that the ecumenical patriarch should be here, while in old Car-grad [Constantinople] the Christian faith is being driven out by the infidel Turks for our sins."[9] It may be doubted whether Jeremiah uttered these words, inhibited as he obviously was by the need to travel home afterward, back into the clutches of the infidels with whom it was his principal function to find ways of co-existing. But the sentiments were put into his mouth by zealous Muscovite scribes who could afford the luxury of hurling distant abuse.

The abject condition of Constantinople (the "second Rome," after the fall of Rome itself to barbarians in the fifth century) contrasted strongly with the situation of Muscovy under Ivan the Terrible, who in the late sixteenth century was busily conquering and devastating the Tatar khanates to the south and east. Already the idea of Moscow as the Third Rome had been mooted by Filofei of Pskov in 1511:

> Your great Russian empire, O pious sovereign, the third Rome, surpasses them in piety and all the pious kingdoms are united in yours. You alone under heaven will be called Christian Tsar throughout the world by all Christians. Two Romes have fallen, and the third is still standing, and a fourth there shall not be.

As Jaroslav Pelikan has observed, "The idea of Moscow as the third Rome was an apt expression for the theological interpretation of Russia's historic role."[10]

It was augmented by the vastly influential teaching of Saint Joseph of Volotsk (1440-1515), who insisted that liturgical worship must be correct in every detail and brought ritual sanctification to the nation. This notion became so deeply embedded that even during the Second World War, after the Orthodox church had endured terrible persecution under Stalin in the 1930s, and then, with the Nazi invasion of 1941, instant rehabilitation in order to galvanize popular support for defending holy Mother Russia, the patriarch in 1943 told a Western bishop that all was well enough with the Russian church: permission to carry out the correct liturgical functions was all that mattered.

The idea of Moscow as the Third Rome did not become general until the eighteenth and nineteenth centuries, and it included not merely an assuming of the role left hanging by a conquered and compromised Constantinople but also the subsumption of the second Rome's insistence on

Western, Catholic corruption. The Third Rome claimed not merely a preeminent place for itself within the Orthodox world but also a stance against the apostate West. As one recent writer has noted, "The religious notion of Moscow as the 'Third Rome' posited a divine world mission for Russia that was enthusiastically adopted by Slavophiles, Pan-Slavs, and ideologists for the Russian autocracy" from the mid-nineteenth century.[11] Russia would lead the world to a purer and higher plane of existence. As Dostoyevsky put it, "To become fully Russian can in the last analysis only mean . . . becoming a brother to all human beings. . . . The mission of the Russian people is certainly all-European and worldwide."[12]

This aspect of Russian identity had been strengthened by several major conflicts with the Western powers of the Baltic regions: with the Teutonic Knights and Prussians, and later with the Swedes, in the 1240s. And it was this folk memory of the victories in those conflicts of Alexander Nevski, replete with the religious overtones of that memory, on which the communists were able to draw during the Second World War. During the eighteenth, nineteenth and much of the twentieth centuries, Russian nationalists and Slavophiles came to see Russia as a civilization apart, preserving true sanctity apart from Western corruption, with a mission to protect the Orthodox populations of the Balkans who found themselves, as Russians had once done, under infidel rule.[13]

It was these strands of thought that, in secularized form, the communists were able to draw on after 1917. Russia's historic (even if not divine) mission was to be the leader in bringing in a kind of secular salvation—socialism—that was destined to conquer the world. For the sake of this, all kinds of personal sacrifices were required in the interests of the higher cause. In the meantime, the immediate task of the Russian people was to lead the lesser peoples of the Soviet Union toward modernization.

During the period of the Soviet regime, the insistence of dissident writers such as Nicholas Berdyaev on the Russian people's "metaphysical nature and vocation in the world"[14] seemed to Westerners almost reassuring. In the post-Soviet era, they seem much less so as the Russian messianic idea has reassumed its religious form. In the mid-1990s, one hypernationalist writer was arguing that the collapse of the Soviet Union had been the work of the devil—the fact that the U.S.S.R. had been a vehicle for Russian leadership apparently counting for more than the mere detail of its atheism and long-time persecution of churches. According to Valeri Khatiushin, "Satan's legions were preparing a five-year bloodbath for Russia, in which Russia, like Christ, would be crucified. In the year 2000 . . . Russia would be resurrected as the leader of the world."[15] Khatiushin hardly represents majority opinion, though the particulars of his apocalypticism are more unusual than the mere fact of it. That he and others like him have a following of any size is the point to be noted and stems from the prevalence of Russian messianism in popular discourse about the meaning of the nation.

The implications of all this for belligerence should be clear. Stalin recognized its usefulness: in 1941, faced with a devastating assault by Nazi Germany, he rehabilitated the Orthodox church, on the basis that it would preach support for the Soviet war effort against the wicked Westerners. Already possessed of a vast fund of a particular kind of historical consciousness among the population, it did so. And it worked. Far more fought the Nazis out of patriotism than out of love for communism. Indeed, where Russian patriotism was lacking (in Ukraine, say, or Latvia), many people sided with the Nazi invaders. Stalin recognized the reality: World War II has always been known in Russia as the Great Patriotic War.

The church continued to act as an instrument of Soviet foreign policy throughout the Cold War. Today it is this religious vision of Russia and its "purpose" that continues to fascinate those Russian political forces that want to rearm, fight to the finish in Chechnya or recreate the Soviet commonwealth, by force, if necessary.

As with Serbian religious nationalism, Russian messianism sacralizes the nation. Unlike its Serbian equivalent, it attributes to Russia a mission of leadership among the peoples of the earth, as a parallel to the historic roles played by Rome and Byzantium.

6

TRIBAL GODS II

The Religious-National Myth of England and Collective Self-Worship

"And Was Jerusalem Builded Here, in England's Green and Pleasant Land?"

The poet William Blake (1757-1827) was nobody's idea of an orthodox Christian believer. Not even his own. But it can hardly be denied that he and his work were profoundly religious. On the one hand, he counts as a Romantic, influenced by that great current of literature, art and intellectual life of his age. On the other, he was something of a mystic, interested in Swedenborgianism and the use of traditional religious terminology for new and unusual ends, particularly in fostering the then innovatory (though now tiresomely compulsory) romanticization of the individual.

In his famous hymn, "And did those feet in ancient time walk upon England's mountains green?" (the correct answer to which question is, incidentally, an emphatic no), he was indulging his taste for the esoteric. Yet the esoteric ideas to which his hymn referred had a long history. And, in the nineteenth century, they had a great future before them. Then, when it seemed to have died down, the vision was reappropriated by the post-World War II generation of socialists to epitomize the aspirations of the Attlee government.[1]

The nineteenth century lasted well into the 1960s and 1970s in my grammar school, which is how I became acquainted with "Jerusalem," since we were required occasionally to sing it in morning assembly, complete with the pledge of the final lines: "I shall not cease from mental fight, nor shall my sword sleep in my hand, Till we have built Jerusalem in England's green and pleasant land." If we ever meant these sentiments, it remains far from clear that we have succeeded. The shopping malls of England, glittering yet litter-strewn, so prosperous yet hooligan-menaced, bring to mind the visions of Hieronymus Bosch far more easily than that of William Blake. Yet in Britain, his hymn remains the anthem of the doughty matrons of the Women's Institute.

Blake, however, had not been creating a myth; he had been referring to one that was already deeply entrenched and giving it a new accent for his age. Broadly speaking, this myth consists of three elements: the Arthur legends and their associated ideas; the special nature of English Protestantism, particularly as expounded in John Foxe's *Book of Martyrs*; and the British Israel theory.

The Arthur legends are well known, and we need point out here only the aspects that bear on our purpose. Arthur, possibly a fifth-century Celtic prince in the southwestern part of Britain, fought against the pagan Anglo-Saxon (i.e., English) tribes from Germany that were invading the island. Many, though not all, of the Celtic inhabitants of Britain had been christianized during the later period of Roman rule, so it is possible to see Arthur's battles on a higher plane, as a championing of Christianity against paganism.

This reading is encouraged by the fact that the Holy Grail forms such an important part of the legends, Arthur's quest for which symbolizes his reaching out for all that is holiest and makes him a Christian hero, despite his personal shortcomings. In the legends, the Grail is a cup containing the blood of Christ and had supposedly been brought to Britain, not long after the crucifixion, by Joseph of Arimathea. The established fact of trade links between Phoenicia and Cornwall during these years lends the story a certain circumstantial plausibility.

After the eventual christianization of the English invaders during the seventh century, English writers came to look favorably on the Celts whom their people had supplanted. The Venerable Bede (c. 673-735) is a prime example: he was sympathetic to Celtic Christian leaders of the past and praised them in his writings, thereby beginning the process whereby later English people would reverse the judgment of their ancestors and co-opt the native Celts as in some sense part of their own identity, just as Americans have done with the Indians or New Zealanders with the Maoris. The Arthur legends gained general currency in England from the twelfth-century chronicles of Geoffrey of Monmouth and strengthened the idea that Britain had a strand of Christianity stretching back to the apostolic period.[2]

About that particular claim, there is nothing unusual: such fantasies abound across Europe, Asia and much of Africa. What gave the English and then, later, British claim added significance and virulent new life was the advent of the Reformation. Like all of the European Protestant Reformers of the sixteenth century, those in England were confronted with the troubling question from apologists for Catholicism: "Where was your church before Luther?" Ingenious English exegetes, however, thought to have found a convincing answer with resounding local credentials. Celtic Christianity, it was alleged, had existed in the island from a very early period. Indeed, it was the supplanting of that faith by norms imposed from Rome as a result of the Synod of Whitby (663-664) that had introduced into the island the corruptions and popish distortions of the true faith that the sixteenth-century Protestant leaders were now intent upon eradicating.

It therefore became irresistible to Protestant exegetes to argue that Celtic Christianity had been pure, by Protestant lights. The Celtic church became, in this revision of history, an early medieval "Protestant institution in all but name, characterized by evangelical purity and wholly independent of Rome."[3] All kinds of virtues and ideas could be projected back onto it—a bogus past brought in to prop up the claims for the present. (This game has been played again, with just as much conviction and just as little support from the extant facts, by New Agers and postmodern Christians.[4])

William Tyndale (c. 1494-1536) took this line of Protestant argumentation, as did the polemicist John Bale (1495-1563) and the famous martyrologist John Foxe (1516-1587).[5] The main purpose of Foxe's vastly influential work, the cataloging of Protestants martyred from 1553 to 1558 under the Catholic Queen Mary I, is well known. He thereby wished, obviously, to bolster the later, Protestant régime of Mary's half-sister, Elizabeth I. But the manner in which he made his argument had a number of subsidiary effects, two of which are of interest to us here.

In the first place is the idea that God is concerned in some particular way with England. The early part of Foxe's enormous work (the most recent complete edition, published in 1870, runs to eight volumes of many hundreds of pages each, in small type) merely chronicles the well-known stories of the Christian martyrs of the early church.[6] But the central and later stages are concerned almost exclusively with English martyrs, both Lollards and others of the pre-Reformation period and then the more well-known Marian martyrs of the 1550s. The message throughout is that God has always had his Englishmen and Englishwomen who will stand for the truth and that Protestantism (or, as with Lollardy, proto-Protestantism) is to be identified closely with Englishness. The Catholic church, particularly during Mary's reign, is portrayed as allied with tyrannical rule, foreign influence on government (for Mary had been married to King Philip II of Spain) and religious persecution. Protestantism, of course, persecuted its rivals just as Catholicism did, but Foxe wished to imply that it did so rather less.

The fervent Protestants John Hales and John Knox had both hailed Queen Elizabeth as a second Deborah, the prophetess of the book of Judges; Foxe identified her as a second Emperor Constantine.[7] All expected her to lead a Protestant crusade against the Antichrist, whom Protestants, lamentably enough, were unanimous in identifying as the pope. And it was true that Elizabethan English people found themselves in constant fear of invasion by the greatest Catholic power of the day: Philip II's Spain. The fighting took place in the Netherlands, where the English helped Dutch rebels against Spanish rule; in Ireland, where the Spanish returned the compliment; on the high seas, where Puritan-financed privateers (or perhaps pirates, according to point of view), plundered Spanish treasure ships; and, in 1588, in fending off the Armada, by which Philip hoped to invade England and re-Catholicize it. By the 1580s, at the latest, English nationalism and Protestant partisanship did seem to be one and the same cause.

To say that Foxe's *Acts and Monuments of the Christian Church* (to give the *Book of Martyrs* its official title) was hugely influential on English thought during the later sixteenth and seventeenth centuries would be a gross understatement of the case. Only the Bible was read more frequently and more avidly. Foxe's work remained constantly in print and was read by all of the fast-growing minority who were literate; through the universal practice of reading aloud, its contents were known also to those who still could not read. Foxe's religious nationalism was an essential ingredient and informed English people's understanding of the ongoing conflict with Spain and of the threat posed, really or merely supposedly, by remaining Catholics in England.

The second, only partly intended consequence of Foxe's book that concerns us here is the advent of postmillennialism. This is the idea that the return of Christ comes only after (i.e., post-) a reign of the saints on the earth. So the kingdom of the saints is ushered in by the saints themselves, as godliness triumphs over wickedness. It should be emphasized that Foxe himself taught no such thing. But his idea that a Protestant crusade against Catholicism would be led by an English monarch and would be successful invited such a development. The Puritan writer Thomas Brightman (1562-1607) developed the new postmillennial view, the later varieties of which fed off Foxe's earlier vision and modified or radicalized it. On into the seventeenth century, English Protestants saw themselves as God's intended spearhead against the Catholic powers.

Because continental Europe remained predominantly Catholic (the Protestant states being mostly, except for the Netherlands and, for a while, Sweden, fairly weak), it became possible to view "continentals" as a whole as possessed of an inferior, backward-looking, Catholic culture that Protestant England was destined to eclipse and then dominate. Since the seventeenth and eighteenth centuries did witness England's (and then, because of the recent union with Scotland, Britain's) rapid elevation to great power status, this vision became all too plausible.

Postmillennialism, after suffering the early misfortune of being taken up by cranks, as well as many of unimpeachable orthodoxy, during the period of the English Civil War, settled down in more respectable forms to become the dominant and Anglocentric theology of Protestants in the eighteenth century. This was so both in its more liberal, deistic forms (the world would get better and better under the distant supervision of a benign Providence) or among evangelical revivalists, such as the Wesleys and Jonathan Edwards (world evangelization would proceed apace until "one nation shall be enlightened and converted, and one false religion and false way of worship exploded, after another").[8] Both kinds of optimistic scenario—and they were neither mutually exclusive nor hermetically sealed off from one another—tended to take the leading role of Britain, its dependencies and their culture more or less for granted.

So it came naturally to the generalized Protestant, evangelical-influenced society of late-nineteenth-century England, Scotland and Wales—that is to say, of Britain at the apogee of its global power—to view the British Empire as the divinely ordained vehicle of progress and right order in the world, and the burgeoning missionary movement as an instrument of spreading the religion and its intrinsically associated culture that had made that power, that progress and that order possible. The British had no compunction, at least not until after World War I, when those certainties began to fade, in using force, whether against rival powers or uppity natives, to advance or to maintain their empire. It is true that they seldom invoked God or religion explicitly to that purpose but rather to the furthering of the culture, law and values that a benevolent God had so clearly chosen to favor and that recommended themselves to reason and to a biblically informed conscience. To the late-nineteenth-century

Englishman, this was obvious: on this scale of values, the Turks were barbaric, the Russians ignorant and elemental, the French either republican and atheistic (if they were supporters of the Revolution) or, if they were not, then papistical, superstitious and backward, like the rest of Catholic Europe. It took the meteoric rise of (mostly) Protestant Germany at the end of the century and the early twentieth to unsettle this easy arrogance and then, after the two world wars, to fracture it beyond repair.

It is far from coincidental that the same period that saw the decline, and then collapse, of the religious-national myth also saw the rapid decline of evangelicalism in Britain. It was not that evangelicals were more fervent than anyone else in supporting the myth, though they often found their own reasons to do so,[9] but their existence was the backbone of the generalized religiosity that succored that myth across wider society.

The third element of the religious-national myth is perhaps the strangest of them all. This is the so-called British Israel theory, first popularized by Richard Brothers (1757-1824). It depends in no small degree on the other two elements—the Arthurian legends and Holy Grail and the Foxe-derived idea of English Protestant specialness—that we have mentioned. According to British Israelism, whose spirit, if not exact ideas, were so perfectly captured in Blake's hymn, the British were and are the lost tribes of Israel. Their connection with biblical history therefore predates the time of Christ. This was why it was natural for Joseph of Arimathea to bring the Grail to Cornwall and for Paul to come to preach the gospel on Ludgate Hill, where the cathedral named after him in London now stands.

Bizarre though these ideas now seem, they were widely credited in the nineteenth century; the publication of Edward Hine's *Identity of the Ten Lost Tribes of Israel with the Anglo-Celto-Saxons* (whoever they might be!) ran to a quarter of a million copies. Even Queen Victoria seems to have subscribed to such notions. Admiral Sir John Fisher, First Sea Lord of the British Navy in World War I, advocated

> a great Commonwealth—yes a great Federation—of all those speaking the same tongue [English]. . . . And I suppose now we have got [sic] Palestine that this Federal House of Commons of the future will meet at Jerusalem, the capital of the lost Ten Tribes of Israel, whom we are without a doubt, for how otherwise could ever we have so prospered when we have had such idiots to guide us and rule us?[10]

Fisher's scornful rhetorical question was fair enough, even if the conclusions that he drew from it work better as dry humor than as the serious historical claim he intended. Nevertheless, it was this, as G. S. Neal comments, that was

> the pattern of most British-Israelites who influenced, or were a part of, the ruling elites of English society. Their beliefs affected their actions, confirming their goals and giving them the tenacity to push forward in their quest for a greater Britain and the coming Kingdom of God.[11]

In plain language, the myth promoted nationalistic bellicosity.

The English (or British) religious-national myth is now almost entirely defunct. It lingered for a while in the Worldwide Church of God, founded by Herbert W. Armstrong (1892-1986) in America. That church found ways to extend the coverage of the myth to the United States, as an Anglo-Saxon-founded country that had, effectively, inherited the mantle of Britain. Through its free magazine, *Plain Truth,* it perpetuated a soft sell of the myth and of several other unusual ideas to a wide public, perhaps many of whom little recognized what it was that they were being sold, let alone agreed with it. And the majority even of that church has, since Armstrong's death, decisively set such theories aside and sought instead to reconcile itself with orthodoxy.

But explicit British Israelism and the Worldwide Church of God were merely articulating in an extreme form sentiments that were much more diffuse and widely held. The myth has declined roughly in parallel with Britain's place in the world during the twentieth century. The present writer suspects, though has no way of proving, that the main residue of that myth in the present is the persistent anti-foreignism and counterevidential belief in British superiority manifested by the country's soccer hooligans. (The hooliganism, though not, generally, the attitudinizing that underlies it, has recently spread to a number of other countries.) But such behavior is the mere Gibraltar and Rockall of what was once a powerful set of ideas; for all other purposes, the myth is now as dead as the British Empire.

IDOLATRY AND WARFARE

Of the three examples we have discussed here, the Serbian is by far the strongest, though the other two have also been of critical importance in predisposing the populations that imbibed them to fight. But these three are not alone, even if they are the most eye-catching. Other, somewhat weaker but nevertheless important, cases might have been chosen.

Polish nationalism, for instance, has for long built on widespread Catholic Marian devotion among the population to posit a special relationship between the Virgin Mary and the Polish nation. While even very moderate Polish nationalists might counter this observation by pointing out that far more of Poland's wars in recent centuries have been defensive than offensive (an objection that opens the whole debate about what we mean by Polish nation[12]), it should be said that the Marian-Polish myth nevertheless fostered, effectively, rebellions against Russian rule, such as that of 1831 and 1848. Concerning the former, the poet Adam Mickiewicz envisioned his native land as the "Christ of the nations":

> And they [Russian authorities] martyred the Polish people and laid it in the grave, and it descended into darkness. But on the third day the soul shall return to the body and the nation shall rise from the dead and free all the peoples of Europe from slavery.[13]

The American national myth, while largely secular, nevertheless also possesses important religious elements, so that it is not meaningless to speak of an American religious-national myth. As recently as the Cold War, popular support among Americans for a stern military posture appealed to something far more specific than mere opposition to godless communism; it rested on a religious view of America's special place in the world. In part, that view was inherited from the English myth that we have already described. (That was why Armstrongism could flourish in a modest way in the United States.) But it also contained some specifically American elements.

One of these elements stems from the earliest Puritan settlers of New England. John Winthrop (1588-1649), the first governor of Massachusetts, gave perhaps the most famous expression to the Puritans' sense of American destiny:

> We shall be as a city upon a hill, the eyes of all people are upon us, so that if we shall deal falsely with our God in this work we have undertaken, and so cause him to withdraw his present help from us, we shall be made a story and a byword through the world . . . till we be consumed out of the good land whither we are going.[14]

That last phrase consciously evoked the Israelites' journey to the Promised Land; the Puritan settlers believed themselves to be the recipients of a sacred trust to build a Zion in the New World, untainted by the corruption and bondage of the Old. As one recent historian has explained,

> Other peoples had their land by providence; *they* had it by promise. Others must seek their national origins in secular records and chronicles; the story of America was enclosed in the Scriptures, its past postdated and its future antedated in prophecy.[15]

The idea of a city on a hill has endured as part of the common language of American politics, frequently in secularized form, but often enough with its religious content left largely intact. The novelist Herman Melville gave voice to the secular version of this messianism in one of his characters: "The political Messiah . . . has come in *us*. . . . Almost for the first time in the history of earth, national selfishness is unbounded philanthropy; for we can not do a good to America but we give alms to the world."[16]

The Puritans' theocratic ideals barely survived the seventeenth century; however, the notion of America as a godly commonwealth and a refuge for the godly of all nations has long outlasted it. One 1854 publication was titled *Armageddon; or, The . . . Existence of the United States Foretold in the Bible, Its . . . Expansion into the Millennial Republic, and Its Dominion over the Whole World.* And if such works appealed only to a fringe audience, it was nevertheless true to say that by the mid-nineteenth century, "the standard American identification of the United States [was] as 'God's New Israel'"; one preacher addressing a congregation after the assassination of President Lincoln in 1865 told his audience that "the Hebrew Commonwealth, 'in which all the families of the earth were to be blest,' was not more of the whole world's concern than is this Republic."[17]

The strength of religion in American life and the huge influence of American input on the modern missionary movement has reinforced, since the mid-nineteenth century, the idea of the United States as a chosen disseminator of Christianity and of Christian civilization—values that must be fought for. During the First World War, it was the "progressive" (i.e., the politically and theologically liberal) clergy, rather than the conservatives or the emerging fundamentalist constituency, that

> pictured America, the Christ-nation, as God's chosen instrument for this moment in divine history, sacrificing itself in Wilsonian service to humanity and leading the armies of righteousness to victory. They announced that the war would at last "Christianize" America and the world.[18]

Such language continues to recur in popular and sometimes, via the occasional presidential blooper about a "crusade" for freedom, in official public discourse, and on both sides of the political spectrum. Not a few Christian Americans, when sending their sons to Iraq or Afghanistan or otherwise lending their support to the "war on terror," make no sharp distinction between a war for America and a war for Christianity.[19]

In practice, all the examples of religious-national myths that we have selected for discussion here have demonstrably been guilty of fostering belligerence and exceptionally warlike qualities in the populations that have imbibed them. These exceptionalist cases stand guilty of the secularist's accusation against religion: that it is a principal cause of war.

Even here, however, it should be said that religious-national myths are idolatrous; they function by co-opting religion for collective self-worship. That this is utterly unbiblical and foreign to genuine Christianity goes, or should go, without saying. Even so, the religious skeptic will hardly be impressed by this since, from a skeptical viewpoint, the distinction between orthodox (or genuine) faith and heresy is arbitrary or even self-serving for the person making such distinctions. Even the skeptic must allow, however, that it is by no means evident that the wars that religious-national myths foment would disappear if the illusory religious legitimation were taken away. The religion is manufactured and co-opted precisely for purposes of serving as "moral combat gear."[20] The combat came first; the religious myth to legitimate it, afterward.

That being so, the complicity of religious myths in warfare demonstrates little more than what is apparent anyway: religion, as the ultimate source of moral and spiritual authority and justification, is irresistible as a court of appeal for those who wish to use it for selfish or self-justificatory ends. And this is as true in ordinary social and political life as it is in international relations or the conduct of warfare. At its most mundane level, the misuse of religious or pious-sounding arguments for personal ends is familiar to every reader of this book. Whether or not such human abuses of religion thereby discredit religious faith itself is, of course, an entirely different matter.

Nothing I have written in these two chapters should be taken as denigratory of patriotism. For patriotism—that is, a genuine love of country or homeland, warts and all, for what it really is rather than some mythic version—is a sentiment that all should cultivate and feel, just as surely as we should show love and duty to families or to neighbors. For we can love our families the more without loving others the less. (Indeed, it is demonstrable in theory and in practice that such love is not only no bar to but the condition for, and root of, general philanthropy and the love of others.) Nationalism, however, is another matter, for it opens the doorway to all manner of misunderstandings about the past and therefore also of the present. More ominously, nationalism is full of potential to incite us to mistreat or disfavor others as either inferior or as in some way an impediment to our nation. Religious-national myths go much further even than this. If taken seriously, they are blasphemous and idolatrous. As logic could predict in theory and history indicates in fact, they will lead us time and time again into calamitous warfare.

7

SO WHAT CAUSES WAR?

When did war begin? The account of Abel's murder by Cain outside the gates of Eden, in Genesis, suggests that violent conflict is a direct result of the fall of humanity and the deepening spiral of sin consequent on estrangement from the presence of God. Abel's sacrifice of an animal had been accepted by God; Cain's offering of crops had not. Was this an archetypal religious quarrel? If so, Scripture clearly disapproves it. In any case, it is not, by any stretch of the imagination, a bid by one party to force religious conformity on others. No juggling of the facts can make this a quintessential microcosm of the later Crusades, or of *jihad* or of the sixteenth-century wars of religion. The fact that, in this story, Abel was a "keeper of flocks" and Cain a "tiller of the soil" is likely to have been significant, as is the fact that Cain is punished for his brother's murder by being condemned to be a "restless wanderer on the earth"—precisely the fate that his and his brother's pastoralism had been designed to rescue them from.[1] All historians and archaeologists are agreed that the first human beings were hunter-gatherers and that when the earliest agrarian societies developed during the first few millennia B.C., one of the agrarians' priorities was to protect themselves against the still-nomadic majority, who might break in to steal their crops or to kill their carefully tended domestic animals for food. Farmers and hunters, then, were in conflict from the outset. It seems likely that people first began to tend crops and domesticate animals when the wild herds had been hunted to near extinction. In the process of becoming pastoralists, they ceased to garner their livelihoods from just any piece of nature; they became rooted instead to particular pieces of land, of which they now claimed exclusive possession, along with the crops that grew there, and of the animals they tended. The incentive for hunters, who remained outside of such arrangements, to ease their steadily more arduous lot by raiding settled peoples was strong.

What, then, should we conclude from the account of Cain and Abel? That violence flows naturally from the first appearance of property? That God favors a benevolent, primeval anarchy over a society of property ownership and thought for the morrow? These would be doubtful readings. The fact of literacy is in itself conclusive evidence that the Scriptures were produced in, by and for settled societies. The punishment of Cain for his brother's murder was the loss of such slender security as settlement provided. A better reading of the story might be that violence within the agrarian community (such as a crop grower killing a keeper of herds) so endangered its internal order that the perpetrator should be returned to the lawless lands without.[2]

Even so, the great historian Roland Bainton observed that, except for the Assyrians, all the peoples of the ancient world "had the myth of a one-time warless world in a lost age of gold," in which "the earth freely yielded her increase without the toil of man," in consequence of which there had supposedly been "no need for private property, no temptation to introduce slavery, and no reason for recourse to war."[3] The civilizations of antiquity, then, seem to have been at one in perceiving at least some connection between the first appearance of work and private property (that is, of agricultural cultivation and the tending of flocks rather than simply gathering food and sustenance from the wild or hunting) and the phenomena of violence, enslavement and sin.

SETTLERS, RAIDERS AND THE MILITARY CASTE

The discernible facts of archaeology lend at least some support for this view. The military historian John Keegan points to the "very early appearance of fixed defenses at the first agricultural sites" such as those at Jericho (the world's oldest still-inhabited town) as evidence that the emergence of warfare was roughly simultaneous with the appearance of settled, agrarian societies, since the latter "learned to protect themselves against the raiders who emerged without warning from the wilderness beyond the borders of the cultivated lands to pillage and slay." It was the defensive needs of these societies that created the first armies, which could act as "counter-attack forces, funded out of the agricultural surplus" and able to carry the battle into the raiders' own territory.[4]

"Funded out of the agricultural surplus": the historian Patricia Crone argues persuasively that it was because early agrarian societies were bound up in such conflicts that they necessarily came to be dominated by military elites, who could protect them from the depredations of marauding hunter-gatherers.[5] The raising and funding of armies was only the first step in the dynamic, for this demands social specialization: "The division of labor between producers and maintainers of order is thus one conducive to a highly unequal relationship." If those who specialize in protection and keeping order are funded or fed, whether through tribute, taxes or some other mechanism, by those who continue to specialize in the production of food, then nothing prevents the former from using their access to, and expertise in, weaponry from turning that position into a monopoly and using it for "forcibly extracting" whatever can be extracted from those whom they are ostensibly protecting. This, says Crone, is

> what one might call the dilemma of the golden goose: one cannot specialize in the production of wealth (or for that matter children) without becoming both highly desirable *and* defenseless; the very fact that labor is divided up dictates that gold-bearing creatures are weak.

The emergence of a military caste, she concludes, "almost invariably" turned agriculturalists "into miserable *peasants*, that is to say rural cultivators whose surplus was forcibly transferred to a dominant group of rulers."[6]

Virtually all pre-industrial, agricultural societies answer to this description. Such societies are dominated by their military needs. The specialization of which Crone speaks should not lead us to suppose that all states possessed regular, professional armies—merely that military force remained, most of the time, the preserve of a minority who were the ruling caste, able to tax and expropriate at will, subject only to the constraint of keeping the golden goose alive and laying eggs. Even so, settled, agricultural states were more likely to possess standing armies than were the peoples living closer to a state of nature. The more ferocious of these latter, however, were more likely to *be* a standing army, in that "all males were warriors" and "there was no distinction between lawful and unlawful bearers of arms."[7] The Huns, Bulgars and, quintessentially, the Mongols all constituted militarized people groups that presented the severest challenge to the settled states that they attacked and, in many cases, overwhelmed. As Keegan observes, "Historically, war has been a dirty business . . . a predatory affair."[8] The motivation of the earliest warfare, and of many later ones besides, was simple: it was the desire to possess food, livestock, artifacts, slaves, women and land.

The Chinese defended themselves against the nomadic raiders of central Asia by constructing the Great Wall. At the other end of the Eurasian land mass, the Romans policed the Rhine-Danube frontier of their empire with a large, extremely well-disciplined army "as a permanent condition of the empire's survival."[9] Between them were the barbarians. And much of the history of the past two millennia can be read as one of slowly whittling down both the strength and the compass of the unsettled lands that once stretched from the great North European plain, across the steppes, to Siberia. The Cossacks and the tribesmen of the Caucasus and central Asia were simply late examples of the freebooting raiders who, at various points throughout the Middle Ages, had devastated Europe, Persia, the Middle East, China and India.

The process was more complex than a mere onward march by the obviously more viable, more civilized settled states, however. The nomads and raiders had the same advantage that criminals and terrorists do today: they generally held the initiative. To ward off an aggressor is always, by implication, to invite him to attack somebody else or to bide his time until later. Only eternal vigilance—and vigilance in strength—can keep him away forever. And few societies have the will and the resources, and fewer still the concentration and the ability, to remain vigilant for very long. Even the Romans and the Chinese were overcome eventually.

And this brings us to consider what was the real advantage of the settled peoples, such that history has long since moved decisively in their direction, rather than in that of the nomadic raiders. What happened after Rome fell to the barbarians? Kievan Rus' to the Mongols? The southeastern Balkans to the Bulgars? The Middle East and North Africa to the Arab tribesmen? Asia Minor to the Turks? China and India to the Mongols? The various barbarian chiefs converted themselves into settled rulers, fleecing the subjects whose lands they had conquered. At first, there was often appalling bloodshed, most notably anywhere captured by the Mongols. Indeed, Genghis Khan was reported to have been open about his motives for warfare, which he loved for its own sake. "The greatest pleasure," he said, "is to vanquish your enemies and chase them before you, to rob them of their wealth and see those dear to them bathed in tears, to ride their horses and clasp to your bosom their wives and daughters."[10] If he was almost unique in his ability to act on these desires, then he was hardly alone in having them in the first place.

But eventually, the rulers settled down to enjoy the fruits of their conquest. And, although a few doggedly took back all of the booty, slaves and women they could haul to wherever it was they had come from, most preferred instead to enjoy those fruits in situ. By doing so, they became settled themselves and gained a vested interest in the maintenance of order. Successful poachers, if they are successful to the point of driving out the gamekeepers, eventually become the new gamekeepers. The barbarian chiefs who had invaded the western Roman Empire in the fifth century asked for and were given, by whichever trembling, powerless man in Rome continued to cling to the mere title of emperor, the dignities of Roman consuls and prefects in the territories they had conquered. (And why should the barbarians want such baubles? Because barbarians know, in their souls, that they are only barbarians; their ability to terrorize the civilized with the threat of violence consoles them, for a moment, at least, for this irksome fact. The same dynamic applies, in this limited respect, to the hooligans in our streets as much as to the Huns of Attila.) Except in Britain, the barbarian incomers went on to assimilate linguistically with the Romanized populations they had invaded. Several centuries later, the Bulgar warriors who conquered the Slavic agrarians of the eastern Balkans similarly adopted the language of their subjects. Though the Muslim Arab tribes who invaded the Middle East and North Africa in the seventh century kept and spread their language, they were nevertheless "barely acquainted with anything that we should recognize as government," and so, recognizing that their new position as conquerors of an empire meant they could no longer remain free of such knowledge, they extended tolerance to Christians and Jews at least partly because "only Christians commanded the necessary administrative expertise to make government possible."[11] The Turks who passed from Central Asia through the Middle East and conquered Asia Minor ceased to be roaming mercenaries; instead, they founded what we call the Ottoman Empire. Like the Arabs before them, they happily co-opted Christians and Jews into their administration. The Mongol invaders of India went native and became the Moghuls, while the Mongols who had invaded China found that they had merely established a new dynasty in the endless succession of dynasties. In several of these cases, the conquering nomads eventually adopted the religion of those they ruled, until their identity was merged with that of their subjects.

It is this phenomenon that gives real weight to Crone's analysis about military castes fleecing agricultural peasants down to subsistence point as a kind of inevitable equilibrium in the premodern world; the military caste was, often enough, an invader or the descendants of invaders, offering self-interested protection against potential fresh invaders. Where the military caste was native, it needed to adopt broadly the same procedures if it was to survive and keep out foreigners.

But the phenomenon also explains why the settled territories won out in the end and the lands of the wild peoples were reduced further and further. Put simply: the latter were parasitic on the former. And, on the occasions where they succeeded in their depredations to the point of capturing the settled territories, then they found that their interests were now those of settlement.

On the other side of the equation, the interests of the settled peoples lay in ensuring that the wild lands on their borders became settled, too, and populated preferably by themselves but, failing that, then at least by neighbors prepared to treat the land on which they lived as property and who had a concomitant vested interest in ongoing stability. Time after time, the military ventures of premodern states—of Romans against barbarians, of Franks against Saxons, of Germans against Wends, of Muscovy against the Mongol-descended tribes, of English kings against Scots raiders—were fought to establish such a state of affairs. Either way, the tendency of such conflicts, in the long term though not always in the short, was to convert nomads or predatory raiders into agricultural settlers.

Clearly, this pattern is rather too simple: during this very long process, many settled peoples were converted into migrants and predators as a result of being uprooted and forced to flee from other, fiercer predators. Such was the pattern of the so-called Great Migration of Peoples (or *Völkerwanderung*) that brought about the collapse of the Roman Empire: the agricultural Germanic tribes were impelled westward by flight from the Huns, who had crossed into Europe from Asia. Those Germanic tribes fled into the Roman lands where, having wrested control from (or, in southern Britain, displaced) the natives, they settled down as farmers. The Slavs did the same, moving as invaders from the region of the Pripet Marshes across eastern, central and southeastern Europe but then settling down there as pastoralists.

Variations on this pattern characterize the settling of America, in which European pastoralists came to the New World as, in effect, raiders. Once in possession of land, they settled down again as farmers, though a few, on the frontiers, continued as wild people for a little longer. (What else are Westerns all about?)

In summary, therefore, we can say that religion was hardly a principal, or even a significant, cause of military conflict in the ancient world. Where the key motivations for conflict were to be found in anything other than the simple taking of booty, women and slaves, it tended to be located in "quarrels over personal, family or group prestige, territorial control, access to markets or commodities or by the need to achieve security."[12] In Europe after the fall of the Roman Empire, warfare was also frequently driven by arguments over legal and dynastic rights.

It is no mere distortion or sermonizing, then, to lump most of these types of causation together under the category of human greed, or else, where that is too harsh a judgment, of the need for security. We can say that wars were overwhelmingly the outcome of competition for control of resources. But early warfare was not caused primarily, or even secondarily or tertiarily, by religion. That came later. And, as we have seen in earlier chapters, even then religion was frequently a cover for the baser motivations we have been describing here.

Mass migrations aside, competition for power and resources continued to be the principal cause of warfare for as long as most states were governed by single individuals with the power to make war or peace. That was because the need for popular legitimation of conflict—the need to sell a particular war to the population that was being called on to fight it and sacrifice for it—was less pressing. In that circumstance, wars were frequently fought for the territorial aggrandizement or dynastic advantage of the ruler. The only public to which he needed to sell such a conflict was, for the most part, the principal nobility or leaders of his military caste: they needed to be persuaded that there was something in it for them. William of Normandy's invasion of England fits such a case exactly: dynastic conflict; territorial aggrandizement; rewards for leading military supporters.

It was this reality that Immanuel Kant pointed to in his hugely influential tract of 1795, *Perpetual Peace.* In this work, he argued that for sole rulers, "it is the simplest thing in the world to go to war," because war does not require of the ruler "the slightest sacrifice so far as his banquets, hunts, pleasure palaces and court festivals are concerned. He can thus decide on war, without any significant reason, as a kind of amusement."[13] By contrast, he insisted, states whose governments were more or less accountable to the populace would seldom fight. In his view, representative government, or democracy, was inherently peaceful: "If . . . the consent of the citizens is required in order to decide whether or not war is to be declared, it is very natural that they will have great hesitation in embarking on so dangerous an enterprise. For this would mean calling down on themselves all the miseries of war."[14]

Among neoconservatives and liberals alike, Kant's view has become the new orthodoxy since the end of the Cold War. Francis Fukuyama was so convinced of it that in the early 1990s, he famously argued that all states were now embarking on capitalist liberal democracy and, in consequence, history (in the sense of violent upheavals) was coming to an end.[15] To say that this analysis has not quite been borne out by subsequent events would be something of an understatement. Even so, President George W. Bush felt able to insist, in a speech at the White House on December 7, 2004, that "free nations are peaceful nations."[16] Western liberals, it should be said, tend to focus on the big picture implied by the Kantian argument, neoconservatives on the particular details of the moment. The former emphasize that if all countries are liberal democracies, peace will be assured; the latter focus on the threat to freedom posed in the present moment by rogue states and are unafraid of using force to bring about regime change in order to democratize them. Both are mistaken.

The Restraints on War

That Kant wrote just as Europe was being embroiled in more than two decades of fighting, as a direct result of the French Revolution and its call for *liberté, egalité* and *fraternité,* was unfortunate. It also counts against

Kant's thesis that it is precisely those states in the Muslim world today whose governments are most susceptible to popular pressure that are also the most belligerent.[17] Populations that feel aggrieved, with whatever degree of justification, are likely to be kept pacific only if ruled by an individual or group with a vested interest in keeping the peace. In Kant's time, as now, it seems, the utmost violence is produced by the egalitarians' struggle to suppress the supposed historic causes of warfare. Neither is Kant's description of princes flippantly declaring war entirely uncontroversial; it may have fitted the eighteenth-century princelings who never personally went into battle. But in respect of some periods of history, it is little better than a caricature. If a medieval war was dynastic, princes stood to lose their thrones, their estates, their families and their lives. The fifteenth-century Wars of the Roses, for example, decimated the English nobility; the fighting mostly passed the peasant population by, unless they were unlucky enough to be in the path of an army.

Even so, the medieval situation, whereby settled (that is, agrarian) societies were inevitably dominated by a military elite, contained a certain internal contradiction. On the one hand, the military caste was necessary to fend off the wild people; the serfdom or its near equivalents of ordinary people was the heavy price that had to be paid for at least that much security. On the other hand, the rulers had the opportunity and the incentive to use their preeminence and expertise to make war on one another, in order to enlarge their domains or to muscle their way to power over one another. The very mechanism, therefore, that was supposed to secure order stood in perpetual danger of securing disorder, with the potential to devastate those economies and populations that the nobility supposedly existed in order to protect.

And the restraint on that dangerous potential was, often enough, religion. As Keegan notes, "The rise of the great monotheistic religions of Christianity and Islam caused the European and Near Eastern peoples that embraced them to agonize over the morality of killing fellow children of God for centuries."[18] Religious authorities, usually tied closely to their secular counterparts (a phenomenon whose unseemly causes and consequences we shall analyze in the next chapter), frequently acted to hedge military activities about with a range of restrictions or prohibitions:

> Elaborate legal codes . . . required the doing of penance for shedding Christian blood—forty days' penance for even wounding a fellow Christian, done by the Norman knights after the victory of Hastings—and the avoidance of war-making during the Christian year's penitential seasons, Advent and Lent. Islam went further. The Prophet's prohibition of fighting between Muslims was taken so seriously by the devout that, during the civil wars of the early Caliphate, contestants recruited armies of infidel slaves to do the fighting on their behalf.[19]

The Islamic traditions also mandate good treatment of prisoners and forbid looting and the killing of women and children—the last of which proscriptions modern Islamist terrorists have chosen to forget.[20] The various faiths were united in upholding the virtues of peace and mercy in general, even as they lamentably sanctioned departures from those virtues in particular instances. And, of course, those particular departures generally suited the secular rulers with whose interests they were often bound together.

But not always. Religious and secular leaders not infrequently came into conflict. And, though the latter could generally overawe the former (a kind of natural equilibrium of the kind that Crone notices in the economic sphere), it did not always work out that way. In any case, *pace* Hollywood and secularist school textbooks, premodern rulers were not religious skeptics, enforcing on their subjects the strictures of a faith in which they themselves scarcely believed. Kings, too, often feared to anger God; only a few ignored such considerations entirely. Most faiths taught that it was a sin to make war on co-religionists, and, if we today consider that a trifling or even a prejudiced restriction, it nevertheless acted frequently as a significant brake on the propensity of rulers to embroil themselves in military conflict.

Clearly, some religions acted as a more serious brake than others. Islam relied more on the popular sense of Muslim group solidarity, the *ummah,* to maintain peace among believers than it did on any formal religious hierarchy, for Islam has no real equivalent to an institutional church. Within the Byzantine world, the patriarch was very much subject to the emperor; even so, religious considerations did, on occasion, moderate the military appetites of Orthodox rulers. In particular, Orthodox monarchs were aware that they were not supposed to fight one another.

In the Catholic West, Augustine's recrudescence of the pagan Cicero's just war theory, and his attempt at creating a theology for it, broke from Christian tradition. They did this in simultaneously sanctifying war while attempting to curtail its frequency and its effects. It cannot be denied that the just war theory has played a major role in critiquing warfare ever since, even among its practitioners. Each and every soldier, and each and every general, is at least potentially asking, in the midst of campaign, troubling questions: "Is what I am doing right? Is it legitimate?" And that has frequently acted as a restraining influence. In the late Middle Ages, the Catholic church's Peace of God campaign acted as a further important dissuader, in certain cases and for a limited period, on the practice of war. A series of church councils between 989 and 1016 sought to prohibit private warfare by exacting from likely disrupters of the peace oaths to be taken on sacred relics and volumes of the Gospels, swearing that they would neither attack clergy or travelers, nor steal from the peasantry nor "encourage any kind of brigandage or violence." Districts that violated these provisions were to be laid under the interdict of the church.[21] Though it did not stifle all warfare, the movement nevertheless had a significant effect throughout the eleventh century in France, Italy, Spain and Germany.

This development in turn led on to the ideal of Christian knighthood, in which the true warrior was supposed to respect his enemy, defend the weak, honor women, refuse to harm noncombatants and in general take every care to ensure that the barbaric necessity of his trade—that of killing people—was rendered as civilized as the fact of its grisly core would allow. The code of knightly chivalry may appear, to a later age that has debunked honor, as so much hokum. But if so, it was a socially useful, even a necessary, humbug. James Bowman's comments on this phenomenon are worth quoting at length:

> Poets, romancers and historians assisted in effecting the assimilation of knighthood and demands of honor and pride to a religion whose Founder was supposed, rather awkwardly, to have identified the latter as being among the most serious of sins. . . . The Christian knight, like so many other features of the religion he professed, was something of a paradox, but he proved to be immensely influential right down to the Renaissance and beyond. . . . He was an important part of the reason why Western ideas of honor developed along quite different lines from honor in other parts of the world.[22]

It was an ideal that, as he says, "reached its highest stage of development with the Crusades and their aftermath."[23]

The most significant distinctive feature of Western Catholicism, however, was neither the just war theory nor the Peace of God nor ideals of Christian knighthood and chivalry. Rather, it was the simple fact of the papacy's independent power base. By its relative freedom, for most though not all of the Middle Ages, from subjection to royal authority, the church was able to act as a moral counterweight to secular power. The predisposition of the military caste to war making was thereby subject to the check or, at least, to the meddling of an independent religious authority that could not easily be shrugged off.

The Catholic church's successes in this regard should not be overstated. And the papacy sometimes added to its other corruptions that of declaring war on its own account. But the point we are making here is that in the Middle Ages, religion was seldom an actual cause of warfare; if anything, it served to restrain it. Certainly Niccolò Machiavelli, in the early sixteenth century, thought so. According to this most influential and unchristian of political and military theorists, the adoption of Christianity by all European states had reduced people's motivation to defend themselves against one another, because the consequences of defeat in war were so much more humane than they had been in the ancient world.

> For in those [pre-Christian] days men who were defeated in war were either slaughtered or condemned to perpetual slavery. . . . When a city was captured, it was either completely destroyed, or the inhabitants were expelled, robbed of all their possessions, and sent to wander through the world. And fear of these consequences caused the men of those days to keep the arts of war in constant practice. . . . But nowadays most of those fears are lost.[24]

Machiavelli bewailed the fact that in his time, "most men think more of going to heaven by enduring their injuries than by avenging them." "The world," he moaned, "has become effeminate and heaven disarmed" by Christianity, or rather, by what he savingly insisted was a "false interpretation" of the faith. If people understood the faith correctly, they would see that "religion permits us to defend and better the fatherland . . . to love and honor it and to prepare ourselves to be the kind of men who defend it."[25]

Edward Gibbon, the famous eighteenth-century historian of the late Roman Empire and a religious skeptic, argued along similar lines. He put the worst possible face on the early stages of the alliance between church and state, that is, during the fourth and fifth centuries. But his disapproval stemmed not from the fact that martial values were foisted on the faith of the Prince of Peace but from the pacifying influence of Christianity on the traditional Roman belligerence that he so much admired. According to him,

> the introduction, or at least the abuse of Christianity, had some influence on the decline and fall of the Roman empire. The clergy successfully preached the doctrines of patience and pusillanimity; the

> active virtues of society were discouraged; and the last remains of military spirit were buried in the cloister: a large portion of public and private wealth was consecrated to the specious demands of charity and devotion; and the soldiers' pay was lavished on the useless multitudes of both sexes who could only plead the merits of abstinence and chastity.[26]

This is the exact converse of the principal modern attack against religion: that it causes war. To be fair to Gibbon, he was reflecting the views of those pagan Romans of the late empire who constituted such an important part of his field of study. Many even earlier critiques of Christianity, from the period before it ever became the dominant religion of the Romans, had been predicated on the same insight: that Christian faith would undermine the martial virtues that had built the empire in the first place. Celsus, the late-second-century pagan writer, had attacked Christianity on exactly these grounds:

> If everyone followed your [i.e., the Christians'] example, nothing would prevent his [i.e., the emperor's] being left all alone and deserted while all earthly affairs fell under the sway of the most lawless and uncivilized barbarians, and no one on earth heard anything about your religion or the true wisdom.[27]

If that last part of Celsus's prognosis has proved to be spectacularly wide of the mark, the immediately preceding point—that widespread adoption of the Christian faith would let the empire fall "under the sway of the most lawless and uncivilized barbarians"—seems chillingly prophetic in the light of fifth-century events. And that accuracy was the central argument of Gibbon's attack on Christianity.

All of this should give any postmodern secularist pause for reflection: the critique of Christian faith as fomenting violence is the exact antithesis of the reasons for which it was rejected by pagan Romans or even by the Enlightenment rationalist Gibbon. Nevertheless, even though the two critiques are mutually contradictory, neither of them is entirely misplaced. We shall look, in the next chapter, at how early Christianity shed much of its pacific nature during the course of the fourth and fifth centuries as part of the price of making itself compatible with the ethos of the Roman order, thereby becoming a fit partner, politically speaking, in the process of governing that order. So militarists had a right to complain, before the church's metamorphosis and politicization, about Christianity's softness; pacifists have some cause to complain about the church's role during the centuries since.

POPULAR WARS

For Machiavelli, as for all his contemporaries, it was axiomatic that the prince or ruler held, and should hold, sole power over making war and peace. The expansion or security of the ruler's realms was the principal purpose of war in the central and late Middle Ages and continued to be so until the advent of the Reformation brought other considerations into play. Until then, religion hardly came into the matter; if the ruler did not prescribe one particular faith for his subjects, then it was practically irrelevant to issues of war and peace. If he did, then he might refer to religion as a justification for his wars, but it was bound to play a subsidiary role; his command was enough to force subjects to obey. For ordinary people who were neither noble nor wealthy, this dynamic continued to hold good, in large measure, even during the sixteenth and seventeenth centuries. Even during the religious upheavals of those years, if rulers decided to change their realms from Catholic to Protestant (or, in some cases, back again) or to make war on another state supposedly in the name of religion, few of the weak and powerless failed to comply. We pay so much attention to the bold minorities who went against the flow that we can forget to attend to the wider picture.[28]

But where war is not a matter simply of a sole ruler's will and so of his self-interest, then, when armed conflicts do occur, they are likely to come about either in propagation of the frameworks that give meaning to the lives of the populations that are fighting or else in defense of those frameworks if they are perceived to be under threat. This becomes true even where sole rulers are constrained by the need to work up at least some degree of popular enthusiasm for a war—say, through conveying a sense that we are being threatened or by fostering resentment and outrage at the putative enemy or of zeal for some cause. Elizabeth I may have been a powerful ruler of England, but she was greatly helped by being able to work on the rising tide of nationalism (a very new phenomenon then) among her subjects, in enabling her to stand up to the might of Philip II of Spain.[29] In more recent times, where the population as a whole, or wide sections of it, hold real influence over government, then the working up of such enthusiasms is absolutely necessary, or else no conflict can take place.

These meaning-giving frameworks are, in general, an amalgam: culture, language and ethnicity, religion, social and economic arrangements, and law. These are the things that delineate our sense of group belonging, of corporate and family identity, of meaning and, in the case of economic and legal arrangements, even our sense of material security. If we can be persuaded that these things are somehow endangered, then most of us will, at some point or other, be prepared to fight for them rather than lose the things that are most precious to us.

It is for this reason that belligerent leaders need to work up a sense of grievance or of threat in the populations they wish to galvanize into military action. The grievance or threat may sometimes be real, but it will nevertheless be the task of the demagogue to heighten it or to concentrate attention on it for prolonged periods. As war reporter Chris Hedges puts it, "The goal is to show the community that what they hold sacred is under threat. The enemy . . . seeks to destroy religious and cultural life, the very identity of the group or state."[30] Hedges is speaking here specifically of nationalist rhetoric but, mutatis mutandis, the same dynamic applies to socialist class warriors and, on occasions, to certain kinds of religious leaders. It is tempting to play the grievance card in such cases or else declare that we are involved in a life-and-death struggle in which the entire future of our society is at stake.

The problem is inherent in the shift from societies ruled by a monarch, prince or emperor to societies with some form of popular rule. The former frequently enforced one form of religion as an instrument of what Marxists used to call social control. But, if the ruler was strong enough and the realms large enough, he or she could frequently do without this device, as the Romans, Chinese, Khazars, Ottomans and, later, the Habsburgs all did. Loyalty to the ruler—a loyalty cascading down the generations and cemented by similar mechanisms all the way up the social ladder—sufficed to hold the edifice of power together.

But as these kingdoms and empires either disappeared or else transformed themselves, in recent centuries, toward some approximation to popular rule, so personal loyalty to social superiors needed replacing by some abstract principle that underpinned the state and gave a rationale as to why this (rather than that) is my state and why its borders encompass these people and territories but not those. To be sure, such rationales were not—are not—easy to come by. And none of them will be convincing to everybody. The United States has been particularly fortunate in holding together a highly diverse population by means of loyalty to a constitution enshrining abstract principles, but it has done so only at the price of constant and exaggerated inculcation and through catechizing in schools and elsewhere. Even then, the tacit acceptance of the cultural norms of Protestant Christianity by Catholics, Orthodox and non-Christians alike has been necessary to hold it all together, along with periodic social paroxysms of one kind or another (the Know-Nothings, the Ku Klux Klan, anti-evolution, Prohibition, the bitter debate over abortion, the rise of the religious right) when those norms have appeared to be under threat.[31]

For many states that moved toward popular rule, the absence of any basis for logical coherence, once personal loyalty to monarchy was taken away, led to the break-up of the state. The consequent searches for new bases of legitimacy have been the cause of most of the major wars of the past two centuries, as nationalism and socialism have vied with one another in rushing to fill the void left by monarchy—a void they were partly responsible for creating. To take merely one important example, most of the instabilities of the Middle East, including the ferocious disagreement over the state of Israel, are attributable to the central fact that the region has not yet settled down in the wake of the collapse of the Ottoman Empire. More than eighty years after that empire's final demise, it is by no means clear to the populations of the Middle East which replacement states, and with which frontiers, might be considered legitimate by the populations that live in them. The existing states are obviously not legitimate; their borders are mere straight lines drawn on maps by British and French imperialists (with the mostly willing connivance of the Americans, it should be said) to suit themselves. Everything that has happened in the interim—from British and French mandates; to the new monarchies installed by those same foreign powers; to the local strongmen such as Nasser, Assad and Saddam Hussein who overthrew them—has been a mere succession of stopgaps, each as unstable as the last. And that instability is a result of perceived illegitimacy by the restive populations who inhabit the successor states to the Ottoman provinces. Arab nationalism and socialism (flirting with the Soviet Union during the Cold War) have contended to be the meaning that Middle Easterners have been invited to attach to their lives and to the states within which they live. Now Islamism has moved into that position with a vengeance, threatening the old, non-Islamist régimes with overthrow and focusing popular resentment at outsiders with a critique rooted in religious rhetoric. A shared religion, though it threatens minorities such as Druze, Assyrian and Coptic Christians and Jews, seems to offer a basis for legitimacy to replace the old empire. The fact that it has been the overarching meaning to the lives of much of the population—and that that meaning is now under threat by the unwelcome intrusion of Western secularism—only adds strength to the Islamists' appeal. In the modern Middle East, we see a prime example of the willingness of people to fight on behalf of the frameworks—moral, religious, social, but ultimately cultural—that give structure and meaning to their lives. We also see, in the same example, how the transfer in the direction of popular rule leaves minorities—ethnic, religious and linguistic—perilously exposed to oppression and violence.

This is not difficult to understand. If we look at the more belligerent rhetoric even within Western societies at the present, it is immediately apparent that it is the meaning-bearing frameworks for which people are prepared to fight. In those frameworks, religion forms sometimes a more, sometimes a less important part. But it is the framework itself for which people can be motivated to fight, either as part of a moral crusade or if that framework is perceived as being threatened in some way by outside forces. That is why President Bush reminded his audience, during his second inaugural address in January 2005, that

> we have seen our vulnerability, and we have seen its deepest source. For as long as whole regions of the world simmer in resentment and tyranny . . . violence will gather, and multiply in destructive power and cross the most defended borders and raise a mortal threat.[32]

Our way of life is under threat. The conclusion is that it can be defended best by universalizing it.

The president can in no way be criticized for seeking to defend the culture of those who had just elected him. Mistake, if mistake there is, comes not in seeking to defend the framework of meaning but in failing to recognize that the other side perceives its actions in the same light, that the itch to universalize one's own framework is the same thing as threatening to destroy all others—and that that resolve is a recipe for calamitous war.

In this circumstance, many, and particularly Westerners, have concluded that the traditional cultures and religions are the problem, that they are the generators of war and that we would be better off without them. This is no place to reiterate arguments I have made at length elsewhere.[33] Suffice it to say here that this conclusion is both a misunderstanding and a mistake. It is a misunderstanding because it fails to acknowledge that the attempt to abolish metanarratives is just one more metanarrative; that compulsory "freedom" makes traditional modes of life and the perpetuation of traditional cultures impossible; that the insistence on driving religion out of the public square and locking it indoors is not tolerant; that the clash of civilizations has not been averted or resolved but victory merely claimed for itself by one of the combatants on the grounds that it is, to its own satisfaction, at least, a kind of *über*-combatant. It is a mistake because, as we see on the news every day, the attempt to achieve these things is productive of extreme violence and because it threatens the frameworks of meaning of those who cannot easily live without them or without the social and economic security that those frameworks make possible. If we insist on following this route, then war will become, and remain, more popular rather than less.

War as Its Own Cause

One final point needs to be made about the origins of and palliatives for armed conflict: war can also be its own cause. There have always been classes of warriors who live to fight; for whom the adrenalin rush of combat has become a fix; for whom the thrill of exerting violent power over others, using in the process the grisly expertise they have acquired by practice, has given a sense of status and purpose that they could not easily find elsewhere; for whom the camaraderie of battle has made mundane friendships and even the vital relationships of family and marriage seem pale by comparison. This, as we noted earlier in this chapter, was what Genghis Khan understood well and exemplified to the uttermost degree. But far less accomplished warriors than he have shared in the same emotions and motivations. As Hedges notes, "The rush of battle is a potent and often lethal addiction, for war is a drug."[34] It was for exactly this reason that many fighter pilots after World War II deliberately took up dangerous sports, such as motor racing or mountain climbing; the thrill of danger was too hard to give up.

There have been many more for whom the vicarious thrill of witnessing or hearing of combat makes war a matter of fascination or pride. Popular wars (popular, that is, in the sense we have been describing here) can, if they have been victorious, leave a legacy of whole populations for whom the sense of communality and purpose necessarily created by war has become appealing by dint of its ability to push more mundane pressures to one side in the light of the urgency of the cause. Hedges records how even those who suffered bombardment and siege in Sarajevo often found themselves, shortly afterward, pining for "that common sense of struggle, . . . the opportunity to be noble, heroic" and to "rise above our smallness and divisiveness."[35] Most British people who experienced the Second World War, whether as civilians or in a military capacity, cannot do other than account it as the central experience of their lives, dividing their whole experience of life into a before and an after. Not all who pine for the vanished sense of collective belonging and common purpose of the war years are deluded militarists; a paler version of the same thing occurs in many places every time there is unusually severe weather. Hardship and danger, however caused, bring us together, prod us into acting sacrificially and put the petty struggles of every day into perspective.

This necessary defense mechanism, however, is not without its dangers. For the propaganda that is necessary to sell war to ourselves, on those occasions when its occurrence is a pressing necessity and sacrifice has become imperative, has rebounded on its objects and created a myth in which the horrible appears beautiful for its own sake. The ethos of ancient Rome or of the Nazis exemplifies just this. It may be true that we need a pool of young men who are ready for grim and sacrificial service in time of war. If so, they will not emerge willy-nilly at the danger hour merely because we need them; the military virtues will need to be accorded a wider place of honor in the society as a whole, or we shall find that we have no supply of such people in time of need. But a careful balance needs to be struck between cultivating such a sensibility and ensuring that it does not provoke the catastrophe against which it is intended to provide.

For the militarist fallacy, deriving though it does from any society's necessary self-defense mechanisms, is a major contributory cause of subsequent conflicts. Keeping its false demands in permanent check while nevertheless keeping the spirit of communal sacrifice and shared purpose in reserve for dire emergencies is a difficult balancing act to manage.

8

EVEN MARX WAS RIGHT SOMETIMES

For much of my career, I have taught Christian history, sometimes to students preparing for church ministry or missions, sometimes to those involved in a wider range of courses of study. And it has been a regrettable necessity to make plenty of space on the syllabus for studies of violent conflict. For the first three centuries of its history, Christianity was spread exclusively by persuasion and was persecuted for its pains, initially by the Jews but later, from 63, by the Romans. The persecutions of the early centuries, in which thousands of Christians died, would probably count as religious conflict, even though the victims were all on one side. But during the course of the fourth century, after the church had been embraced by the state, this early picture changed drastically. Whereas in 300 Christianity in the Roman Empire was still an illegal, persecuted sect, from 312 to 313 onward it gained toleration and official support. By 400, it was the de facto state religion of the empire and was beginning to persecute dissent.

This process, and the theological shifts that accompanied it (in order to justify it), will be examined in the next chapter. For now, we shall pay attention to the effects of those shifts in creating the possibility of Christian wars. For once Christianity in general and a specific church in particular becomes the metanarrative[1] of a given political community, it is almost bound to end up sanctifying that community's wars and even, because it defines the state's culture, causing them. That is because one of the principal causes of conflict between and within states is over the issue of what shall be its governing story, its meaning. What will be its official creed, whether religious or secular? Will the state be a monarchy? An empire? A republic? A democracy? A nation state? The answers to all of these questions imply a particular set of relationships between the individuals who live in the state and a particular stance vis-à-vis the outside world. And so for Christianity or some variety of it to be the metanarrative of a state is to make it more or less inevitable that certain kinds of wars will be fought supposedly in the name of Christianity.

Are such wars the fault of Christianity itself or merely of those versions or distortions of Christianity that allow the faith to be so used? Where other religions operate as the metanarratives of particular societies, are wars fought in the name of those religions—Islam, Hinduism, Shinto, Judaism—the fault of those faiths?

Marx: Religion as Opiate

Marxism, itself a modernist metararrative and implacably hostile to all religion, has a particularly interesting angle on such questions. We have already seen how the godless creeds of modernity, Marxism prominently among them, have been responsible for the most lethal wars in human history. It may come as a surprise, then, to learn that Karl Marx proves an unlikely and entirely accidental ally of Christians in demonstrating that religion is not, in itself, the cause of all the wars attributed to it. This is not because he had the slightest interest in distinguishing between one religion and another or between legitimate and illegitimate expressions of original Christianity; he considered all religious claims equally spurious. Rather, it stems from his assertion that religious claims are a mere cover for more base motives. Although this is untrue in many cases, it is clear that religion has been and still is so used. One need look no further than the sudden religious convictions asserted by Saddam Hussein, who was generally understood to have been an atheist, when he wished to galvanize the support of Muslims behind himself in confronting the Western powers over his occupation of Kuwait.

To be sure, Marx and his followers resolutely denounced religion as a form of "false consciousness" that, in their eyes, perpetuated the subjection of the working masses. Religious belief had to be challenged, ridiculed and opposed, they argued, because it stood in the way of two central communist goals. In the first place, religion bolstered existing capitalist society, and so it obstructed the achieving of a socialist revolution. In the second place, faith in God hindered the attaining of a truly socialist society even after the revolution had occurred. "The abolition of religion as the illusory happiness of the people," he wrote, "is the demand for their real happiness. The demand to abandon the illusions about their condition is the demand to give up a condition that requires illusions. Hence criticism of religion is in embryo a criticism of this vale of tears whose halo is religion."[2]

These sentences come from the same passage in which Marx described religion, famously, as "the opium of the people." This aspect of his critique—the parallel with the addictive, false euphoria of drugs—is almost certainly leveled against evangelicalism. Most particularly, it appears to be aimed against nineteenth-century Methodism in Britain and the United States and against pietism in the German states. Pietism and evangelicalism were particularly strong among the working classes in the new industrial towns. They promised a reward in heaven ("pie in the sky by and by," as their detractors would have said), which consoled their adherents for the poverty, hardships and squalor of the present. Black American religion, on this theory, fulfilled the same function, during both the period of slavery and its aftermath, as exemplified in the lyrics of spirituals: "Nobody knows de trouble I've seen; nobody knows but Jesus"; "Sometimes I feel like a motherless chile, a long ways from home"; "Deep river, my home is over Jordan."[3] By making the unbearable bearable, by being what Marx called "the spirit of spiritless conditions," pietist and evangelical religion fended off the revolution that was necessary and inevitable and would rectify the wrongs of the present.

Accordingly, Marxists set about trying to disabuse workers of their religious beliefs. After the communist takeovers in Russia, in China, in eastern Europe and elsewhere, Marxist governments persecuted religion in various degrees. Perhaps the most ferocious of these persecutions were in the Soviet Union during the 1930s, in Albania under Enver Hoxha and in China during the Cultural Revolution. One suspects that the continuing situation in North Korea is scarcely better than any of them. Far from coincidentally, the regimes of Stalin, Hoxha and Kim Il-Sung all instituted personality cults, the fervor and extravagant claims of which amounted to religion in all but name.

Marx: Religion as Legitimation of Social Order

Yet there is at least some merit, some of the time, in Marx's insistence that religion is a projection, into an imaginary heaven, of a person's or a group's or a state's *real* aspirations. And *real,* for Marxists, means economic and political. More important than religion's emotional-consolatory function ("opium of the people") is its power function. People, Marx argued, sublimate their material desires into something spiritual. They rationalize their wants and end up saying that these are part of the natural or rather, divine, order of things. To say that kings rule by divine right, according to Marxists, means merely that the person speaking supports royal power, presumably because the speaker is one of those who benefits from the hierarchy of landholding that a traditional monarchy represents. If someone at the bottom of the heap (say, a peasant) were to express the same view, it must be because he has believed the verbal trick that religious statements entail and so has mistakenly given consent to his own oppression. Whereas religion as emotional consolation ("opium") gave indirect legitimation to the status quo, the power function of religion gave direct legitimation to the present social order.

It must be admitted that many theologies and churches have done exactly this. Let us look at an early example that illuminates Marx's point. Eusebius of Caesarea, the fourth-century bishop, was one of Constantine's favored churchmen. Eusebius idolized his imperial master, impressed beyond words that he had put an end to the persecution of the church and had showered it instead with all manner of legal privileges and social advantages. According to Eusebius, "Our emperor derives the source of his authority from above." This might be thought to amount to no more than the apostle Paul's dictum that "there is no authority except that which God has established. The authorities that exist have been established by God" (Rom 13:1). Yet Eusebius goes further—much further. It is the emperor's divinely appointed task to bring "those whom he rules on earth to the only-begotten Word or Savior"—that is, to promote christianization. Thereby, "he renders them fit subjects for [Christ's] kingdom." Most pertinently of all for our theme is Eusebius's description of how the godly emperor does this: "He subdues and chastens the adversaries of truth according to the usages of war."[4]

Needless to say, there is not a hint in the Gospels or in the history of the early church that Christianity is to be spread "according to the usages of war." The idea that it should be stems entirely from Eusebius's exaggerated appreciation of Constantine's protection of the faith. Neither can his claim be defended by Paul's statement that the ruler "does not bear the sword for nothing" but "is God's servant, an agent of wrath to bring punishment on the wrongdoer" (Rom 13:4), for the most elementary knowledge about the background to that epistle shows it to be written under the rule of Emperor Nero, who never favored Christianity and, from 63 onward, persecuted it ferociously. Paul's teaching can only refer to the duty of secular rulers to uphold civil and, ideally, moral order, not one particular faith.

Eusebius's most significant remark, however, comes in what follows. "He [i.e., Constantine] frames his earthly government according to the pattern of the divine original, feeling strength in its conformity with the monarchy of God." The use of the term "monarchy" refers to the idea of divine kingship in Scripture, but it also simply means "the rule of one." "For surely," says Eusebius, "monarchy far transcends every other constitution and form of government, since its opposite, democratic equality of power, may rather be described as anarchy and disorder."[5]

This is not the place to reproach Eusebius for failing to be a democrat.

Nobody before the modern world was.[6] Most premodern political discourse warned of the specter of "equality of power." Archbishop Parker warned Queen Elizabeth I's chief minister, Lord Burghley, in 1573 that if presbyterian agitators were not speedily suppressed, "it will fall out to a popularity [i.e., popular rule], and as wise men think, it will be the overthrow of all the nobility." "Democracy" was a word whose connotations were as obviously bad in the past as they seem to express obvious approval today. Eusebius cannot be faulted merely for thinking what everyone else thought.

However, it is not out of place to point out that his explicit approval of Roman monarchy as a system marks a reversal of Christian rhetoric about the empire before his own time. Back in the late first century, when the book of Revelation was written, Rome, the city set on "seven hills" (Rev 17:9), had been "Babylon, the mother of prostitutes," who was "drunk with the blood of the saints" (Rev 17:5-6). The same identification had been made even earlier by the apostle Peter: the church "who is in Babylon [i.e., in Rome] . . . sends you her greetings" (1 Pet 5:13). The imperial authorities rightly suspected the Christians of disloyalty, and that was why, until Constantine's time, those authorities had persecuted them. And, the more the emperors had persecuted, the more the Christians had persisted in identifying the empire as the enemy of God. In lauding the emperor and the imperial form of government, Eusebius was reversing more than two and a half centuries of Christian discourse.

Most telling of all is Eusebius's insistence that Constantine "frames his earthly government according to the pattern of the divine original." In the heavens, he says, there is a pattern of government—and Constantine has copied it faithfully. That is why the emperor is to be obeyed and supported.

This, Marxists would say, and with strong justification, is pure projection. The existing order in the state projects its values and ways of doing things into (an imaginary) heaven. This is reflected so that the rulers can tell their people: "Do this. Obey me. This is the will of God." And the religious leaders will say "Amen."

As the historian Peter Heather has observed, "These were not claims asserted merely by a few loyalists in and around the imperial court." During the fourth century,

> Religion and Empire rapidly reached an ideological rapprochement. Roman imperialism had claimed, since the time of Augustus, that the presiding divinities had destined Rome to conquer and civilize the world. The gods had supported the Empire in a mission to bring the whole of humankind to the best achievable state, and had intervened directly to choose and inspire Roman emperors. After Constantine's public adoption of Christianity, the long-standing claims about the relation of the state to the deity were quickly, and surprisingly easily, reworked. The presiding divinity was recast as the Christian God. . . . The claim that the Empire was God's vehicle, enacting his will in the world, changed little: only the nomenclature was different. Likewise, while emperors could no longer be deified, their divine status was retained in Christian-Roman propaganda's portrayal of God as hand-picking individual emperors to rule with Him, and partly in His place, over the human sphere of His cosmos.[7]

Heather is highlighting the reworking that needed doing on the side of the Roman authorities and political system. Yet the reworking on the Christian side was far greater and overturned the whole direction of Christian rhetoric and theology up to that period.

Through much of the succeeding centuries, religion has supported social order. Not just any social order, in the Pauline sense—order above anarchy, the upholding of morality, the punishment of thieves and murderers—but the specific social order existing in the particular time and place that espoused that form of religious belief. The society of the Middle Ages was based on a pyramid of landholding. It is far from coincidental that the medieval Catholic church was heavily hierarchical, thereby mirroring the feudal hierarchy that it hallowed, rationalized and justified. The social order found its summit in the king, prince or emperor, descended through various layers of nobility via country knights and squires, down to yeomen and finally reaching the serfs at the bottom. Similarly, the ecclesiastical order ran from pope down through cardinals and archbishops, to bishops, to archdeacons, to parish clergy and finally to the laity. To this, the later Middle Ages posited a "great chain of being," with its summit in God, descending through cherubim and seraphim, through archangels and angels, to human beings, and down to the lower creatures, with earthworms at the bottom. Church and state were merely reflecting the order of the creation; it was all an expression of the will of God, the divine order, against which it was sin to rebel.

When the economic order began to change, with the rise of cities and commerce, then religious ideas began to change as well. The Reformation can be—and by Marxists, was—understood as expressing the material, economic aspirations of the commercial middle classes in religious form. Not the personal authority of the pope but of a printed text, the Bible; not an artistic and dramatic liturgy that has visual appeal for the illiterate peasants but sermons and a stress on literacy, such as accompanied business and town life; not ceremonies and magic but reason and abstract concepts (justification by faith, predestination, imputation of sin and righteousness), using the language of legal fiction that came naturally to lawyers and those who had to deal with them; not saints' days and celebrations but regular work discipline and sober sabbath observance; not spur-of-the-moment almsgiving to paupers but measured, organized charity through trusts, hospitals and, most of all, schools; not an absolute ban on lending money at interest (usury) but a pragmatic permission for it, of the kind that would facilitate business. And a greatly truncated church hierarchy, reflecting the greater though far from complete egalitarian mode of urban, commercial existence.

And who, the Marxists asked insistently, became Protestants at the time of the Reformation? The urban trading classes, that's who. To be sure, the different kinds of Protestantism—Lutheran, Calvinist, Anglican—varied in their social appeal. But the point to note is that each variety picked up most strongly among the social milieu to whose interests it was most attuned: support for episcopal government in the Church of England was strongest in the countryside and among landowners and strongest of all with the chief landowner, the monarch. (James I famously observed, "No bishop, no king.") Conversely, the presbyterian-minded Puritans found their support in the clothing towns and among the London merchants. Lutheranism, likewise, found most support in the German cities, but its high view of sacraments guaranteed at least some enthusiasm among peasants. The austerity of Calvinism, on the other hand, restricted the appeal of the Huguenots in France almost exclusively to lawyers and business people.

And so on. The pattern could be extended through history. It could be extended well beyond Christianity to embrace the other major faiths and most minor ones. In each case, Marxists would argue, with some reason, a given set of religious ideas and a particular church project the values of the socioeconomic group that supports it into an imaginary heaven and then, having done so, insists that those values are "the will of God" or of "the gods" whose existence has been conjured up for the purpose.

The trouble with this explanation is that, all too frequently, it works. For some years, I observed an academic who taught senior-level classes in sociology of religion advertise his course each May to juniors by giving them a little test. He would describe four ministers in a certain town, giving brief social and educational backgrounds about each. Then he would list the four denominations to which they belonged. Then he would ask the students to call out which man was a pastor in which church. In all of the years I observed him doing this little promotion for his course, I never observed a student call out a wrong answer. Even the weak students got it right.

WARS OF RELIGION OR WARS ABOUT ECONOMICS?

There is much that could be criticized about this kind of reductionism, and at some points (we shall indicate where presently), it breaks down badly. However, in so far as it has validity—and there is much to be said in its favor—it means that conflicts of religion really turn out to be about something else. The religious wars of the sixteenth and seventeenth centuries, Marxists would argue, are battles between the landed aristocracies of the premodern world and the bourgeois of the modern age. The former used Catholicism or sometimes a high form of Protestantism as their justifying ideology; the latter used the ideas of the Protestant Reformers, especially of Calvin and his successors. The banner of religion was mere camouflage for upheavals that were economic and social. Clear-sighted realism about the actual causes of social conflict, civil war or revolution, Marxists argued, was the monopoly of their own creed.

Perversely, then, Marxism ends up exculpating religion for supposedly religious conflicts at the same time as it blames religion for keeping ordinary people subjugated to traditional rulers. It does this because its atheism assumes that human beings cannot be taken seriously when they claim to be motivated, whether for charity, self-sacrifice, service of others or even warfare by religious beliefs. To the Marxist, religious beliefs are necessarily false. Therefore, the person who claims to be acting from religious motives must be either deluded, self-deluded or attempting to delude others. If deluded, then the Marxist must enlighten him. If self-deluded, then Freudian explanations must be resorted to. If deluding others, then his actions are exposed as a mask for oppressing those others. In fact, the second category might well be subsumed under the third by the more brutal Marxists. For who would want to delude himself, unless he were loath to admit that the religious beliefs in question were actually a vehicle for serving his own material and social interests?

Accordingly, the Marxist historian Christopher Hill spent a lifetime demonstrating, to his own satisfaction, at least (though views like his were the academic orthodoxy of my schooling and student days), that the conflicts over religion in late sixteenth- and early seventeenth-century England, conflicts that came to a head during the English Civil War of the 1640s and 1650s, were the "English revolution." Many non-Marxists conceded and still concede that those wars were, in part, a bourgeois revolution against the landed society of the late Middle Ages, which the king represented and was attempting to perpetuate. But Hill, as a Marxist, went further. For him, the idea of class conflict was the defining, explanatory grid for the events of that and every era. The various strands of Puritanism and sectarianism, he insisted, represented different socioeconomic interests, which would have clashed anyway, with or without their supposed and competing religious legitimations.[8] Religion was vital to the various actors principally because it enabled them to claim the moral and spiritual high ground for themselves and to articulate an insistence that their preferred settlement was the one most in accord with the Will that made the universe.

In this scenario, the religious element of the English Civil War, which struck contemporaries so forcibly as an important causative element, is transformed into what Marxists claimed all along about religion: it was just so much hokum, justifying and legitimating baser, material instincts.

It has to be said, though, that the Marxist model of analysis is a two-edged sword for Marxists and Christians alike. For Marxists, their atheism is laid on a foundation that paradoxically ends up excusing religion for most of the wars waged in its name. For Christians, the problem is that their different churches seem to have been debunked; if the various ecclesiastical bodies can be shown to have arisen, or to have taken the forms they did or even to be adhered to in the present, overwhelmingly by people whose material interests were or are served by those particular church structures and those particular theologies, then how can one continue to take them seriously? They can be blown over at will by the first skeptic who says, "You're only saying that because . . . "

Alas, the major historic, confessional churches can be shown to have functioned largely on this basis. Catholicism legitimized, by and large, the hierarchical society of the Middle Ages. With the approach of the modern, commercial world, it resisted commercialism and the social structures that went along with it. In conflicts within states, it found its greatest support among the most economically and socially traditional sectors of society and so was favored by most, though not all, monarchs. Where those sectors remained politically in the saddle throughout the sixteenth and seventeenth centuries, Catholicism remained in the saddle with them and sanctioned the absolutist monarchies of post-1648 Europe. In so doing, it strengthened resistance to commercial modernity in those countries, thereby perpetuating the relative economic backwardness of that larger portion of western Christendom that remained Catholic. Even so, Catholicism had to redefine its relationship with secular rulers after 1648, to recognize the papacy's diminished power to make and unmake rulers. A further crisis came in the late nineteenth and early twentieth centuries, when creeping economic change eroded Catholic power even in the heartlands of southern and central Europe, leaving the church in acute danger of finding no viable secular polity of which it approved and by which it could be endorsed. Its most devoted following was now among the most backward sectors of society (especially the peasantry of southern Europe) or among those who had suffered from modernization (small traders and traditional craftsmen). Finally, after flirtations with right-wing militarism, emanating from its continuing support among the sectors within historically Catholic societies who were most unhappy with the capitalist or socialist direction in which most of Europe was by then headed, this led to something of a self-reinvention of the church at the Second Vatican Council (1962-1965).

The same general pattern emerges with the Protestant churches from the period of the Reformation onward. Luther was the most theologically conservative of the Reformers, and the Lutheran churches followed in his wake. Calvin, Zwingli and Bucer advocated a more radical break theologically with the Catholic past, and won support from those sectors of society furthest removed from feudalism. Accordingly, Lutheran societies included at least some—most notably the Hanseatic ports—that were more commercial than their Catholic counterparts but less so than the areas that became Reformed. The Church of England was a somewhat more complex case; from the beginning, it was contested between various factions, yet the same pattern showed itself all the way through: the most traditionalist people, theologically and in terms of their attitude toward ecclesiastical hierarchy, were generally from among the most economically and socially traditional sectors of society and from the areas least economically developed; the Puritans, by contrast, were predominantly from the most commercialized elements and regions.

In all cases, the preponderant religion reflected preexisting (i.e., pre-Reformation) economic differences and reinforced those differences during the centuries that followed. The confessional churches, it can be said, provided the various states with their metanarratives—with those large, overarching explanations of what this society and life for every individual within it are all about.

How does all of this relate to our theme of religious warfare? Because, where Christianity in general and a specific church in particular becomes the metanarrative of a given political community, it is bound to end up sanctifying that community's wars and even, because it defines that state's culture and social structure, causing them. To argue in all seriousness that, for example, the dreadful Protestant-Catholic wars of the sixteenth and early seventeenth centuries were not caused by religion because Catholicism was a cloak for a quasi-medieval social order and Protestantism a cover for a commercial society: such an argument is as fatuous as the inquisitor's plea that the church killed no one because victims were handed over to the secular arm for punishment or that killing heretics by burning justified the claim that blood was not shed. The fact is that confessionalist, state-embracing churches have been implicated in warfare down the ages. And they have been implicated precisely because they have been state-embracing, culture-defining sanctifiers of a particular social order. Here Christianity stands guilty as charged.

And not only Christianity. Bernard Lewis, one of the foremost historians and analysts of the Middle East, sees the problem as general among the major faiths:

> In the teachings of the monotheistic religions, it is not God calling on mankind to help Him against His enemies; it is mankind, or rather some parts of it, calling on God to help them against their enemies, to adopt their enemies as His. They are, so to speak, recruiting God. . . . The same approach is often adopted in modern times, as for example in the many hymns and anthems and special military prayers in which God is requested, or sometimes even instructed in somewhat peremptory terms, to save our King, Queen, Kaiser, Tsar, republic, or country, and of course to frustrate our enemies by adopting them as his own.[9]

Such sentiments might have been expressed by a Marxist or by the kind of post-Marxist currently prominent in our media and education systems with a skeptical smirk. But a pious Christian might make the same point, with an air of appalled outrage. In point of fact, however, Lewis is a British Jew much favored by American neoconservatives. And for once, they would all be right.

9

THE LORD MIGHTY IN BATTLE—AND THE PRINCE OF PEACE

Religion . . . is incontestably a source of war. . . . All religion leads to war, but the Word of God is not a religion, and it is the most serious of all betrayals to have made of it a religion.[1]

Are some forms of religious faith, especially of Christian faith, more likely to cause war than others? If so, why? And how would we distinguish between what Jacques Ellul called "religion" and "the Word of God"?

Ellul's career was marked by deep and lasting contact with Marxism, which had held an overwhelming appeal for him in his youth and the strength of whose ideas he never entirely escaped. In particular, the Marxist critique of religion seemed to him rather well-founded, if by that term we mean the basis for a social order rooted in the transcendent and expressed through an authoritative human institution.

But genuine Christianity (what he calls here "the Word of God"), Ellul insisted, is not a religion in the sense required, for it cannot, by its nature, be constrained or allied with civil power. I have rather tartly made the same point elsewhere: "Marxism explains everything about religion except, of course, the religious part."[2] Tart or not, I meant what I said. For religious theories about warfare, support for monarchy against oligarchy, or for oligarchy against democracy or for democracy against either or both:

these are not religious except in Ellul's negative sense of that word. They are about "this world," of which Jesus' kingdom, as he told Pilate, "is not." They are attempts to co-opt God for our purposes and, as Bernard Lewis says, "to save our King, Queen, Kaiser, Tsar, republic, or country, and of course to frustrate our enemies by adopting them as his own." By contrast, what is done unconstrainedly by individuals in self-sacrifice, praying in secret, laying down their economic and social interests: this the Marxist analysis has no power to explain. But this is discipleship of the One who taught us to pray in the inner chamber and to give without letting our right hand know what the left is doing. By the very act of being beyond the ability of public or ecclesiastical authorities to oversee or control, this discipleship slips beyond the reach of materialist debunking, too.

It is not that Christians may have nothing to do with politics, art, culture, education, economics or even war. Far from it. Versions of these things that hold sway in a particular time or place may be utterly corrupt or evil, and, where they are, it is part of our calling to rescue people from them and to call for change. But to claim our particular favored brand of them, conditioned as they all are by the circumstances of time, place, accident and culture, as uniquely godly and justified by Scripture, the church or the Christian tradition, is a fallacy. Even a Marxist can show it to be so.

Primitive Christian Apoliticism

Despite the repeated attempts of so many Christians since the fourth century, there is no solid basis in Scripture for a Christian political order, and so none, either, for a Christian theory of war. (This latter point is just as well because, as we shall see in the next chapter, all attempts to construct such a theory break down in the face of what war is.) Neither a political order nor a theory of war was intended by Jesus. Nor were they intended by the church of the first three centuries—and that not merely because the reality of Christians being a persecuted minority made any such theorizing somewhat abstract but because the church fathers and their theology set their faces against any such thing.

Voluntary Christianity (which is to say, the Christianity of Jesus) is not vulnerable to the Marxist critique and its variants that we have been outlining in the previous chapter. Jesus insisted that his kingdom is "not of this world." "If it were," he added, "my servants would fight to prevent my arrest" (Jn 18:36). Though he could have summoned "legions of angels" (Mt 26:53) to assist him when arrested, he did no such thing.

It can be argued, quite reasonably, that the passion of Jesus is not capable of being made a paradigm for all Christian behavior, because the crucifixion and resurrection are central, unique events that were a necessary fulfillment of Old Testament prophecies. This argument runs that Jesus' renunciation of violence is not an in-all-circumstances proscription of Christian participation in warfare.

Naturally, both sides of the debate between pacifists and nonpacifists resort to Scripture to back up their case. Christian pacifists point not just to Jesus' example but also to Jesus' teaching in the Gospels, and in particular to the Sermon on the Mount: "blessed are the peacemakers" (Mt 5:9); "Love your enemies and pray for those who persecute you" (Mt 5:44); turn the other cheek (Lk 6:29). Peter's exhortation, "do not repay evil with evil" (1 Pet 3:9), is also much cited, as is the simple command "thou shalt not kill" (Ex 20:13 KJV). Nonpacifists, by contrast, stress the Pauline observation that the magistrate "does not bear the sword for nothing," Jesus' positive contacts with soldiers and his failure to rebuke them for their chosen profession, and those passages in the Old Testament, such as in Joshua and Judges, in which God mandates the use of lethal force.

In truth, both sides are guilty of eisegesis, that is, of reading into Scripture meanings already decided on in advance, because gleaned elsewhere. At the least, interpretations on both sides can often be somewhat contrived. Against the pacifists, it should be noted that Jesus' commands are directed toward individual disciples in their personal relationships; they are not prescriptions for public policy, any more than the commands to give to the poor constitute a biblical mandate for compulsory wealth redistribution via the taxation system or that private prayer and fasting are to be made obligatory by government. (And yes, it would have to be all or nothing in that list, or else one would be guilty of outright exegetical dishonesty.) Furthermore, the sixth commandment ("thou shalt not kill") is a condemnation of murder as ordinarily understood, not a blanket proscription of all killing under any circumstance whatever; it comes in a context that prescribes capital punishment (Ex 21:12, 14, 15, 16, 17, 23) under a variety of circumstances.

Against the nonpacifists, it should be noted that Paul's statement about the magistrate and the sword is an observation of political fact, not an endorsement or a recommendation. (In the same way, what I have called Jesus' gritty realism about the inevitability of warfare is not an endorsement of fighting, least of all fighting for Christianity.) And the appeal to Old Testament warfare, while it does make problematic pacifist arguments rooted in the character of God, is nevertheless of little use to specifically Christian discussions of the issue. Old Testament Israel was a theocracy: a political entity that one entered by virtue of birth and was ruled by divine law. Christ's kingdom, by contrast, is emphatically different: the whole point of Jesus' intention to contrast the command of Moses, "Do not murder," with his own injunction not even to be angry with one's brother is to radicalize the commandment and to internalize it in such a way as to make it insusceptible of being regulated by other human beings. You can stone adulterers, if you please, but if the command extends to all those who have lustful thoughts, then we are all dead, in theory, at least, for it is far from clear who would remain to do the stoning, as the woman caught in adultery (Jn 8:3-11) found to her relief. Jesus' point is, first, that you—and you and you and I—are all sinners, in need of redemption; and, second, that God sees beyond mere outward observance and demands far, far more than can ever be commanded by publicly enforceable morality. The same is true of prayer, fasting and charity: what happens in secret, in the inner room, beyond any possible control of religious or other authorities, God sees. And that is what counts.

And, with this, falls any possibility of a Christian state whose law is the Bible, however interpreted.

Not only is it true to say, therefore, that the forms of Christianity described and debunked by Marxists in the previous chapter are not biblical, but neither are they in line with the experience of the church in the first few centuries. This point—that the church of the early centuries followed through on what Jesus had been teaching—needs to be emphasized, for my use of the term "early church," here and throughout this book, is not a sort of spiritually brow-beating code for "what Pearse thinks the New Testament says" in some kind of implied opposition to what anyone else thinks it says. On the contrary, it is demonstrably true to say that the Christians of the first three hundred years had nothing to do with politics, with sanctifying war or, for that matter, with criticizing it. Their discussions were concerned with whether *Christians* might take part in warfare; what happened beyond that or what was permitted or forbidden by governments, was, in the most literal sense, none of their concern.

It is not that the early church forbade its members to participate in the structures of government; the Roman authorities, by persecuting Christians and driving them underground, effectively did that forbidding for them. It is that early Christianity was in no sense a program for running society as a whole; it was a program for running the lives of personally committed disciples. That is the reason, for example, for the New Testament's failure to condemn slavery. This failure is supposedly notorious. In point of fact, the modern assumption that it should condemn slavery is mistaken and a result of misreading what early Christianity was about. It is not that the early Christians accepted slavery, except in the rather fatuous sense that one might accept gravity; it was a social reality. It would no more have occurred to them, any more than it would have occurred to any other private individuals in the premodern world, to campaign for this, that or the other change in society or in government policy than it would to try flying to the moon. For "political campaign," "society," "government policy" or "flying to the moon" are all terminology, along with the notions to which that terminology refers, appropriate only to modern, Western societies in the past couple of centuries, in which private individuals are political actors. But that novel circumstance is found nowhere else. Ordinary people in premodern societies were not political actors, at least, not unless, like the Zealots in first-century Palestine, they wished to take up arms in foredoomed rebellion. And that, as we know, is the one thing that Jesus refused to do.

For modern Westerners, even if they belong to the baptistic tradition (Baptists, Brethren, Pentecostals, Mennonites, etc., of one variety or another), it takes a real effort of mind to disentangle ourselves from the Kantian tradition with which we have grown up and that has shaped our thought forms: If a maxim is truly good, we think, then it must be a universal law. As adherents to a believers' church, American Baptists may know that their congregation is the property only of the converted; as Americans, they know they should accept the separation of church and state. But the combined weight of, on the one hand, the Kantian atmosphere that has nurtured them from the cradle and of, on the other hand, the historic strength of evangelicalism in American life and its consequent status as an unofficial civic religion, is too strong for good Baptists (or good Americans) to withstand. In consequence, the world of the early church, or even of the early eighteenth century, is all but inaccessible to them, at least without great and unrelenting effort of mind.

To reiterate, therefore: the early church had no theory of warfare—as to when and how it might be considered just—for the prosaic reason that Christians neither were nor sought to be nor could imagine themselves being in a position either to make or to influence political decisions. At the level of personal decisions, which is where the church did seek influence, it continued strongly to discourage violence and the taking of revenge.

But the church also discouraged Christians from participating in the army. The debate rages, therefore, as to whether this fact stemmed from a principled pacifism (no Christian should ever fight) or from objection to the immoralities of army camp life and to the requirement for soldiers to swear by the Roman gods. But, whatever we might think of those debates (and the evidence can be made to point to either conclusion), what is certain is that Christian involvement in the military was minimal. Only by the late second century do we have any clear evidence of the existence of Christians in the army, and even then the most frequent source of such evidence is the expression of church leaders' disapproval of the fact. Some soldiers who became Christians sought to leave their profession; some were martyred.[3]

THE BIG SHIFT TO CHRISTIAN WARS

Only when, during the course of the fourth century, Christianity found itself at first endorsed by an emperor (Constantine) and consequently no longer persecuted but then actively encouraged and, finally, toward the end of the century, made effectively compulsory—only then did Christian attitudes toward the military begin to change. Not long after the mid-century, Basil of Caesarea (c. 330-379) felt able to write to a soldier with whom he had become acquainted, congratulating him that he was "a man who demonstrates that it is possible even in the military profession to maintain perfect love for God and that a Christian ought to be characterized not by the clothes he wears [i.e., army uniform] but by the disposition of his soul."[4] Everything about this sentence indicates that Basil felt himself to be overturning traditional Christian expectations and his own previous opinions, as indeed he was. His contemporary, Athanasius of Alexandria (c. 296-373), went further and commented, sometime before 354, that "one is not supposed to kill, but killing the enemy in battle is both lawful and praiseworthy."[5]

Ordinary people on the ground detected the changing trends soon enough, and Christians acted out scenes that would have horrified their predecessors in the faith. A recent Scots Catholic historian concedes that in late fourth-century Alexandria,

> the triumph of Christianity had been effected by hordes of often fa-

> natical Coptic monks who would periodically sweep down from their desert monasteries, attacking the pagans and their shrines, and burning any temples left undefended; in 392 A.D. they finally succeeded in burning the Serapium, and with it the adjacent Alexandrian library, storehouse of the collected learning of antiquity. The houses of the city's pagan notables were ransacked in the monks' search for idols; no one was safe. The most notorious outrage was the lynching of Hypatia, a neoplatonic philosopher of the School of Alexandria and a brilliant thinker and mathematician. She was pulled down from her palanquin by a lynch-mob of monks, who stripped her, then dragged her naked through the streets of the town before finally killing her in front of the Caesarion and burning her body.[6]

It all represented an enormous change from the Christian attitudes of two generations earlier. In the first place, the army had become a less hostile environment for Christians after Constantine's accession to power. Sacrifices to the Roman gods were no longer required. In the second place, Christian leaders began to endorse what previously they had condemned. Finally, Augustine of Hippo (354-430), the most influential theologian of the period, recognized that Christianity was now a program for running society, and so he began to formulate a definite theory of warfare and to discuss how, in certain circumstances, it might be considered just.[7]

All of this stood the body of Christian teaching that had been accepted for the first three centuries on its head. But the transformation in the social position of the church had already been stood on its head. Augustine, it might be argued, was merely trying to help theory catch up with practice.

In any case, the Christian leaders' use of Scripture had been undergoing a profound alteration, during the course of the fourth century and even more thereafter, in a way that prepared the ground for a changed view of warfare.[8] The new, state-church exegesis of Scripture appealed to the Old Testament political and judicial arrangements as normative for

Christian states, thereby undoing the spiritualizing and radicalizing thrust of Jesus in the Sermon on the Mount while retaining that teaching's universalizing aspect. But it was hard for the new exegetes to be entirely consistent. If Old Testament laws were to be a model for Christians, then one would find that one was committed to wars of extermination against enemies and nonbelievers, such as those of the books of Joshua and Judges. Even defenders of state Christianity have generally balked at this. Augustine was happy to justify the use of force against misbelievers in a state that was already Christian, but when he cited the book of Daniel in order to do so, he minced his words. He pointed to the example of Nebuchadnezzar who, he said, had "decreed that anyone in his kingdom who blasphemed against the God of Shadrach, Meshach and Abednego should be punished appropriately."[9] But "appropriately" is too coy; Daniel 3:29 gives the king's actual words: "I decree that the people of any nation or language who say anything against the God of Shadrach, Meshach and Abednego be cut into pieces and their houses be turned into piles of rubble."

No wonder that Augustine does not quote the text in question; not even he was willing to say explicitly that misbelievers should be cut in pieces and their property destroyed. Yet, if the method of biblical exegesis is sound, then nothing less will do. If the Old Testament is to stand as a model for a Christian political order and a justification for Christian violence, then this and Joshua 6:21 (the destruction of every living thing in Jericho) or Joshua 8:2 (the annihilation of the people of Ai) not only can but also must be accommodated within it.

To be fair to Augustine, he did come close to this position. In rebutting the objections of a Manicheaen who was "horrified at the wars waged by Moses," he asked, "What is it about war, after all, that is blameworthy? Is it that people who will someday die anyway are killed in order that the victors may live in peace? That kind of objection is appropriate to a timid man, not a religious one."[10]

It was a long way from the Sermon on the Mount. And it is impossible not to notice the content that Augustine was packing into those last two adjectives: it was entirely classical Roman, rather than Christian. In the Roman tradition, "timid" had been a term of contempt and dismissal—the opposite of pride (viewed positively) and manly courage. And "religious," in that usage, referred to the ancient qualities of honor and a willingness to sacrifice oneself to the needs of the empire or of one's family.

It is not that the Roman virtues were always necessarily bad, but they were not the same thing as the Christian ethos. Yet the alliance of church and state demanded that they be made the same thing. If the state needs to fight, as states always have and always will, then there needed to be a Christian rationale for determining when such conflicts might be religiously justified and how they were to be fought.

The Middle Ages and Since

The Middle Ages in the West were dominated by the late classical, Augustinian synthesis of neoplatonic philosophy and badly adulterated Christian thought. And that included, naturally enough, the christianized just war theory. As we saw in chapter 7, even then Christianity acted more often as a force for restraint on war than it did, as in the Crusades, as a catalyst for violence—and that fact is all to the good.

Certainly it provides at least a modest contrast with Islam. We have considered the point in chapter three, so there is little point in belaboring the fact here, but it is undeniable that with the possible exception of some regions of southeast Asia, wherever the faith of Muhammad predominates today, it was originally spread by violence. When, in September 2006, Pope Benedict XVI quoted a Byzantine emperor who had made the same basic point, he provoked fury, including violent fury, among Muslims around the world. While the responses of some Muslim leaders during the furor seemed encouraging in respect of future trends, the comment of the Saudi Grand Mufti Sheikh Abdul Aziz al-Sheikh does not inspire any confidence that a future Muslim empire would permit even access to the simple facts of history: "This is all a lie . . . Islam . . . was spread only through the conviction of peoples who saw the good and justice of Islam."[11]

As we saw in chapter 2, however, the Roman Catholic, Eastern Orthodox and Protestant state churches do not have spotless records in this regard either. The Eastern Orthodox church did not espouse Augustine's theory, on this subject or anything else, but it legitimized the defense of the Byzantine Empire. This might be thought fair enough, and apologists for eastern Orthodoxy can point to the concurrence of most historians that the Orthodox church neither called for holy war nor offered spiritual benefits to Christian soldiers as an incentive to fight, and the clergy were, at least some of the time, quasi-pacifist. Indeed, following a ruling of Basil of Caesarea, soldiers who killed in battle were, in theory, at least, to be excluded from communion for three years. However, lest this lead to unwarranted idealization of Orthodoxy, it should be remembered that the Byzantine emperors held a quasi-priestly status within the church and were seldom above giving religious legitimation to war and offering spiritual benefit to participants. Emperor Herakleios, in the 620s, is recorded to have encouraged his troops, who were about to face the Persians, with the thought that "when God wills it, one man will rout a thousand. So let us sacrifice ourselves to God for the salvation of our brothers, may we win the crown of martyrdom so that we may be praised in future and receive our recompense from God."[12]

Emperor Constantine VII (913/945-959) told his troops, when facing the Muslim invaders, that they must "be the avengers and champions, not only of Christians, but of Christ himself, whom they [Muslims] wickedly deny."[13] It nevertheless remains broadly true that "the use of the phrase *holy war* in a Byzantine context is misleading because *the* Orthodox conception of war failed to incorporate, or actively rejected, crucial aspects of related ideologies."[14] Yet, as we have seen, there were important exceptions to this, and they became more frequent with the passing of the centuries.

Rather like Islam, Eastern Orthodoxy often benefits today from scholarly special pleading on the subject of warfare. Unlike Islam, Eastern Orthodoxy does have something to be said, relatively speaking, in its favor. But such pleading can go too far. Timothy (or, since his conversion to Orthodoxy, Kallistos) Ware, commenting on the dreadful and inexcusable ravaging of Constantinople by the Western Crusaders in 1204 and the "wanton and systematic sacrilege" that accompanied it, suggests that the suffering Greeks "must have felt that those who did such things were not Christians in the same sense as themselves."[15] But this, frankly, is humbug. The Byzantines had visited cruelties as bad and worse on their enemies. Following victory at the battle of Kledion in 1014, for example, the soldiers of Emperor Basil II (976-1025) had blinded ninety-nine Bulgarian prisoners in every hundred. (Each hundredth man was blinded only in one eye so that, with the aid of a rope, he could lead the others back to their home territory.) It has been calculated that of 109 Byzantine rulers over the centuries, just 34 succeeded in dying in their beds, and only a few of the others on the battlefield or in exile. Most were assassinated, starved, mutilated by castration or the gouging out of their eyes, poisoned, suffocated, strangled or hurled from the top of a pillar.[16] And however little the Orthodox church may have been directly to blame for this catalog of barbarism, the notion that the Orthodox world was Christian in a sense that the Latin West was not may safely be discounted.

The record of the Latin West, though, was brutal enough. Lebuin, a missionary to the recalcitrant Saxons of Marklohe in the 770s, told them,

> If you are unwilling . . . there is ready a king in a neighboring country who will invade your land, who will despoil and lay waste, will tire you out with his campaigns, scatter you in exile, dispossess or kill you, give away your estates to whomsoever he wishes; and thereafter you will be subject to him and to his successors.[17]

Charlemagne proved as good as Lebuin's word: he did exactly this, and the Saxons were incorporated into Christendom. In the following century, Saint Methodius induced Prince Bořivoj of Moravia to convert to

Christianity with the promise that "you will be the lord of your lords, and all your enemies will be subordinate to your power."[18] Stephen, the first Christian king of Hungary, sought to impose his new faith on his subjects, but "when he could not convert them by exhortation, he had to suppress them by force of arms."[19]

When Kievan Rus' was christianized from Byzantium in 988, the chronicles record that its prince, Volodymyr, "sent heralds throughout the whole city to proclaim that if any inhabitant, rich or poor, did not betake himself to the river [i.e., to be baptized], he would become the prince's enemy."[20]

During the Middle Ages, it seems, the record of the churches of Christendom is hardly better than that of Islam. The Crusades and the sixteenth- and seventeenth-century wars of religion are particularly notorious examples of savagery that the churches allowed to be legitimized in the name of God.

However, though the churches of the Reformation were not one whit better than their Catholic and Orthodox counterparts, the sixteenth and seventeenth centuries did see two hopeful developments that have resulted in a massive reversion, during the modern period, in the general direction of the early church's stance.

In the first place, the Reformation triggered a multiplicity of breakaway groups of all kinds, as many competing exegetes took it into their heads to expound their own ideas of the real meaning of Scripture or to make a claim for themselves as prophets or theologians. This was exactly what the spokesmen for Catholicism had said would happen if the protest of Martin Luther was allowed to stand without being squelched. However, among the several varieties of state-church Protestantism (Lutheran, Reformed, Anglican) and many varieties of heresy (mystical-revolutionary, rationalist, anti-trinitarian) that emerged, there arose also a number of groups that, while adhering to biblicism and not departing from historic creedal orthodoxy, resurrected the idea that Christianity was for disciples only, not a program for running society. The evangelical Anabaptists embodied this insight and, though their repudiation of wider society was somewhat extreme (a reaction to the apostasy they saw as attaching to any participation in the institutions of Christendom), they proceeded to gather churches on a voluntary basis and forbid their members to serve as magistrates or in the armed forces.

Later sectarians (for radicals of this type were and are sectarians in the sociological sense of that word, even if not in the theological sense) took more nuanced approaches. The English General Baptists of the seventeenth century reiterated most of the Anabaptist teachings and rejected any notion of a Christian state. Yet they were not pacifist, and, at the mid-century, many of them were prepared to fight for secular causes, such as religious toleration and even, during the Leveller disturbances, for manhood suffrage. The Quakers of the 1650s were willing to fight on similar grounds (they were particularly numerous in the New Model Army), though after the restoration of the monarchy in 1660 they became pacifist.

In the second place, the Reformation accidentally brought about a situation of religious pluralism. This was not desired by any of the Protestant Reformers; all endorsed religious persecution and the enforcement of their own brand of Christianity. But the mutual failure of the Catholic and Protestant churches to eradicate one another, or even to force all adherents of the other confession into compliance in some of the states or localities controlled by one side or the other, necessarily created a circumstance in which adherents to the new faith and the old were forced, however unwillingly, to live side by side. Furthermore, the fracturing of state-church Protestantism generated a situation in which, in a few areas at least, rival Protestantisms were obliged to coexist. Finally, the inability of governments to extirpate sectarianism (Anabaptism of various kinds in continental Europe; Baptists, Quakers and others in Great Britain) despite often ferocious persecution left some areas characterized by de facto pluralism. It mostly took a century or two, but de jure pluralism followed.

The Netherlands and Britain were the most pluralist of the lot. The Dutch Reformed had led the revolt against Spain from the 1560s until

1648 and had been obliged to refrain from persecuting their still-Catholic countrymen as the price of gaining their cooperation, or at least their acquiescence, in revolt. Dutch Mennonites had sheltered in the resultant legal uncertainties. The new, fast-growing trading city of Amsterdam found itself host to a wide array of merchants and artisans from many countries and soon found that those economy-enhancing, tax-revenue-producing newcomers included Spanish Jews and Moors escaping the intolerance of their common enemy. And it was sometime around then that the Reformed dream of a monolithic Calvinist commonwealth slid slowly into the mud of a Dutch canal.

The muddled, center-ground nature of Elizabeth I's attempt at reformation in England left the national church eternally contested between competing factions. A small number of Puritans eventually lost patience that they would ever succeed in pulling the tug-o'-war far enough in their own direction and so, from the 1580s onward, splinter groups of them broke quietly away from the Church of England to form their own congregations. Several generations later, in the 1640s, the Civil War had the effect of making the national church presbyterian; in fact, the country was so anarchic that each parish did that which seemed right in its own eyes. Then, after the restoration of the monarchy in 1660, so many of the Puritan old guard found themselves expelled from the Church of England that, alongside the sectarians, they made up too considerable a number to be persecuted with ease. And so, from 1689, they were granted a grudging and limited toleration.

Except for Pennsylvania and Rhode Island, the American colonies all tried persecution, and all failed. That failure was due not to principle but to geography and the sheer ethnic and religious variety of the incomers. Imprisoning them all was not a viable or practical policy. The aftermath of the American Revolution merely enshrined in principle what had for long been necessary in fact. From very early on, it would be true to say, North America has functioned on sectarian principles.

Since these three countries were the dominant forces of modernization, their patterns in this matter, as in so much else besides, have tended to be adopted, in the long term, by the other states of what was formerly Christendom. Those states, as we all know, have hardly been pacific in recent centuries. But after 1648 their wars were not, in general, conceived as wars for Christianity.

This change by states left the churches somewhat more free to pursue directions of their own. The open societies brought about by the modern age have created a novel situation for Christians that contrasts sharply with their historical experience: unlike the first centuries, or the Middle Ages or the Reformation era, private individuals are now political actors, if they wish to be so. The idea of a political campaign is now eminently possible. That still does not give the church as a whole a mandate from God to idolize some historically contingent political credo. We are no more a program for running society as a whole than we were when Jesus delivered the Sermon on the Mount. But it does render the radical separatism of the early centuries or of the Anabaptists somewhat redundant. It is now possible, on the one hand, for individual Christians to get involved in wider society without being persecuted by that wider society and, on the other, without seeking to capture its structures for some christianized project of social coercion, as in the medieval Christendom scenario.

The state churches remained attached to the ideal of Christendom for a long time after the governments on which they depended and that had formerly depended on them had effectively orphaned them. And, by the twentieth century, many other issues, most notably those of theological liberalism, had come along to muddy the waters yet further. Yet, on the issue of warfare, the growing separation of church and state had enabled the churches to begin finding their way back to the situation of the early Christians. Most were not and are not pacifist. But the idea of calling a crusade or a military campaign in the name of furthering the gospel of Christ seems abhorrent and ridiculous to almost all of them. The debate among Christians now is that between pacifists and nonpacifists; fighting for Christendom is not, by and large, on the agenda.

So, though Pope Benedict's predecessors gave their blessing to much carnage in the name of Christ, the papacy has long since been converted to the peaceful advance of Catholicism and, since the Second Vatican Council, has formally endorsed religious toleration for all, including for non-Catholic minorities in preponderantly Catholic countries.

The churches of the Reformation have by now taken the same view for so long that many of their current adherents are surprised to learn that their sixteenth-century founders (Luther, Zwingli, Calvin, Cranmer and the rest) ever thought otherwise—though they certainly did. The world is now so far changed that all churches, regardless of their history and original rationale, must act, in effect, on Anabaptist principles. That is to say that no one is obliged to adhere to them and that they must win their adherents on the basis of persuasion alone. In that circumstance, all churches are, in effect, believers' churches, and the option of fighting for Christianity has been given up. The wheel has come almost full circle.

But the problem is not quite past, and complacency is by no means in order. The low-level fighting in Northern Ireland from the late 1960s to the mid-1990s was sustained on the basis of Catholic-Protestant division, in which at least some members and some clergy in each community were prepared to give succor, sympathy and support to practitioners of violence against the other. And where, as in some parts of eastern Europe, an individual historic church retains even now something like the old monopoly, then the temptation remains for that church to assert ownership of a state or of the population within it. As we have seen in the Balkans, this can be highly dangerous, because it threatens those who, for historic reasons, form part of a different ethnicity—nearly always reflected in membership of a different religious confession—with oppression or expulsion or, if they attempt to resist, with war. It was precisely these circumstances that helped generate the war in Croatia in 1991 and 1992 and in Bosnia from 1992 to 1995. In such circumstances, all Christians must act in concerted ways to prevent disaster and to cajole the dominant church to loosen its hold and abandon its pretensions to define an ethnicity, a state or its polity.

Precisely because there is no biblical basis for a Christian polity, neither is there any basis for a single, Christian-approved secular polity. Running the world is not what Christianity is. So just as we may not pursue a theocracy, neither may we idolize any other series of political arrangements; all of them can be shown to be contingent on the accidents of time, place and culture in which they have arisen and, as we saw in chapters five and six, to absolutize one of them (in practice, it will nearly always be the arrangements of the time and place in which we happen to live or have grown up) is idolatry. We are free to participate in the society around us, to be salt and light in its political, cultural and educational life. And even, perhaps, its military. But we may not absolutize their forms as if they were uniquely Christian, or we misunderstand them and ourselves.

Nations cannot be Christian; only individuals can. If Christians can fight, then it cannot be for Christianity, for that is a contradiction of Christ himself. The question is: can a Christian fight at all, even in a secular cause, say, to protect the weak or to right a monstrous injustice? In the following chapter, we shall consider the answers that have been given to that question, along with the consequences of those answers.

10

CAN A CHRISTIAN FIGHT?

Arguments, especially biblical arguments, about the permissibility or otherwise of Christian participation in warfare have been rehearsed in countless publications, and this is no place merely to repeat them. As far as Scripture is concerned, much hangs on the relation between the Testaments, though that is not quite the end of the matter. Debate rages also over the meaning and scope of Jesus' commands in the Sermon on the Mount and on the distinction between a Christian's actions as a private person and actions in public life, or over whether such a distinction is legitimate.[1]

Our purpose in this book, however, is to examine the relationship, in the past and in the present, between religion, especially Christianity, and war, in order to draw conclusions from that historical experience. How have Christians, in practice, answered the question of whether or not a Christian can fight? And what have been the consequences of those answers?

As we have noticed, in the fourth century, Christianity became allied to particular states. In consequence, the church began to justify warfare, most famously in Augustine's version of the just war theory, thereby creating the possibility of Christian wars. However lamentable that fact may be, there is a certain inevitability about it. For once Christianity or any religion or philosophy is used to legitimize a state or states, then that religion or philosophy is absolutely bound to produce a theory of warfare, if it does not already possess one. And the reason for that is extraordinarily simple: there cannot be such a thing as a pacifist state.

The Security of Tiny States

Many readers will, perhaps, balk at this. Surely this cannot be true? Surely a state could renounce force, declare itself no threat to its neighbors and a neutral in any future conflicts, and others would then leave it alone?

True—but only for about twenty minutes. History knows no example of a state that renounced force, but it knows of many (indeed most) that were too weak to resist aggressors at some point and so have not endured down to the present. There is no sign that this fundamental reality is about to change.

Yet what about the continuing existence of Liechtenstein? Of San Marino? Of the Vatican City, Monaco or Andorra? These are states so obviously small and powerless as to make it inconceivable that they could defend themselves against the forces of Mali on a bad day, let alone against a reasonably well-armed and well-led aggressor. Surely their continued existence demonstrates that states can renounce force and survive?

A moment's reflection, however, indicates that this is not, and cannot be, the case. Every one of those states exists on the sufferance or rather on the goodwill of its neighbors who, from a strictly military standpoint, are in a position to extinguish it or protect it at their pleasure. If Switzerland were to invade Liechtenstein, then Austria would be extremely angry and in a position to do something about it. Conversely, if Austria were to invade Liechtenstein, then Switzerland would know how to respond. And that is without even taking account of other powers, in Europe and elsewhere, who would react negatively to such a development. Of course, neither Austria nor Switzerland is in any danger of being tempted to act in such a foolish manner. The military realities are so self-evident that they have doubtless not needed even to be articulated on the sub-sub-sub-agendas in the military counsels of either country for generations, and both states have got on with more worthwhile things instead, like banking, trade, making chocolate, fostering tourism and quietly preparing emergency plans to deal with real enemies instead.

The same, broadly speaking, is true of the other small states we mentioned. Their protection lies not in their ability to stand up to an aggressor but in ensuring the solicitousness of larger powers for their welfare, say, by making themselves important in trade or other ties. And this has been true also of middle-sized or even of quite serious military powers; during the Cold War, even France and Britain needed the United States to underwrite their security against the Soviet Union.

At the lower end of the power scale, this protection by others is the only reality that counts. Andorra and Monaco continue to exist in the same way and for the same reason that a baby, an invalid, an old person or a pacifist does within civil society: they are recipients of the protection that is exerted by those who are willing and able to do so; that is, by adults generally and by the forces of law and order in particular.

The case of the Vatican City illustrates this fact clearly. Not only does it exist entirely by permission of Italy, but also its territory is exactly as large as Italy allows it to be. During the Middle Ages and down to the nineteenth century, the papal dominions extended to a wide belt of territory across the center of the peninsula. Nor were they in the least defenseless then; some popes led their troops into battle personally. During the nineteenth century, however, the existence of the papal states and of all the other small territories in the Italian peninsula came under threat from the rising tide of Italian nationalism. The nationalists, led by Mazzini and Garibaldi, made a tacit alliance with one of the more powerful Italian states, Piedmont, and declared the aim of uniting Italy in a single, national state. At one point, in 1849, the pope's territories were overrun by these enemies. However, on that first attempt, the pope was reinvested with his lands as a direct result of French military action, which intervened to scatter the nationalists, at least for the time being. (This was not, by the way, because of any Catholic zeal by the government in Paris but partly by a wish not to have a strong, united neighbor—a state of Italy—on its southeastern border and partly by fear that Austria might move in to crush the rebels and then remain in occupation.)

Finally, however, the Italian nationalists succeeded. The small states were all swept away and replaced by a united Italy. Only one exception was made.[2] For a combination of domestic and international considerations—not wanting to antagonize devout Italian Catholic opinion too far and thereby make their new country ungovernable, and not wishing to invite retribution from foreign Catholic powers should the papacy be expelled from Rome—the papal states were kept in existence, but only as a few acres in the center of Rome. There, in the Vatican City today, the papal writ still runs, symbolically guarded by a few men in picturesque uniforms, carrying medieval weaponry. The tourists and pilgrims generate huge economic benefits for the powerful neighbor beyond its walls, thereby giving Italy a vested interest in leaving the frontiers exactly where they are. And the quixotic and picturesque Swiss Guards who patrol them are a ceremonial reminder of the fifteenth and early sixteenth centuries, when popes fielded real armies of Swiss mercenaries.

The Vatican is, obviously, something of a special case. Yet its history illustrates perfectly the hard truth that there can be no such thing as a pacifist state and what is the real significance of the continuing existence of small polities that cannot, realistically, defend themselves.

Just War Theory and Its Problems

So we have vindicated our observation that, once Christianity became entangled with secular government, and the fourth-century Roman Empire and the kingdom of Armenia gradually began to enforce Christian profession on their populations, then it became inevitable that a Christian legitimization of warfare, under some circumstances, at least, would eventually be produced.

Augustine christianized the just war theory of the pagan Roman orator Cicero.[3] According to Augustine, a particular conflict might be considered morally defensible if it was declared for a just cause *(ius ad bellum)* and conducted in a just fashion *(ius in bello)*. Under the first category, the war must be fought to secure justice (i.e., there must be no aggression, revenge, conquest); it must be a last resort after peaceful attempts to resolve a conflict have failed; there must be a realistic opportunity of achieving the aims of the war (no desperate or pointlessly bloody last stands); and the war must be conducted under direction of the ruler, in an attitude of love for the enemy.[4]

It is doubtful whether any of these stipulations could always be met. The first, a prohibition on conquest and revenge, is perhaps the most straightforward. But, as anyone who has attempted to mediate in even a personal quarrel knows all too well, the ability of human beings to insist that "*he* started it!" is almost limitless. As for last resorts, it is usually difficult to determine whether every peaceful attempt at resolution has been tried to exhaustion. Protagonists of war will declare, "Enough!" at an early point in negotiations; supporters of the enemy or self-loathers in our camp will never be satisfied that we tried hard enough or that provocations were sufficient to warrant a military response. In any case, such a doctrine has always run into the severest difficulties in practice. As Roland Bainton has observed, attempts at mediation presuppose "a relative equality of power; the lion does not arbitrate with the lamb. . . . Rome would not submit her own disputes to arbitration, though willing to enforce it upon her subjects."[5] Neither is a realistic opportunity of success always discernible before battle is joined; history has produced some surprising outcomes of military confrontations. The battle of Marathon comes to mind. Augustine's doctrine would presumably have ruled out the defense of the Alamo, yet its bold defenders are generally considered heroes today. Perhaps an undue adherence to the same precept should have induced the British to surrender to Hitler in the late summer of 1940, but it is just as well they did not.

The final stipulation would rule out all rebellions, a sentiment with which all premoderns would have agreed. Even a Nero or an Ivan the Terrible seemed preferable to the anarchy that would ensue if every person arrogated to himself the right to invoke military force. (This is a sentiment still appreciated by many Iraqis who were but recently under the rule of Saddam Hussein and now have yet worse horrors to contend with.) Yet the prohibition offends those of us who think that Bonhoeffer and other Germans involved in the plot to kill Hitler had right on their side.

And what if, like Bonhoeffer and his fellows, one lives under a ruler who commands an unjust war? Must Christians obey the call to arms? Augustine's statements on such questions do not entirely reassure:

> A righteous man, who happens to be serving under an ungodly sovereign, can rightfully protect the public peace by engaging in combat at the latter's command when he receives an order that is either not contrary to God's law or is a matter of doubt (in which case it may be that the sinful command involves the sovereign in guilt, whereas the soldier's subordinate role makes him innocent).[6]

Again:

> Christian soldiers obeyed their emperor despite his lack of belief, but when it came to the issue of Christ, they acknowledged only Him who was in heaven. If Julian wanted them to honor idols or throw incense on the altar, they put God before him. But whenever he said "Form a battle line" or "Attack that nation," they obeyed instantly. They distinguished between an eternal and a temporal master, but at the same time they were subject to their temporal master for the sake of their eternal one.[7]

The exercise of a Christian conscience about matters of warfare, it seems, is the prerogative of the ruler, even if the ruler is not a Christian. As for "sinful commands" embroiling only the giver in guilt, "whereas the soldier's subordinate role makes him innocent," this is the plea of the concentration camp guard: he was only following orders.

Already we are encroaching into Augustine's second category of stipulations: the requirement that war be fought in a just fashion. This is considerably more problematic than the first. Just war requires that a conflict must be fought to reestablish peace (i.e., that it does not encompass the total destruction of the enemy); that promises to the enemy must be kept;

that the force used must be proportionate to the cause of its being invoked; and that noncombatants must be respected, that clergy were not to fight and that there were to be no atrocities.

The terrible truth, however, is that virtually all wars encompass unspeakable acts. Whenever I taught on this subject in theological seminary, I used to ask my class to give me an example of a war that they considered would be justified by Augustine's just war criteria. It was a low and dirty trick on my part. I knew in advance to which example they would point; the combination of national myopia and historical ignorance did the work for me every time: They pointed to the Second World War. A collection of far from perfect but at least acceptable democracies had confronted the utter evil of Nazi Germany. (The less well-informed among them thought that the former had made war in order to prevent the Holocaust, though ordinary British and American people knew little about the gas chambers and concentration camps, and their leaders suppressed information about them until after the war was over.) In response, I used to point out that by far the largest portion of the fighting and the dying took place on the eastern front, where horrifying evil in the form of Nazi Germany confronted horrifying evil in the shape of Stalin's Soviet Union. But, even if we discount that rather large point and address ourselves exclusively to the conflict that my students had had in mind—that is, between the Anglo-American and other Western allies and Nazi Germany and Japan—there remained serious difficulties. I would list for them the serious war crimes perpetrated by the Western Allies: the carpet bombing of cities; the deliberate creation of firestorms in Hamburg and Dresden with effects similar to and death tolls that outstripped those of the atomic bombs on Hiroshima and Nagasaki; the forcible handing over to Soviet and to Yugoslav partisan custody of hundreds of thousands of prisoners who the British and Americans and the prisoners themselves knew full well would be shot by the communists. A just war could not deliver justice in war. "And this," I would conclude, "is our best case of a just war. So what is the theory worth?" And it probably was the best case. That was the point. So what of the rest?

The fact is that war has an appalling dynamic of its own: it drags down the participants, swiftly and surely, into ever more savage actions. The side that is losing will frequently resort to some tactic that had hitherto been out of bounds or off limits in order to put itself back into contention or to damage its enemy in a way that the enemy could never have anticipated.[8] If such tactics are successful, then the enemy will respond with something yet more harsh. War, it has to be said, is war. Though individuals may act morally or heroically within it, there is nothing moral or heroic about war itself. That is precisely why statesmen and individuals of sense and morality do everything in their power to avert it.

And it is this reality that gives the pacifist argument real force. The just war theory is so general in its strictures as to be almost worthless. As for its *ius ad bellum* aspects, most states in most wars have pointed to it as vindicating their participation in a particular conflict. That is to say that, in most wars, both sides have claimed to be justified by it. So what is the use of a theory that can so repeatedly and so easily be pressed into service for mutually contradictory causes?

The Problem with Pacifism

The failure to frame a moral theory sufficiently practical to encompass warfare might be held to imply that pacifism is the most moral recourse in the face of violence. And perhaps it is. However, for reasons that became apparent earlier in this chapter, there cannot be a pacifist state, merely a state that depends on others, possessed of more force or of the willingness to use it. So a consistent pacifism, exercised by a private individual located somewhere in the world that is not, say, Andorra, demands also the retreat from politics into private life. As Evelyn Underhill put it, when advocating a pacifist stance during World War II, "questions of expediency, practicality, national prestige and national safety do not as such concern" the church of Christ.[9]

That view is consistent (if one accepts, for the sake of argument, that the early church was pacifist) with pre-Constantinian Christianity. It is consistent, too, with the stance taken by sixteenth-century evangelical Anabaptism. The Anabaptists called for believers' churches that were entirely unconnected with the state and its necessary concomitant, the use of force.[10] The claims of Christian discipleship were directed to individuals; the faith and its various moral and spiritual demands had no place, therefore, in the public realm. Pacifism dictated or, at least, was a concomitant of a retreat into the private sphere.

But a lot of more recent religious pacifism does not observe this rather drastic self-denying clause. Much pacifism is to be found in churches that are not anabaptistic in either theology or historic roots.[11] It tends instead to be correlated with the prevalence of an outlook borrowed from secular liberalism: human beings are essentially good and amenable to reason; if there is a conflict that threatens or occasions violence, it must be because of misunderstanding between the parties or because of some structural injustice. The solutions are therefore twofold: multicultural engagement to increase understanding and particularly to eradicate real, nonnegotiable cultural differences that might occasion conflict; and political agitation for an ever more egalitarian world in which no one can feel harm done by or nurse grievances that might give rise to violence. Convictions of this kind, rooted in romanticism about human nature and presented in a rhetoric of Christian benevolence, are a long way from historic Christian pacifism. Rather than demanding a retreat into the private sphere, the new pacifism is a political stance, though one that, for reasons we have rehearsed, cannot finally succeed. Secular liberalism does not need to succeed in any traditional sense, however; it is enough for it to generate sufficient self-loathing within the wider society against that society's institutions, particularly its defense mechanisms. Almost no one seriously believes, as a theoretical proposition, that if we cease to defend ourselves, everyone will be nice to us and all will be well. But, by talking about each and every conflict in which we are potentially or actually engaged as if sweet reason could somehow make it go away, we defend ourselves without conviction, undermine our security, despise those whose job it is to defend us and tie them up in ceaseless government inquiries and red tape. And so on.

This rather distasteful aspect of some modern pacifism is merely circumstantial, however. For many convinced pacifists are fine and brave people who are obviously not afraid to dirty their hands or put themselves in harm's way in their attempts to minister to the injured and dying. They do as Jesus would do. The stretcher bearers of Third Commando, "one of Britain's toughest Second World War units," for example, were pacifists who, as John Keegan has observed, "were held by the commanding officer in the highest regard for their bravery and readiness for self-sacrifice."[12]

The core difficulty of a consistent pacifism, even of this admirable kind, is the danger of elevating personal moral purity of the self above the sometimes desperately urgent need of the weak for protection. In civil society, where a madman is on the rampage with a gun (and this is far from being a merely hypothetical scenario; it is enacted somewhere, several times each year), then a principled unwillingness to use lethal force to stop him is not moral purity but moral narcissism. It is to place the self or a view of the self above the lives of those who could have been saved by determined violent action to defend them. What we mean is that a repudiation of force in all circumstances is not merely an abdication of moral responsibility (as if life-and-death issues should be decided by such abstract, pompous-sounding phrases); it is an abandonment of victims—real people—to their fate. And in exactly the same way, a refusal to use force to stop the soldiers of Genghis Khan, Hitler, Stalin and Pol Pot from wreaking what carnage they will is, to put no finer point on it, not necessarily the optimal moral stance. As George Orwell insisted in 1942, during the Second World War, "Pacifism is objectively pro-Fascist."[13] That is, perhaps, a harsh way of putting the matter, but Orwell was insisting that the entirely foreseeable consequences of an action or decision for inaction are an inseparable part of the moral choice. Without millions of people willing to use countervailing force against monstrous violence and injustice, the entire human race (or those, at any rate, who survived) would be forever condemned to inhabit the nightmare worlds those monsters sought to create.

THE IRRESISTIBLE FORCE AND THE IMMOVABLE OBJECT

Where does this argumentation leave us? We already know that those who defeated Hitler were an alliance of a state that was in every way as bad (Stalin's U.S.S.R.) with tolerable democracies that nevertheless, as we have already noted, perpetrated frightful crimes in the process and aftermath of the fighting. So, when we are done second guessing our parents and grandparents, what *should* they have done?

But, if this issue seems hard enough, our problems are only beginning. The technologies of the second half of the twentieth century have generated weapons capable of destruction so fearful that the dilemmas become yet worse. Paradoxically, nuclear arms kept the peace during the Cold War; the threat of mutually assured destruction (rightly called simply M.A.D.) concentrated minds wonderfully.

These weapons violate virtually every principle of the just war theory: that war be fought to secure justice; that there be a realistic opportunity of achieving war aims and an attitude of love for the enemy; that a party that is at war use proportionate force and not encompass the total destruction of an enemy; that noncombatants be respected. For this reason, John Stott, that most influential of Christian teachers, was a nuclear pacifist during the Cold War, even as he subscribed to traditional just war theory. It was, in his view, the Augustinian doctrine that rendered any use of nuclear weapons utterly impermissible.[14]

And yet, in this terrifying new world the state that does not have nuclear weapons is effectively disarmed when locked in serious confrontation with the state that does possess them. No one seriously doubts that, had the Western states of the Cold War era renounced the use of nuclear weapons, then they would eventually have succumbed to communism.

What can the Christian conscience say in the face of this awesome dilemma? For the logic is at one with the principle of warfare: a refusal to use violence hands the world over to the person who will. If those with moral consciences make such a renunciation, the world will be run by those with no moral conscience. And so it is with nuclear weapons. Yet how is the use of nuclear weapons—the incineration alive of countless men, women and children—compatible with a moral conscience? Of course, it is not.

The Cold War passed off without the use of these fearful weapons, thanks to their powerful deterrent effect. The possession of them by each side forefended their use by either. Indeed, it deterred a lot more than this. So scared were Western allies and Soviets of the possibility of escalation that these major protagonists did not engage in armed combat with one another directly. Instead, they sponsored proxy wars around the globe, directed against one another's interests and supporters.

But deterrence cannot work unless each side is certain that the other really would, in extremis, use the dreaded weapons. The claimed willingness cannot be a mere bluff. And therein again lies the insoluble dilemma for Christians. We are called to live by the Sermon on the Mount in the midst of a world whose operating principles were correctly identified by Machiavelli. No wonder that the apostle Paul cried out, "What a wretched man I am! Who will rescue me from this body of death?" (Rom 7:24). Even the person who desires to escape from sin finds that warfare's logic of evil is inescapable.

Now communism is, North Korea and Cuba aside, little more than a memory.[15] Yet the danger is not diminished but rather increased. The end of the Cold War has produced greater instability and generated the frightening likelihood that weapons of mass destruction (W.M.D.)—nuclear, chemical or biological—will be used, somewhere, sometime. The logic of deterrence needs now to operate not just between two sides but between many. Even here, however, it will probably work, for to risk attack would be, in every sense, M.A.D. The real problem in the post-Cold War world is not that a nuclear warhead may come via intercontinental ballistic missile over the polar ice caps; it is far likelier to be smuggled into an elevator in Manhattan by suitcase, delivered by a suicide bomber who cannot even be identified, far less deterred, and whose organization is but a proxy of a proxy of a proxy and probably, therefore, not under the final control of the weapon's originator. What measures might be justified or even possible in fending off such a threat? How, and against whom, would one legitimately and proportionately strike back in the event of a failure to do so?

And even now we are not done. If these terrible dilemmas are the new reality at the level of weapons of mass destruction, the new realities at the bottom end are almost as ugly. The developing world is awash with cheap weaponry; a Kalashnikov can be bought for just a few dollars in many conflict-prone countries. Land mines are a cheap and moderately reliable defense of a front line in a poor country, yet their effects linger for decades, killing and maiming people long after the conflict is over. Perhaps worst of all, many armies in sub-Saharan Africa use child soldiers, youngsters who have been kidnapped and brutalized at a young age by forced participation in extreme violence.[16] Though their deeds are often despicable, they might be viewed as victims as much as those who are killed as a result of the violence they inflict.

Yet a large and growing proportion of the population of sub-Saharan Africa is now Christian. How should the Christian African respond to these realities? If land mines are not used, then the side that forswears them stands to lose to the militia that has no such scruples. Worse still, what does one do when child soldiers swoop on a village to gouge, maim and murder women and children? If one shoots them down, one is killing children who have been stolen from their parents and brutalized. If one holds fire, one is yielding up more women and children to be put to death in an unspeakable fashion. Does Augustinian theory have an answer to this?

This is what is meant when we say that warfare has its own dynamic of evil, dragging its participants ever downward—that war is war. We can and should try to regulate it, to humanize it by treaties like the Geneva

Convention. This has been attempted in different ways over the centuries: traditional codes of honor among warriors; quasi-legal systems like the Kanun of Lek Dụkagjin that limit in scale while simultaneously permitting blood revenge in tribal and clan societies; the ideal of knightly chivalry; pagan and Christian ideals of just war; religious and other taboos like places of sanctuary or against fighting on certain days or in certain seasons; modern technocratic mechanisms like the Geneva Convention or international war crimes courts. But we can never hope to be more than partially or temporarily successful. Always, some parties will find it in their interests to ignore such conventions, or else the ever-changing technology of warfare will render some of their provisions redundant.

We should secure interstate cooperation to capture and punish people who are guilty of atrocities and massacres, even though that process is visibly subject to politicization and can smack of mere victor's justice. In other words, such processes, codes and interventions are vulnerable to becoming just one more instrument of conflict. When, to take just one example, the Bosnian Muslim leaders (1992-1995) realized that international forces would occasionally intervene against the Bosnian Serb army when it shelled civilians, the Muslim high command took steps on several occasions to ensure that this happened. Local, religious and international attempts at containing the worst aspects of warfare are no more than mitigations, but they are all we have.

Just as criminals will always possess at least one advantage over the forces of law and order—that of holding the initiative—so the appalling dynamic of warfare will always eat away at the conventions, treaties, codes and law courts designed to limit and constrain it, leaving attempts at regulation one step behind. It is not that the attempt to hold it within bounds is a waste of time but rather that war can never be sanitized; it is the most fearful of human activities. And no system can take away from individuals, Christian or otherwise, the responsibility for what they, in their own persons, will do, which orders they will obey and which disobey, even at the cost of their own lives.

SEEING THE DILEMMA: LUTHER KING AND BONHOEFFER

Having seen the impasses to which pacifist and nonpacifist arguments lead us, where might we go from here? Certainly, I have no easy answers in my pocket. But we might pause to consider the thoughts and actions of two thinkers who have attempted, with no small degree of persuasiveness, to take account of the weaknesses of the traditional positions and to cast around for a basis on which Christians might act.

Martin Luther King (1929-1968) was essentially a pacifist but urged that this was not equivalent to a passive stance in the face of evil. Inspired by the example of Gandhi in British India ("Christ gave us the goals, and Mahatma Gandhi provided the tactics"), he took the view that reform could be attained by black American Christians as they outmatched the capacity of their oppressor, white America, to inflict suffering by their own ability to absorb it.[17] This would happen until a large enough body of opinion among white Americans was shamed into abandoning the mistreatment of black people.

> But be ye assured that we will wear you down by our capacity to suffer. One day we shall win freedom, but not only for ourselves. We shall so appeal to your heart and conscience that we shall win *you* in the process, and our victory will be a double victory.[18]

At a cost that included King's death by assassination, the strategy worked, at least insofar as the state of the law was concerned, and reform was achieved.

Dietrich Bonhoeffer (1906-1945) was a minister in the Protestant state church in Germany and a committed opponent of Hitler. Though a prolific theological writer and an influential pastor, he has been best known since his death for two things. In the first place, he is the author of an astonishingly insightful devotional book, *The Cost of Discipleship,* which takes the form of a commentary on the Sermon on the Mount and in which he cuts through all of the cant that so frequently surrounds such expositions. In the second place, he was involved on the periphery of the failed plot to assassinate Hitler.

Bonhoeffer's initial thoughts seem to have been similar to those held later by King. However, as World War II proceeded, Bonhoeffer came to the conclusion that the Nazi leaders could not be shamed into abandoning its ways—that Hitler and his henchmen had consciously and irrevocably chosen to pursue the path of evil to its end. That being so, Bonhoeffer reluctantly came to the conclusion that, in order to save life, Hitler must be killed.[19] The plot misfired, and Bonhoeffer and most of his co-conspirators were arrested and eventually executed.

Why were Gandhi and King largely correct in their calculations about the capacity for change among, respectively, the British colonialists and white Americans, while Bonhoeffer also correctly despaired of any such change among the Nazi leaders? It is strongly arguable that the former two groups were largely affected by a Christian-informed conscience, while the latter group was inured against it. That is not to say that the British ruling classes in the 1920s to 1940s or white Americans in the 1960s were all actively committed Christians—far from it. But those groups had been brought up, educated in and continued to be surrounded by environments in which Christian ideals were highly influential. And, in consequence, they were susceptible of having their consciences pricked. Religious influence, once again, acted as a force for the disarming of conflict.

All three men (and it must be remembered that Gandhi was not a Christian) eventually died for their beliefs. Gandhi was assassinated, after independence for India had been achieved, by a hardline Hindu who was outraged at the concessions made to Muslims. Bonhoeffer was hanged, just days before the end of World War II, by the Nazis. And King was shot dead (at the same age as Bonhoeffer—thirty-nine) by a white racist who was determined to stop the reforms that the Baptist preacher was in the process of achieving.

It is significant that neither Bonhoeffer nor King was martyred specifically on account of his Christian faith. And Bonhoeffer had been engaged in a plot to kill someone: the Führer. If Christians can, in certain circumstances, legitimately fight (and I think they can), then that fighting clearly cannot be for the faith. It can only be for secular causes: to defend the weak from slaughter; to fend off an imminent attack; and perhaps, in limited circumstances, to right a grotesque wrong. And this is so not merely because fighting for Christianity would leave us guilty as charged by the secularists (and thereby spoil the argument of this book) but because, as the teaching of Jesus, the doctrines of the early Christian fathers, the Anabaptist insights about the church, Bonhoeffer's *Cost of Discipleship* and King's *Strength to Love* all testify, faith in Christ is something for which we can only die—not kill. To fight under the delusion that one is thereby promoting Christianity is to lose sight of what Christianity is, just as to fight a war under the delusion that the conflict can be covered and sanitized by some ethical system is to lose sight of what war is. As Jesus told Pilate, "My kingdom is not of this world. If it were, my servants would fight to prevent my arrest" (Jn 18:36). It is arguable that soldiers were numbered among the wider circle of Jesus' disciples and undeniable that even his inner circle possessed swords (Lk 22:38). But his servants did not fight because, as we all know, to have fought for Jesus by releasing him would have undone the central purpose for which he had come. The kingdom of God is not something for which we can fight; to attempt to do so is, by definition, to undo it.

Christians may fight to save or protect others but not to secure the promotion of or even the protection of their faith by the public authorities. Even then, as we noticed with the case of World War II, which my students understandably but wrongly considered to be so cut and dried, wrong actions, even war crimes, may be committed by the right side, and it may be the duty of Christian combatants to refuse to participate in them, even at the cost of being arrested or executed by their own side.

For the Christian must always insist on doing the one thing that no sensible military policy can possibly countenance: keeping his conscience in his own hands. Armies depend on the automatic, prompt and wholehearted carrying out of orders—a reality that, as we have seen, Augustine well understood. The soldier, in normal military practice and in Augustinian theory, hands over his conscience to the commanding officer on enlistment. No armed forces can be organized around the principle that the individual combatant can select which orders to obey.[20] Yet, I would contend, it is precisely this that a Christian may not do; the obedience and willingness of the Christian to follow orders must always be more provisional and tentative or, at any rate, less absolute, than traditional theories allow. And this is no different from the age-old problem for Christians when confronted by state power and identified by the apostle Peter in Acts 4:19 and Acts 5:29: "We must obey God rather than men."

General Sir Mike Jackson, Chief of the General Staff in the British Armed Forces, who admits to "a quiet and simple faith," admitted that one cannot make an easy distinction between oneself as a private person and as a soldier obeying orders:

> You would be in internal conflict, if you said, "My duty requires me to do this but my judgment tells me I should not." Either your duty prevails . . . or . . . your conscience . . . prevails and you say "I cannot do that, so I will have to leave."[21]

Easier said than done, of course, especially if one is a junior soldier in the heat of battle, when decisions that are matters of life and death have to be made in split seconds for oneself and some other person; often, when one cannot be sure who the other person is: friend or foe, man, woman or child.[22]

As we have seen, the objections to pacifism are overwhelming in the face of radical evil in the world, while theories insisting that war can be just do not stack up. Furthermore, Christian attempts to steer between the difficulties of pacifism and those of just war theory break down into implausibility. Warfare destroys and breaks down not only human lives and bodies, human relationships and communities but all of the moral and theological categories by which we ordinarily attempt to codify, measure and regulate those things. It is an evil so radical that (in my judgment) it frequently does not even give us the option of washing our hands of it and walking away. For the weak and defenseless cry out for protection. Warfare, let it be said, is the most intractable of problems to which, neither in theory nor in practice, is there any convincing moral solution. "War," as the great American General William Sherman, commander of the Union forces in the Civil War, aptly reflected in old age, "is hell." And let none of us pretend otherwise.

11

THE RELENTLESS WAR AGAINST FAITH AND MEANING

In the end it comes to this, that if you want to exorcize conflict then erase history and eliminate difference. But be well assured that any such policy will be the occasion of the most ferocious conflict.[1]

My friends include two very different men. One is a pacifist Mennonite leader whose humility, shining example and character have been an inspiration to me over many years. The other, whom I came to know quite recently, is a remarkable man whose work once entailed spending long periods of time underground in a bunker in Missouri, for the purpose of defending us all by babysitting fifty Minuteman nuclear missiles, along with the codes that he was authorized, in extremis, to enter in order to fire them. The conclusions I have reached in the previous chapter will, it is to be feared, sadden both of them. And that, in turn, saddens me. But I hope that they, along with other Christians of all kinds, will agree that war is the most fearful of human activities, from which we should daily pray that we might be delivered; the world is a violent place, whose terrors and mortal concerns will always impel many good people, including Christians, to consider force as a means to defend all that they hold most precious or sacred.

Aside from the usual chaos of the world of human beings—in rebellion against God, at loggerheads with one another and frequently torn by violent conflict—peace everywhere has come to be threatened in recent decades by a new phenomenon. And that is the growing military, political and cultural domination of the world by a novel kind of Western society, more prosperous and more cut off from traditional cultures and their values than our ancestors could ever have imagined.

This circumstance—domination by those who have no real comprehension of the dominated—is one highly conducive to instability and war. To be sure, where those wars are between Westerners and non-Westerners, they are, by now, almost always asymmetrical in nature. Indeed, the recent coinage of the term "asymmetrical conflict" is a clear enough indication of how novel is the prevalence of this phenomenon, as of the circumstances that have given rise to it. Non-Western forces cannot hope to stand up to the armaments and technology of the Americans, of NATO or of the Israelis on the battlefield. The Western military behemoths have vast resources at their disposal, resources easily capable of winning the kind of set-piece battles that their enemies are understandably unwilling to fight. So the question arises as to why, despite such odds, Islamists and others are so often willing to take on the Westerners at all.

WAR AND THE WESTERN THREAT TO TRADITIONAL CULTURES

As we have seen, aside from human greed for power and for things, the principal cause of warfare throughout history has been conflict over the shape of society itself, in terms of its meaning, its traditions or perceived traditions, and its culture. Where that is perceived to be under threat, people will be willing to fight. And religion, historically and in the present, has been one of the biggest single frames of meaning, a principal conduit of tradition and one of the major shapers or even definers[2] of culture.

In this respect, principled irreligion in the first half of the twentieth century functioned in the same way as religion itself—though as the key to some radical, alternative meaning and novel culture, such as communism and fascism. Those totalitarian creeds made no bones about their own bellicosity. For them, warfare was either a virtue if it was in the right cause (communism) or a virtue in itself (fascism) because a proving ground for Nietzschean heroes and pure races.

The godless ideologies killed their scores of millions, and now they, in their turn, are dead. But godlessness is not dead in the postmodern West. Far from it. It has merely abandoned its own former metanarratives. The new atheism is every bit as anxious to distance itself from its communist and fascist antecedents as I have been in distancing genuine Christianity from the ghastly distortions of the Christendom period, an exercise with which the large majority of contemporary Christians would concur.

But for Christians, the exercise bears a rather different aspect to that in which the atheists are engaged. The Christians can point to three centuries of their faith in which no believers were engaged in constraining anyone to belief or in justifying warfare, still less in fighting wars in the name of their faith. They can point to a continuing tradition, even during the Christendom period, of Christians who did not endorse fighting for the faith or in forcing belief. And, in recent times, those Christians have once again become the overwhelming majority.

Secularists have problems of a completely different magnitude. Their history is much shorter, for one thing. Many states in the past have been, in effect, secular, but none has been secular*ist* and anti-religious on principle, except the regimes whose nature and pedigree we considered in chapter 1. To be sure, contemporary secularists repudiate the fascist and communist ideologies, yet they have nothing to put in its place. Their quarrel with communism and fascism, they would argue, is one with their quarrel with religion. The trouble with all of them is that they believe something to be true. Claims to higher-order beliefs, they insist, are inherently arrogant and oppressive. Those claims and the beliefs that underlie them are the principal cause of war.

The solution? To banish such beliefs to the margins of society wherever they are found. Only so do we have any chance of peace.

The new version of secularism, then, is every bit as bossy as its communist and fascist predecessors; it has become what I have called elsewhere the "metanarrative of antimetanarrativism" and the "absolutizing of relativism"[3]—not simply a denial of meaning but a denial to which all must submit.

This assumption has by now become so all-pervasive among Westerners as to be almost platitudinous. Take the example of Chris Hedges's recent book, a volume whose more positive aspects we have already had cause to notice: *War Is a Force That Gives Us Meaning*. The title alone should be a danger signal, suggesting as it does the possibility that war is always wrong *because* it gives meaning, in the sense we described in chapter seven. In fairness, it should be said that Hedges mentions several times that he is pointing out merely the danger that war can be an appealing activity because it "gives meaning to sterile lives."[4] That would be an acceptable line of argument, because it implies that the solution is to have lives invested with real meaning instead. However, he does not attempt to show that wars are fought only by hollow cyphers of people with otherwise "sterile lives," for that would be a completely unsustainable argument that flies in the face of common experience. And he nowhere spells out what real meaning or meanings might or should save us from the possibility of war. He thereby leaves open the suspicion that, in his view, meaning is itself the problem and the cause of militarism—that it is something to which we should not aspire. This suspicion seems to be confirmed when he opines that "once we embrace a theological or ideological belief system that defines itself as the embodiment of goodness and light, it is only a matter of how we will carry out murder."[5] The problem turns out to be not so much that war gives us meaning but that a belief in meaning will lead to war—that only the embrace of meaninglessness can deliver peace.

The trouble with this is that all belief systems (certainly all traditional ones) consider themselves to embody the truth (or, if he insists, "goodness and light")—that they are better than their alternatives. Yet it is this elementary fact, according to Hedges, that makes the carrying out of murder or preparing for war inevitable. To avert that danger, it seems, one must embrace no belief system.

Hedges, whose book is otherwise stuffed full of many helpful insights and moving testimonies, has not said this in so many words, but his meaning is nonetheless clear. The sad thing about his kind of analysis is that it is no longer even controversial in the West. The equation between belief system and violence is virtually taken for granted.

And it is the need to rebut this mistaken notion that is the principal reason for writing this present book. Religions are unavoidably a belief system. Yet that elementary fact, according to postmodern Westerners, makes faith of any kind a prelude to warfare. When *jihadists* enact appalling terrorist acts in our cities and religious violence explodes around the world, Westerners consider themselves confirmed in making such an analysis. But it is a profound mistake, even so.

Against this misreading, we have made four main arguments. In the first place, it is clearly demonstrable that the attempts to replace religion with secularism, whether old style (communism and fascism) or new style (compulsory meaninglessness), have not stemmed or even eased the flow of blood in the world but rather have increased it.

In the second place, given that reality—that religion is not so easily dispensed with—it becomes imperative to inquire what kinds of religious beliefs are more likely, or less, to promote violent conflict. And the historical record indicates that primitive Christianity, along with its echoes down the centuries and in the present, is what its Founder intended when he said "blessed are the peacemakers." That is because, although Christianity is certainly a metanarrative that claims to be the truth in a sense that postmodern Westerners have lately come to find unacceptable, primitivist Christianity, as distinct from its later, Christendom-era developments, does not seek to impose itself and so is not a program for running society as a whole. Even if its followers are not necessarily pacifists, they will not fight for that religion. The problem with meaning and belief systems, then, does not lie where Hedges insists that it does—with the fact of their existence. Rather, it lies in the insistence on universalizing them.

In the third place, the contemporary wars in which religion is implicated are, for the most part, fought for the cultures and cultural values from which a particular faith is, for whatever historical reasons, inextricable. Secular metanarratives, whether communism, fascism or even liberal, free-market democracy, do not escape this circumstance. They are, in effect, secular religions for which people will fight.

Fourth, there is no possibility of abandoning all ideas of truth; even the attempt to abandon it has become, in the West, a new and crushingly oppressive truth of anti-truth that its protagonists are incessantly seeking to universalize. And that attempt at universalizing the repudiation of traditional cultures along with their associated religions is generating new, persistent and ferocious forms of warfare.

Bloody Secularism

Secularism and the various creeds it propagates have introduced fundamental destabilization into domestic and international affairs, rendering warfare a more persistent problem than it ever was in the past. The Italian historian and political scientist Emilio Gentile concludes that

> the greatest and most inhuman massacres, which involved the mass slaughter of millions of victims at the altar of deified political entities, were inflicted during the [twentieth] century by political movements that operated very much as . . . intolerant religious movements.[6]

Martin Wright agrees that "the striking development in war in the past two hundred years is not its growing destructiveness, but the way it has increasingly become the instrument of doctrinal conviction." And, by doctrine, he is referring not to religious dogma but to secular, political tenets. The reason for the development he notes is that political utopianism "approximates war to revolution" and "blurs the distinction between war and peace," a distinction he correctly describes as "the foundation of civilized life." Political utopianism has been responsible for "every war in Europe since 1792," all of which, with the partial exception of the Crimean War, were initiated out of "some doctrinal motive, asserting some horizontal right against some vertical legitimacy." To those who doubt this, he proffers the statistic that "since the American Declaration of Independence in 1776, every war between great powers, with three exceptions and those before 1860, has led to revolution on the losing side."[7]

The assertion of "some horizontal right against some vertical legitimacy" is the factor that unites almost all Western meddling in non-Western space, from neoconservative pressure on dictatorships that have fallen foul of Washington or London to the tying of feminist values or birth control to aid programs or the activities of the Western-payrolled United Nations and its offshoots.

In that case, misrepresentations of the past are, it seems, acceptable in order to score a point. So, in a prominent magazine one writer, as part of his assault on the prominence of Christianity in American political life and on President George W. Bush in particular, opined that

> history judges religious zealots harshly, particularly those wielding state power. The Crusades slaughtered millions in the name of Jesus. The Inquisition brought the torture and murder of millions more. After Luther, Christians did blood battle with other Christians for another three centuries.[8]

To describe these claims as dubious would be an understatement. It seems certain that "millions" were not killed by the Crusaders; it is quite certain that the Inquisition did not have victims in anything approaching such numbers; the period of religious warfare ushered in by the Reformation was bad enough but did not extend beyond a century and a half.[9] Neither is the evangelicalism and Catholicism of so many Americans today even close to asserting its right to political and territorial hegemony in the manner of the Crusaders or of the Reformation-era warriors for Catholicism and Protestantism. (Such comparisons are similar to those made by some journalists who likened the riots in Budapest in September 2006 to the Hungarian uprising of fifty years earlier: ignorant, ridiculous, mindlessly sensationalist and an insult to the memory of the dead.) Nor is non-Western and especially Muslim resentment of Westerners provoked by too much Christianity on the part of the latter but rather by the godless secularism and hedonism that Kuttner seems to approve. Other than that, our man is right on the money.

The riposte by Mark Noll is well justified: "Apart from a loose grasp of historical fact, assertions like these betray an incredible confidence in the moral power of merely secular norms, which in actual historical situations have never lived up to the claims made for them."[10]

As we have seen, the secular norms did "slaughter millions" during the twentieth century. World War I was sold to a doubting American public as the "war to make the world safe for democracy"; its aftermath saw the rise of totalitarianisms in one country after another, a danger that, later on, during the 1930s, President Franklin Delano Roosevelt's economic strategy was consciously attempting to stave off within the United States.[11] In chapter one, we considered the enormous numbers of casualties inflicted in wartime, such as during two world wars and the Russian and Chinese civil wars. But even this does not take into account the many millions persecuted for decades after the communist takeovers, or the vast numbers (estimates range between five million and fifteen million) who perished in the manmade famine created by Soviet collectivization of agriculture in the early 1930s or the millions more (perhaps up to thirty million) who starved to death when the experiment was repeated a generation later in Mao's China. Even in recent years, several million are believed to have died from the same causes in North Korea.

However, there are important differences between early twentieth-century secularism's rejection of the divine image in humanity, along with the consequences of that rejection, and the same rejection by contemporary Western secularists. The fascists and communists made an idol of collectivism: because human beings were not created in the image of God, individual human lives did not matter if they stood in the way of attaining a supposedly perfect ideal society in the future. Hence the warfare of the "armed doctrine." Postmodern Western secularism, by contrast, is highly individualistic. Its extreme squeamishness about risking the lives of its own citizens stems not from its more than half-forgotten Christian legacy about each person being created in the image of God (Western states kill many hundreds of thousands of unborn babies in the womb every year) but rather from the loss of belief in many of the things (honor, duty, confidence in an afterlife) and the serious erosion of others (family, patriotism) for which young men were traditionally prepared to risk death. This world being all there is, and life being one long party of consumer goodies, few have any strong sense of a cause worth either killing or dying for, not even the defense of the endless party. The fact that the United States is rather less prone to this particular weakness than are the other Western powers almost certainly owes something to the relative strength of religious belief among Americans, especially among the less affluent groups from whom most soldiers are recruited.

Doubtless these facts add confidence to the secularists' assertion that irreligion, when combined with Western individualism, demotivates people for war and so is inherently peaceful. However, the theory does not work out in practice. Postmodern secularism is also an "armed doctrine." As we have noticed, the crusade to "erase history and eliminate difference" is generating massive conflict all around the world.

According to journalist and military specialist Ralph Peters, it is "globalization" that has kick-started many of our current woes. What all mean by that term—and so we must presume Peters's concurrence in it—is the worldwide spread of free markets, westernized media, consumerism and the human rights ideology. As his choice of language shows, Peters is too dyed-in-the-wool American to have much sympathy for those he dubs "our enemies," but his analysis of what is happening and why is, nevertheless, realistic. With the end of the Cold War, he points out, the old ideologies are dead. In the new world that has arisen from their ashes, globalization has

> revived old identities of faith and tribe in traditional societies, [and so] such default allegiances [have] become worth fighting for again. Men are once more killing to please an angry god or to avenge (real or imagined) ethnic wrongs. . . . Iraq has been a terrible disappointment to those who believed in the galvanizing power of our ideas. Instead, we unleashed the killing power of faiths struggling for supremacy and the savagery of ethnic strife.[12]

That is not the way I would have put it, but the essential recognitions are there: the aggressive export of the Western model ("our ideas") generates violence from those who perceive that model as a threat to the traditional and, to them, preferred meaning of their society, and to the viability of the *ethnoi* and of the cultures that they have historically enshrined.

The Gods of War and the Prince of Peace

We have argued here that certain forms of religion are more prone than others to lead to war. And the strongest and most persistent connection between religion and belligerence or nonbelligerence is the issue of whether or not a religion claims or possesses a corner on some state polity and the population that lives within that polity. If it does, then it is a potential, even a likely, cause of conflict at some point. And this is as true of Hinduism as it is of Christianity, of Confucianism and Buddhism[13] as of Shinto, Judaism or Islam.

The religion may explicitly justify and legitimate the polity—specific forms of government of the state in which it exists—as with the absolutist monarchy of France in the seventeenth and eighteenth centuries or the princes and, later, tsars in the Russian lands at almost any period before 1917. Where this is the case, then the state's quarrels inevitably become the church's quarrels, too; the state's wars are furthered by religious leaders. This is bad enough, but still a relatively mild circumstance, for it could be argued that the wars would have happened with or without the church's blessing; the church was a useful tool in advancing conflicts that had not been occasioned by religion.

Religion is even more deeply complicit in warfare in circumstances where the church is as strong as and sometimes stronger than the state, as in the case of the medieval West. There, the direction of influence is reversed, and the church's quarrels are likely to become those of rulers. It is at least arguable that the Crusades are an example of this phenomenon.

Where a theocracy has been achieved, as in Iran after 1979, then the religious leaders are the rulers. Though Iran has been involved in only one major conflict since then—the decade-long war against Saddam's Iraq—it is indisputable that the often suicidal fighting technique was driven by religious zealotry. And the country has been funding a variety of armed militant groups, including Hezbollah in Lebanon, whose purpose is to make holy war.

Modern Iran is something of an exceptional case, even among Muslim societies. In Islam, as in many other faiths, such as Judaism and Hinduism, there is no formal hierarchy and institutional church as such whose interests might need protecting or advancing. This renders the connection with a specific polity slightly different. Rather, those faiths rely much more strongly on identification with a population, whose faith the ruler is obligated to reflect and uphold. Here, the rule of thumb to be observed is that the stronger or more despotic the king or other ruler, the more likely he was to be religiously tolerant and to rely on his own mere power to keep order. Conversely, the weaker he was, the more he needed to appeal to the dominant religion to help keep order. This implied a deal with religion: support my power, and I will impose the one true faith on all, or at least make life hard for misbelievers. But that in turn implied religiously motivated warfare, if the faith in question faced serious challenge either from minorities within the polity or from enemies of another faith without.[14]

The Ottoman sultans in the later stages of the empire's existence began to need this deal. Until the nineteenth century, they had been at least moderately tolerant of their Christian subjects. But, as the empire declined, the Porte needed to play the Islam card with its Muslim subjects to keep loyalty, in a way that had not been necessary in the days of Suleiman the Magnificent (reigned 1520-1566). At that point, it began to mistreat the Balkan and Armenian Christians and found the powers of Christian Europe intervening to protect them.

Israelite religion was similarly pugnacious during the Old Testament period and under Roman occupation, when hopes were not entirely farfetched that a popular uprising might throw out the invaders. But after those risings (66-70 and 132-135) had been bloodily squelched and the population dispersed, Judaism was forced to come to terms with its status, throughout the long centuries of the Diaspora, as a sect in the sociological sense, a permanent minority for whom it was unrealistic to form the basis for public polity. And so, though frequently persecuted, it became peaceful. It is open to debate whether Judaism today is always peaceful; the Israeli state is essentially secular, yet, because it remains the focus for Jewish religious aspirations, it would be true to say that devout Jews are often key political players in pushing Israel toward belligerence.

Islam, as a faith, functions by virtue of its hold on a particular population and its claims to exclusive power to shape the polity under which that population lives. For this reason it is, as John Keegan rightly observes, "by origin the most militant of polities."[15] And that militancy has been, by and large, reflected throughout its long history, down to the present. Where Muslims are important minorities, as in India or western Europe, religiously inspired rioting and corporate self-assertion are frequent. At the extreme end of the spectrum, Islamist terrorism has emerged. Between 7 percent and 15 percent of British Muslims surveyed in 2001 thought the 9/11 attacks on America were justified; between 13 percent and 24 percent thought it was acceptable to go and fight for the Taliban.[16] Four years later, in 2005, a quarter of British Muslims claimed "some sympathy" with the "feelings and motives" of those who carried out the 7/7 attacks in London; 6 percent considered them to be fully justified.[17] (These aggregated figures will, obviously, have been higher among young people and lower among their elders.) And one recent study of suicide attacks concludes that "a tradition of combative martyrdom . . . is stronger in Islam than in any other main religion" and "seems to provide a rationalizing narrative for the perpetrators, their families, and constituencies without which an organization that banks on popular support could not run S[uicide] M[ission]s."[18]

Comparable belligerence by Christian minorities of similar size in predominantly Muslim countries is not exhibited. On the contrary, most of them live in considerable and, in the light of recent experience, justifiable states of anxiety. They had been safer under strong kings in the past, whose reliance on mere power had allowed them to be tolerant toward their minorities. Christian anxiety has led to a draining away of the Christian population from the Middle East during the twentieth century—from around 20 percent in the 1890s to 3 to 4 percent by the 1980s—mostly through emigration.[19]

Christianity, as we have seen, has not always itself been tolerant. But again, we must note the correlation between the connection with state power and the propensity for religious violence. Unlike Islam, Christianity began with no aspiration to become the metanarrative of any state. The teaching of Jesus could hardly have been more clearly designed to render such a connection impossible. Nevertheless, from the fourth century onward, that connection was made anyway, with all kinds of implications for theology and biblical exegesis, which we have been able to do no more than allude to in chapter 8. Christianity therefore generated justifications for war and, with the passing of the years, religiously inspired persecutions—of Jews, pagans and those the church deemed heretics—and religiously motivated wars.

Even then, though, the pacific elements in Christianity could not be suppressed; Gibbon's argument that the late Roman Empire's military ethos was damaged by adopting the faith is a theory that remains worthy of consideration when attempting to account for the barbarian invasions. As state-embracing religions go, even the corrupted and, as Anabaptists might insist, apostate Christianity of the Middle Ages was at least somewhat more pacific than its alternatives. James Bowman warns against the easy caricatures of that period:

> The ideologies of scientific progress have taught us to think of the medieval Christian centuries in terms of the Crusades or the Inquisition or the censure of Galileo. We forget what a progressive force the Church represented in the world it inherited. . . . We have only to think again of the custom of "honor killing" in the honor cultures of Pakistan and India to get an idea of what a revolutionary force Christianity was. . . . There has always been a sense, even in Christianity's most martial phases, of a contradictory tension between the life and commandments of Jesus and the bloodthirsty deeds so often done in His name—a tension that doesn't exist, naturally enough, in other traditions.[20]

Bowman's point, though valid, remains a mere mitigation of the underlying problem—a problem that remains in parts of historic Christendom, even now, where ancient churches have become entangled with modern nationalism in new strategies to maintain exclusive or near-exclusive purchase on entire population groups. As David Martin explains, this is dangerous

> where . . . religion mediates . . . ethnicity and vice versa, and where the markers of identity, whatever they are, provide in *special definable* circumstances the preconditions of conflict and are in turn mobilized and reinforced by that conflict. Among those special definable circumstances is the collapse of empires.[21]

We may not take all that seriously each and every manifestation of nationalism that claims religion for its justification as a bona fide example of religious war. Where Martin's judgments in respect of the recent Balkan conflicts are crushing, they are nevertheless just:

> It would do no harm to remember that the rival leaderships in Serbia and Croatia and the middle-ranking strata in Bosnia consist of *apparatchiks* who have transferred themselves from loyalty to the proletariat to loyalty to the ethnic group. Their piety is their survival.[22]

Eastern Europe partly aside, however, Christianity has long since been moving back, in recent centuries, toward its roots. Even now, only a minority of Christians are pacifists, but almost none of them thinks in terms of fighting for Christianity, let alone seeking to spread the faith by military conquest. The hysteria of remarks such as those by Kuttner stems more from the fear that if Christianity becomes too influential, it may temper the recent permissions for hedonism at home in the West, not from any seriously held belief that Baptists in Missouri are likely to seek a theocracy similar to that in Iran or to inflict 9/11-style attacks on the godless.

Such rhetoric also involves a verbal trick. The term *fundamentalist* was coined during the second decade of the twentieth century to refer to a particular view of biblical inspiration. It later became debased by journalists to refer to any traditional Christian position, on any topic, of which the person speaking disapproved. As it became clear, nearer the century's end, that there were believers in other faiths who would not simply roll over and die when faced with the secularist West's new shibboleths, the epithet was transferred to them too. So it is now possible for a speaker to refer to "the dangers of fundamentalism" generally, in a way that implies that inherently violent radical Islamists ("Muslim fundamentalists") are somehow to be evaluated in the same category as the Pentecostals round the corner to whose cultural values the speaker has taken a dislike. Those who use such rhetoric are in serious danger of giving the game away: that their target is not religious violence; it is religion.

THE INEVITABILITY OF WAR

World War I was supposed to be the war to end wars. As we have seen in the years since, the end is nowhere in sight. Throughout history, all the states that have come into existence have done so through violent conflict, invasion, war, civil war and revolution. The "velvet divorce" that sundered Czechoslovakia into two without a drop of blood being spilled is remarkable for its exceptionalism; the norm is quite otherwise. And yet we remain strangely persuaded that peace is the normal, default state of affairs in human life, with war as an abnormal irruption—notwithstanding that the Scriptures and all of history warn us otherwise. How did we come to be so persuaded? Did we think that the kingdom of heaven had arrived along with our shopping malls and fitted kitchens? Keegan observes our wonderment with astonishment of his own:

> Our daily diet of news brings us reports of the shedding of blood, often in regions quite close to our homelands, in circumstances that defy our conceptions of cultural normality altogether. We succeed, all the same, in consigning the lessons both of history and of reportage to a special and separate category of "otherness" which invalidates our conceptions of how our own world will be tomorrow and the day after not at all.[23]

Warfare may be, by its nature, outside of all our attempts to delimit it ethically; it may be a theological problem; it may be a moral outrage; but it is not, socially, abnormal. Only those who have grown up with the assumption that all problems can be solved, all poverty eliminated, all human behavior sanitized by technocratic means could ever have thought otherwise. Human beings are as sinful—even in a prosperous, free-market economy, even in a democracy—as they have always been since the Fall. If some individuals behave better than others, it is for the same reasons that are observable throughout history: character formed by long habit; that kind of commitment to particular relationships that we call love; and, more often than not, a life of religious faith. As we see daily, prosperity does not make people good. And, though it does give them a vested politicoeconomic interest in the perpetuation of order, they will nevertheless resort to military solutions if that order or their own stake within it is seriously threatened or undermined.

We have been so comfortable for so long, and in thrall to the incantations of technocracy and the "to every problem, a solution" legacy of the Enlightenment, that we forget what normal human existence has been like throughout history or remains still, outside of our consumer bubble. At least, we forget all this until those who have concluded that violence is the only way to grab our jaded attention bring horrifying death to our skyscrapers, subways and shopping malls.

Our very language has accommodated itself to this amnesia. The word *violence* has only recently acquired its current, generic sense.

> Originally it referred only to criminal violence. . . . But its modern sense makes it difficult if not impossible for us any longer to express the distinction, so central to cultural honor, between good and bad, right and wrong, just and unjust fighting. Even conservatives today will disapprove of "violence" on television, as if the context of violence, whether it is justified or not in a particular situation, were unimportant.[24]

The controlling assumption of the consumer bubble is that violence is never justified. But those whose lives are more desperate than our own will refuse to see things in this light. Neither will those whose cultures are more threatened than we who dominate the world's airwaves, economy and education could ever understand. Indeed, we do not even observe the "never justified" precept ourselves. And, as 9/11 has made quite clear, nor can we afford to.

People will always fight, if not from greed, then to defend what they have; if not from cultural arrogance and the desire to impose their ways on others, then from fear of losing their culture, its structures and mores to barbarians from without. "Whatever brings people together will also separate them, and will under definable circumstances foster enmity rather than amity."[25] But one of the things that "brings people together" and, for that reason, is capable of separating them and fostering enmity is religion, especially where it enshrines and is enshrined by a particular culture. In such cases, to identify "religion as *the* cause of *the* trouble, . . . makes virtually no sense whatever."[26]

Erasing History, Eliminating Difference

Sense, though, is not much in evidence in the current campaign to emasculate traditional cultures and lock religion indoors in the cause of world peace. Apart from the obnoxiousness of this project, even viewed in the abstract, it is just one more metanarrative crying out for universalization and therefore productive of violent conflict between its promoters and those who resist it. It is perhaps no accident that Kant's imperative ("Act only according to that maxim by which you can at the same time will that it would become a universal law") came to prominence at precisely the time that state-sponsored Christianity was becoming finally untenable. The new, secular maxim has eventually come to replace its state-church predecessors. Early on, it reinforced the tendency of the new, revolutionary ideologies to adopt the form of secular religions.

Keegan summarizes the matter well:

> The armies of the French Revolution were bombarded with propaganda about the . . . duty of all citizens to bear arms . . . to overthrow the aristocratic order wherever it was found, not only so that the Revolution might be defended at home but so that its liberating principles might be implanted wherever men were still unfree.[27]

The quasi-religious tone and the drive for universalization are exactly correct. Those last two lines sound uncannily familiar, as if from the mouth of political leaders far more recent than the French Revolution. The various revolutionaries—nationalist, egalitarian and socialist—of the period from the late eighteenth to the early twentieth centuries consciously encouraged an aura of "violent 'collective effervescence'" around "the world of modern politics" that amounted to "a numinous experience."[28] The Italian cultural historian Adriano Tilgher, writing in 1938, noted the same phenomenon:

> We witnessed the birth of new deities [*numines*] with our own eyes. . . . For very many of our contemporaries State, Fatherland, Nation, Race, and Class are objects not just of enthusiastic veneration but also of mystical adoration. . . . The twentieth century promises to add a few interesting chapters to the history of religious wars (which the nineteenth century believed were over).[29]

Universal political doctrines, whether religious or secular, socialist or capitalist, austere or consumerist, end up establishing de facto empires, proclaiming "beyond the confines of the empire there is no salvation." This is as true of the new crusade for universalizing liberal democracy or of its antithesis, the Islamic *jihad,* as it was for socialism during the twentieth century, for nationalism and republicanism during the nineteenth century, or for Catholicism or Protestantism during the wars of religion. Whether the salvation proposed is religious or secular makes no essential difference to the equation of peace and war.

Although Martin Wright notes that since the end of World War I, frantic efforts have been made to demarcate the distinction between peace and war and to define precisely what might constitute an act of war, "in practice the borderline has become more smudged than at any time since the Wars of Religion."[30] And, we might add, for the same reason: doctrinal war, resulting from political utopianism, makes any peace a mere tactical truce. It matters little, in terms of the consequences for peace or war, whether the protagonists proclaim that "the survival of liberty in our land . . . depends on the success of liberty in other lands"; promote the Clinton doctrine of "humanitarian [military] interventions"; divide the world into the *dar al Islam* (house of Islam) and *dar al harb* (house of war); or exhort "working men of all countries" toward "the forcible overthrow of all existing social conditions."[31] Supporters of any "armed doctrine" unavoidably intend, as Burke put it in respect of the French Revolutionaries, either "to force mankind into an adoption of their system, or [else] to live in perpetual enmity" with them until they do so, making "a schism with the whole universe" in the meantime.[32]

Indeed, the consumerist West has made "a schism with the whole universe." Its own protestations notwithstanding, it is a force for belligerence in the contemporary world. It has, in effect, undertaken a relentless war to "erase history and eliminate difference." Having succeeded at home, it is now in the process of extending its crusade (I choose my words advisedly) abroad, utilizing its massive dominance of the global economy, global media and communications, political and even military structures. When this accumulation of power is brought to bear against traditional belief systems, especially religions, along with the cultures that enshrine them and are enshrined by them, the resultant explosion of violence is unsurprising.

Take a look around. Inside the West, religion is locked relentlessly indoors. Increasingly, its adherents are given no place to hide even there, as their children must be yielded up for compulsory socialization in secular schools; careers are made subject, formally or informally, to opinion tests so as to exclude traditionalists; social, state and even legal support are withdrawn from marriage in one Western country after another. In Europe, enforcement of the new anti-morality is a precondition for a state to join the European Union.

And outside the West, economic, political, financial and cultural muscle are used by Western powers to secularize; aid programs and international organizations are used to promote birth control, abortion and easy divorce; advertising by multinationals promotes sexualized clothing. The consequent eruptions of anger are wars for religion.

But whose religion? At whose door must the blame be laid? The traditional religions and cultures of the earth? Or the religion of repudiation and secularism that deconstructs the social, economic and familial structures of those cultures, as surely and incessantly as it deconstructed its own Western-Christian heritage; that "kills what it sees, and only sees by killing"?[33]

Secularist Western consumer society has generally sought to portray itself as peace-loving. After 1989, admirers of Western capitalism became fond of citing "Michael Doyle's Kantian analysis supporting the proposition that democratic states do not fight each other."[34] The neoconservative intellectuals have uniformly equated all nondemocracies with the fascist and communist totalitarianisms and insisted that *they* (the non-Westernized states) are essentially violent, while *we* (capitalist democracies) are inherently peace-loving. Whether this is precisely what Kant meant may be doubted, but the attempt to claim him for authority is perhaps not entirely farfetched.

Yet the view that secular Western populations are essentially peaceful, and peaceful because secular, correlates not at all with the view from the non-West. There, Western secularism is perceived as threatening and aggressive. By its incessant and relentless expansionism, it is the cultural, moral and philosophical nihilism of Western consumerism that is generating warfare all around the globe.[35] "Erasing history" and "eliminating difference"—Martin's phrases—is precisely the project on which Western secularism is embarked at home and abroad. And, as Martin has warned, it is "the occasion of the most ferocious conflict."

The instincts of Western liberals in this situation have been a little more complex than those of their neoconservative opponents, but they arrive at the same place in the end. They have frequently felt torn between the desire to denigrate capitalism (as supposedly complicit in non-Western poverty) and a rueful appreciation of it (because of the abandonment of traditional moral strictures that the superabundant wealth created by capitalism has made possible). And, although they have often blamed any belligerence by non-Westerners, whether Islamist or otherwise, on the injustices that must, it is supposed, be the inevitable concomitant of Western opulence, liberals almost unanimously point also to the economically underdeveloped, superstitious advocates of traditional cultures and traditional morality as the principal culprits in fomenting violence and warfare. In this view, religion is primarily about "policing boundaries, demonizing the other, subserving the malign powers of hierarchy and primal cohesion."[36] It is best done away with or ignored.

This last alternative—of attempting to ignore religion and refusing to take its claims seriously—was attempted by the Clinton administration, as Madeleine Albright makes clear in *The Mighty and the Almighty.* The *Washington Post* summarized:

> On her watch, U.S. foreign policy made every effort to ignore religion. . . . It seems absurd that America's leaders self-consciously pretended that religion was not an important world force. But according to Albright—and it is hard to see why she would overstate the case—the Clinton team insisted privately, not just publicly, that the Balkan crises, the Israeli-Palestinian conflict and, yes, al-Qaeda's August 1998 bombing of two U.S. embassies in East Africa were "not about religion."[37]

In summary: both sides of the political spectrum in the West have generally insisted that the secular consumer society is an essentially peaceful project that, if it could be universalized, would be a panacea for warfare. Though conservatives and liberals have often differed sharply over the West's uses of force, the tendency is nevertheless to see Western military adventures as either in fact (neoconservatives) or else in principle (liberals) merely defensive—a corrective to "fundamentalist" violence or terror emanating from outside the safe prosperity of the West. The invasion of Iraq proved polarizing inside the United States and Britain, but military actions in Kosovo in 1999 and, immediately post-9/11, in Afghanistan were far less so.

Conclusion

Religion certainly is one of several important causes of war, both in the past and the present. But we need to recognize that its alternatives have proved uniformly catastrophic as a remedy for war. The alternative metanarratives on offer to us at the present—universal Islam and the universal antimetanarrative of consumerist secularism—are no alternatives. The monarchies and empires of the past could often afford the luxury of allowing real alternative metanarratives to live side by side, their contradictions unresolved, and so decline to promote or generate religious warfare. In the early twenty-first century, it is by no means clear that their populist successors, who must claim to reflect "the people" in order to establish their own legitimacy, have found the means to repeat this trick.

Old-style, state-embracing, polity-defining religion, most eye-catchingly in its Muslim form, vies for the soul of the world with the inheritor of Enlightenment, secular, political utopianism. A victory for either side would be a disaster for humanity, yet the struggle between them is making life ever more intolerable, dangerous and violent. Only real tolerance—the tolerance of different kinds of polity and the cultural space that makes them possible—can save us from further descent into madness. And to that end, Christians, who know from Scripture and from their own painful, error-ridden past that their faith is not a basis for governing society as a whole but a private choice and a transcendent calling, have far, far more to contribute than most.

NOTES

Introduction

[1]It is interesting that his choice of words, even as he expressed his contempt for religion, indicates more than a desire to use bad language. (He might, after all, have resorted to sexually obscene terminology.) He clearly wanted a term that would express a condemnation more categoric and all-consuming and invoke a judgment more fearful than any that this world could deliver—as well he might in respect of the 9/11 atrocities. And so he is forced into using or abusing religious language, even in the act of repudiating religion. See Ben Fenton, "This Is War and We'll Win It, Say Pentagon Staff," *The Daily Telegraph,* September 12, 2001 <www.telegraph.co.uk/news/main.jhtml?xml=/news/2001/09/12/wpent12.xml>.

[2]Cited in Os Guinness, *The Dust of Death* (Leicester: Inter-Varsity Press, 1973), p. 54.

[3]"Sixty-eighters": the generation of student and associated radicals of 1968.

[4]The term used by the Second Vatican Council to mean "bringing up to date."

[5]Gilles Kepel, *The Revenge of God* (Cambridge: Polity Press, 1994), pp. 1-2.

[6]"Religion Does More Harm Than Good—Poll," *The Guardian,* December 23, 2006.

[7]<http://humanist.toronto.on.ca/ImagineNoHeaven.html>

[8]Michael Portillo, "If God Is Talking to You, Too, Mr. Cameron—Don't Listen," *The Sunday Times,* February 25, 2007.

[9]Liverpool has named its airport for John Lennon; the management has chosen its motto—part ghastly kitsch, part atheistic sneer—"above us, only sky."

[10]"When Elton Met Jake," *The Observer,* Sunday, November 16, 2006.

[11]"No Religion and an End to War," *The Guardian,* January 1, 2007 <www.guardian.co.uk/science/story/0,,1980978,00.html>;<www.edge.org/q2007/q07 _12.html#dawkins>

[12]A. C. Grayling, *The Heart of Things: Applying Philosophy to the Twenty-First Century* (London: Orion Publishing, 2006).

[13]<http://ffrf.org/timely/dawkins.php>

[14]*The Guardian,* September 15, 2001.

[15]Sam Harris, *The End of Faith,* 2nd ed. (New York: Norton, 2005), pp. 236-37.

[16]<http://www.edge.org/q2007/q07_5.html#harriss>

[17]Hector Avalos, *Fighting Words: The Origins of Religious Violence* (Amherst, N.Y.: Prometheus Books, 2005), p. 29.

[18]James K. Wellman Jr., ed., *Belief and Bloodshed: Religion and Violence Across Time and Tradition* (Lanham, Md.: Rowman and Littlefield, 2007), pp. 7-8.

[19]Philip Jenkins, *The Next Christendom* (New York: Oxford University Press, 2003), pp. 163-64.

[20]Samuel P. Huntington, *The Clash of Civilizations and the Remaking of World Order* (New York: Simon and Schuster, 1997). According to Huntington, alliances in the post-Cold War world are mostly between states and societies that share a common, long-run-of-history culture. Similarly, wars are mostly between groups belonging to different civilizations. While this situation can lead to "long-range" conflict, most local wars are therefore on the geographic frontiers, where one civilization (e.g., Catholic Europe or the Orthodox world) ends and another (e.g., the Muslim world) begins, as in the Balkans or the Caucasus.

[21]"Faith, Reason and the University: Memories and Reflections" (Rome: Libreria Editrice Vaticana, 2006), p. 2.

[22]<http://news.bbc.co.uk/2/hi/europe/5352404.stm>

Chapter 1: The Bloodiest Century of All

[1]John Keegan, *War and Our World: The Reith Lectures 1998* (London: Pimlico, 1999), p. 9.

[2]Fyodor Dostoyevsky, *The Best Short Stories of Fyodor Dostoevsky,* trans. David Magarshack (New York: The Modern Library, 2005), p. 128.

[3]<http://users.erols.com/mwhite28/wars19c.htm#Taiping>

[4]The website <http://users.erols.com/mwhite28/warstat1.htm> gives an excellent compendium of estimates, by a wide range of reputable historians, of fatalities in modern conflicts, showing where scholars differ from one another, what median estimates are, differentiating between military and civilian casualties, and so on.

[5]<http://users.erols.com/mwhite28/warstat1.htm#Russian>

[6]Roland H. Bainton, *Christian Attitudes Toward War and Peace* (London: Hodder and Stoughton, 1960), p. 224.

[7]Keegan, *War and Our World,* p. 62.

[8]Ibid.

[9]Cited in Orlando Figes, *A People's Tragedy: The Russian Revolution 1891-1924* (London: Pimlico, 1997), p. 641. Two decades and millions of deaths later, Trotsky became a victim of his own scornful repudiation of the doctrine of the sanctity of human life. Having fallen foul of Stalin's régime and living in exile in

Mexico in 1940, he was assassinated, with an ice axe to the head, by Stalin's agents.

[10]<http://138.23.124.165/exhibitions/che/essay_002.htm>

[11]Writing in 1920; cited in *War,* ed. Lawrence Freedman (Oxford: Oxford University Press, 1994), pp. 121-22.

[12]Benson Bobrick, *East of the Sun: The Conquest and Settlement of Siberia* (London: Heinemann, 1993), p. 442.

[13]Cited in *A Documentary History of Communism,* ed. Robert V. Daniels, 2 vols. (London: I. B. Tauris, 1987), 1:117.

[14]Cited in Figes, *A People's Tragedy,* pp. 524-25.

[15]Richard Pipes, ed., *The Unknown Lenin: From the Secret Archive* (New Haven, Conn.: Yale University Press, 1996), p. 50. The emphasis is Lenin's. A kulak had originally meant a rural moneylender; under communist usage, it came to mean any peasant who was slightly more prosperous or enterprising than his peers.

[16]Ibid., p. 749.

[17]Cited in Norman Davies, *White Eagle, Red Star: The Polish Soviet War 1919-1920 and "The Miracle on the Vistula"* (London: Pimlico, 2003), p. 157.

[18]Pipes, a prominent historian of the Russian Revolution, emphasizes this point in his autobiographical *Vixi: Memoirs of a Non-Belonger* (New Haven, Conn.: Yale University Press, 2003), p. 236. The bogus distinction is held to by those who wish "to admire communism without bearing the burden of Stalinism." Pipes quotes Molotov, Stalin's henchman, who, in his years of retirement, was asked whether Lenin or Stalin was "the more severe." He replied, doubtless with at least some hyperbole: "Of course, Lenin. I recall how he scolded Stalin for his softness and liberalism."

[19]Cited in Robert Conquest, *The Harvest of Sorrow* (New York: Oxford University Press, 1986), p. 234.

[20]Cited in Freedman, *War,* p. 99.

[21]Ibid., pp. 67-68.

[22]Cited in Figes, *A People's Tragedy,* p. 535.

[23]As Bernard Lewis notes in respect of Islam, "The presumption is that the duty of jihad will continue, interrupted only by truces, until all the world either adopts the Muslim faith or submits to Muslim rule." *The Crisis of Islam* (London: Weidenfeld and Nicolson, 2003), p. 25.

[24]Paul Johnson, *The Intellectuals* (London: Weidenfeld and Nicolson, 1988), p. 71. Known, admittedly to opponents, as "the red terror doctor," he wrote to the Prussian government in 1849 to inform them: "We are ruthless and ask no quarter from you. When our turn comes we shall not disguise our terrorism." Nor did they, as the twentieth century was to prove.

[25]Cited in George Watson, "The Cycle of Terror," *Quadrant Magazine* 48, no. 12 (December 2004).

[26]Maximilien Robespierre, *On the Principles of Political Morality* (1794) <http://www.worldfuturefund.org/wffmaster/Reading/Communism/Robespierre%20Quotes.htm>

[27]Maximilien Robespierre, *On the Moral and Political Principles of Domestic Policy* (1794).

[28]Cited in Daniels, *Documentary History of Communism,* 2:181.

[29]*On the Principles of Political Morality*; Jean-Jacques Rousseau, *The Social Contract,* 1.7.

[30]Robert Conquest, *Reflections on a Ravaged Century* (New York: Norton, 1999), p. 4.

[31]Ibid., pp. 7, 81.

[32]Simone de Beauvoir, *The Prime of Life,* trans. Peter. Green (Cleveland: World, 1962), p. 30.

[33]Chernyshevsky was a Russian materialist philosopher; that is, he insisted that this material world is all that exists and, that being so, it must be turned into a utopia.

[34]Conquest, *Reflections on a Ravaged Century,* pp. 10-11.

[35]Quoted in Ciano, *Diario 1939-1943,* entry for April 11, 1940 (1946).

[36]Benito Mussolini and Giovanni Gentile, *The Political and Social Doctrine of Fascism* (London: Leonard and Virginia Woolf at the Hogarth Press, 1932), 2.3.

[37]Robert Soucy, *Fascist Intellectual: Drieu La Rochelle* (Berkeley: University of California Press, 1979), p. 336.

[38]Ibid., pp. 337, 341.

[39]Ibid., p. 351.

[40]George L. Mosse, *Masses and Man: Nationalist and Fascist Perceptions of Reality* (New York: Howard Fertig, 1980), p. 210.

[41]Ibid., pp. 208-9.

[42]Sheila Fitzpatrick, *Everyday Stalinism* (New York: Oxford University Press, 1999), pp. 115-38.

[43]Cited in Martin Gilbert, *Second World War* (London: Fontana, 1990), p. 466.

Chapter 2: In the Long Run: Religion as a Cause of War

[1]The Christian population of the Middle East continues to plummet, emigrating or apostasizing in the face of violence and intimidation. In India, Christians are subject to occasional violence and to constant vilification in, for example, Bollywood productions as promoters of Western immorality.

[2]Tacitus *Annals* 14.30.

[3]It should not be supposed, from this account, that such royal decisions were made on a whim or without careful sounding out of the likely responses of leading subjects. Premodern kings were nowhere close to being the absolute rulers of their kingdoms that twenty-first-century Westerners are inclined to imagine.

[4]Examples include Rene Weis, *The Yellow Cross: The Story of the Last Cathars 1290-1329* (London: Penguin, 2001); Stephen O'Shea, *The Perfect Heresy: The Revolutionary Life and Death of the Medieval Cathars* (New York: Walker, 2000); Jean Markale, *Montségur and the Mystery of the Cathars* (Rochester, Vt.: Inner Traditions, 2003); and the recent translation of Otto Rahn's 1933 legend of the Cathars and the Holy Grail, *Crusade Against the Grail* (Rochester, Vt.: Inner Traditions, 2006). Rahn was a romantic, obsessed with esoterica and the supposed secret connections between them; he was recruited to the SS shortly after writing this work, though he later became disillusioned with Nazism.

[5]William Urban, *The Teutonic Knights: A Military History* (London: Greenhill, 2003), p. 49.

[6]Eric Christiansen, *The Northern Crusades* (London: Penguin, 1997), pp. 86-89.

[7]J. N. D. Kelly, *The Oxford Dictionary of Popes* (Oxford: Oxford University Press, 1990), p. 153.

[8]<http://users.erols.com/mwhite28/warstatv.htm#Ellas>

[9]Reginald Haynes Barrow, *The Romans* (Harmondsworth, U.K.: Penguin, 1949), pp. 33-34.

[10]John Boardman, Jasper Griffin and Oswyn Murray, eds., *The Oxford History of the Classical World* (Oxford: Oxford University Press, 1986), p. 405.

[11]<http://users.erols.com/mwhite28/wars19c.htm#Napoleonic>

Chapter 3: Islam and the Abode of War

[1]Peter G. Riddell and Peter Cotterell, *Islam in Context* (Grand Rapids: Baker, 2003), p. 212.

[2]Bernard Lewis, *The Crisis of Islam* (London: Weidenfeld and Nicolson, 2003), p. 24.

[3]Ibid., p. 28.

[4]Marshall G. S. Hodgson, *The Venture of Islam*, 3 vols. (Chicago: University of Chicago Press, 1974), 1:177.

[5]Quoted by Efraim Karsh, "The Perfect Surrender," *The New York Sun*, September 25, 2006 <www.nysun.com/article/40266>.

[6]*Sahih Bukhari*, vol. 1, book 2, number 35 <http://www.usc.edu/dept/MSA/fundamentals/hadithsunnah/bukhari/002.sbt.html>

[7]Riddell and Cotterell, *Islam in Context*, pp. 33-39. It is possible, as the *hadith* suggest, that Umar was murdered by a Persian prisoner, but suspicion lingers

over Ali ibn Abu Talib, the eventual fourth caliph, as being behind the assassinations of both his predecessors.

[8]Richard Fletcher, *The Cross and the Crescent* (London: Penguin, 2003), p. 13.

[9]N. A. Newman, ed., *The Early Christian-Muslim Dialogue: A Collection of Documents from the First Three Islamic Centuries, 632-900 A.D.: Translations with Commentary* (Hatfield, Penn.: Interdisciplinary Biblical Research Institute, 1993), p. 14.

[10]Patricia Crone, *God's Rule* (New York: Columbia University Press, 2004), p. 367.

[11]Samuel H. Moffett, *A History of Christianity in Asia,* 3 vols. (Maryknoll, N.Y.: Orbis, 1998), 1:329, 336-37.

[12]W. G. Clarence-Smith, *Islam and the Abolition of Slavery* (Oxford: Oxford University Press, 2006), p. 6.

[13]*Qur'an* 9.29, trans. Yusuf Ali.

[14]Cited in Richard Fletcher, *Moorish Spain* (London: Phoenix Press, 1994), p. 106.

[15]Jacques Ellul, *Anarchy and Christianity* (Grand Rapids: Eerdmans, 1991), pp. 24-25.

[16]C. W. Previté-Horton, *The Shorter Cambridge Medieval History,* 2 vols. (Cambridge: Cambridge University Press, 1952), 1:151-52.

[17]B. Z. Kedar, *Crusade and Mission: European Approaches Toward the Muslims* (Princeton, N.J.: Princeton University Press, 1984), p. 98.

[18]Ibid., pp. 98-99.

[19]The choice of this term is emphatically not a piece of Protestant blame laying; it is a simple demarcation of the fact that on the Christian side, the Crusades were a Western, not an Eastern Orthodox, event. Neither are the reasons for Eastern Orthodox noninvolvement to be found in any supposed moral superiority of the Byzantine world but in the more usual causes of victimhood or nonaggression in history: military weakness.

[20]Cited in Norman Cohn, *The Pursuit of the Millennium* (London: Paladin, 1970), pp. 67-68.

[21]Significantly, the Crusaders did not call themselves by that name, nor did they call their military campaigns Crusades; those titles were conferred on them only subsequently. They described themselves as pilgrims and their enterprise as going on pilgrimage.

[22]Bernard Lewis, *Islam in History* (Chicago: Open Court, 2001), p. 412.

[23]Cited in Robert Irwin, *For Lust of Knowing: The Orientalists and Their Enemies* (London: Penguin, 2006), p. 10.

[24]Geoffroi de Villehardouin, *Memoirs of the Crusades,* trans. Frank Marzials (London: J. M. Dent, 1908), pp. 1-2, 5. Indulgences (the promise of absolution from sins in return for fighting in the crusade) would, over the next three centuries, become yet further debased, to emerge in the form—sins forgiven in exchange

for cash down—that Luther denounced, with such memorable results, in 1517.

[25]Regine Pernoud, *The Crusaders,* trans. Enid Grant (London: Oliver and Boyd, 1963), pp. 98-99.

[26]<http://users.erols.com/mwhite28/warstat0.htm#European>

Chapter 4: Where Religion Plays an Ambiguous Role

[1]<http://news.yahoo.com/s/afp/20050926/od_afp/russiareligionmilitaryoffbeat_050926150901>

[2]Caroline Finkel, *Osman's Dream* (New York: Basic, 2005), p. 110.

[3]John V. A. Fine, *The Late Medieval Balkans* (Ann Arbor: University of Michigan Press, 1994), p. 412.

[4]Jason Goodwin, *Lords of the Horizons* (London: Vintage, 1998), p. 31.

[5]Charles A. Frazee, *The Orthodox Church and Independent Greece 1821-1852* (Cambridge: Cambridge University Press, 1969), pp. 28-29.

[6]Ibid.

[7]Ibid., p. 43.

[8]Ibid., pp. 49, 52.

[9]Ibid., pp. 46-47, 50.

[10]Ogier Ghiselin de Busbecq, *The Turkish Letters,* trans. Edward Seymour Forster (Baton Rouge: Louisiana State University Press, 2005), p. 40.

[11]Ivan Roots, *The Great Rebellion 1642-1660* (London: Batsford, 1966), pp. 62-66, reflects some of the confusion experienced by contemporaries.

[12]G. E. Aylmer, *Rebellion or Revolution?* (Oxford: Oxford University Press, 1986), p. 41, in reviewing the plethora of factors that prompted people to take sides, notes that "if we try to look at the country as a whole and at all social groups and classes, the divisions can be related to the religious issues of the previous eighty or more years and to the constitutional difficulties of the 1610s and 1620s." In effect, this is to direct our gaze at long-term cultural and religious casts of mind rather than at the recent, trigger events that will have been fresh in the minds of the combatants.

[13]See, e.g., Lawrence Stone, *The Causes of the English Revolution 1529-1642* (London: Routledge and Kegan Paul, 1972), pp. 144-45.

[14]Derek Hirst, *Authority and Conflict: England 1603-1658* (London: Edward Arnold, 1986), pp. 224-27, strikes the right balance between the various religious and nonreligious factors that caused people to take one side rather than another.

[15]Elizabeth Fox-Genovese and Eugene D. Genovese, *The Mind of the Master Class: History and Faith in the Southern Slaveholders' Worldview* (New York: Cambridge University Press, 2005), p. 473.

[16]Ferdinand Jacobs, *The Committing of Our Cause to God* (Charleston, S.C.: A. J. Burke 1850), p. 20, cited in ibid.

[17]Cited in Mark A. Noll, *A History of Christianity in the United States and Canada* (Grand Rapids: Eerdmans, 1992), p. 318.

[18]Mark A. Noll et al., *Christianity in America* (Grand Rapids: Eerdmans, 1983), p. 262.

[19]Ibid., p. 314.

Chapter 5: Tribal Gods I: The Phenomenon of Religious-National Myths and the Cases of Serbia and Russia

[1]Such myth making is present every time a speaker uses "we" or "us" to refer to medieval antecedents, for the collective consciousness of people in the Middle Ages (their "we") referred to the locality, the village and the extended family at the micro level and to the entire religious community (Christendom, Islam, the Jewish people) at the macro level. Their nearest approach to the kind of large-scale, mutual, collective belonging that we mean by modern national consciousness was what we would nowadays call a tribal sense of identity. That was the content of "nation" in the biblical sense, the kind of meaning still reflected in, for example, "the Iroquois nation." The literature on nationalism and its development in recent centuries is vast. For a summary of this argument, see Meic Pearse, *Why the Rest Hates the West* (Downers Grove, Ill.: InterVarsity Press, 2004), chap. 6.

[2]It was the assassination of Archduke Franz Ferdinand in Sarajevo in 1914 that had triggered the diplomatic meltdown between the great powers, a process that had led to the outbreak of the war.

[3]"What wilt thou now choose to be thy kingdom? Say, dost thou desire a heav'nly kingdom, Or dost thou prefer an earthly kingdom? If thou should'st now choose an earthly kingdom, Knights may girdle swords and saddle horses, Tighten saddle-girths and ride to battle—You will charge the Turks and crush their army! But if thou prefer a heav'nly kingdom, Build thyself a church upon Kosovo. . . . And to all thy warriors and their leaders Thou shalt give the sacraments and orders, For thine army shall most surely perish, And thou too, shalt perish with thine army." *Propast Carstva Srpskoga* <http://home.earthlink.net/~markdlew/SerbEpic/thefall.htm>

[4]*Car Lazar ai Carica Milica* <http://home.earthlink.net/~markdlew/SerbEpic/militsa.htm>

[5]*Mušić Stefan* <http://home.earthlink.net/~markdlew/SerbEpic/stefan.htm>.

[6]In fact, however, the process has been going on over centuries and is far more complex than we can enter into here. For a good overview, see Noel Malcolm, *Kosovo: A Short History* (London: Macmillan, 1998).

[7]Peter J. S. Duncan, *Russian Messianism: Third Rome, Holy Revolution, Communism and After* (London: Routledge, 2000), p. 11.

[8]Jaroslav Pelikan, *The Christian Tradition,* 5 vols. (Chicago: University of Chicago Press, 1977), 2:297-98.

[9]Ibid.

[10]Ibid.

[11]Marshall Poe, *"Moscow, the Third Rome": The Origins and Transformations of a Pivotal Moment* (Washington, D.C., 1997), pp. 11-12, in David G. Rowley, *"Redeemer Empire": Russian Millenarianism,* <http://www.historycooperative.org/journals/ahr/104.5/ah001582.html#FOOT43>.

[12]From a speech on Pushkin in *Writer's Diary,* August 1880, cited in *The Portable Nineteenth-Century Russian Reader,* ed. George Gibian (New York: Penguin, 1993), p. 434.

[13]See, e.g., Geoffrey Hosking, *Russia: People and Empire 1552-1917* (London: HarperCollins, 1997), pp. 368-371; Tim McDaniel, *The Agony of the Russian Idea* (Princeton, N.J.: Princeton University Press, 1996), pp. 76-77.

[14]Nicolas Berdyaev, *The Russian Idea* (New York: Macmillan, 1948), p. 193.

[15]Valerii Khatiushin, "Esli Poimem—Spasemsia," *Molodaia Gvardiia* 3 (1995): pp. 27-40, summarized in Rowley, *"Redeemer Empire."*

Chapter 6: Tribal Gods II: The Religious-National Myth of England and Collective Self-Worship

[1]Kevin Jeffreys, "Rebuilding Postwar Britain: Conflicting Views of the Attlee Governments, 1945-1951," *New Perspective* 3, no. 3 (March 1998) <www.users.globalnet.co.uk/~semp/conflict.htm>.

[2]This latter idea (the origins of British Christianity during the apostolic period) originates probably with Gildas (c. 504-570), who wrote that "these islands . . . received the beams of light, that is, the holy precepts of Christ, the true Sun . . . at the latter part, as we know, of the reign of Tiberius Caesar [died A.D. 37], by whom his religion was propagated without impediment, and death threatened to those who interfered with its professors" (*Works* 1.8) <http://www.fordham.edu/halsall/basis/gildas-full.html>.

[3]Ian Bradley, *Celtic Christianity: Making Myths and Chasing Dreams* (Edinburgh: Edinburgh University Press, 1999), pp. 91-92.

[4]A number of recent books have claimed Celtic Christianity as a historical precursor of modern feminism and of the green movement. This would all have been news to saints Columba, David and Patrick.

[5]Bradley, *Celtic Christianity;* Glanmor Williams, *Reformation Views of Church History* (London: Lutterworth, 1970), pp. 39, 47, 57. Bale believed the Arthurian legend that Christianity had been brought to Britain by Joseph of Arimathea, so that the Britons "took the Christian faith at the very spring or first going forth

of the Gospel when the Church was most perfect and had most strength of the Holy Ghost." Foxe, though, gave less credence than did Bale to the chronicles of Geoffrey of Monmouth. See ibid., p. 53.

[6]John Foxe, *The Acts and Monuments of the English Martyrs*, ed. Josiah Pratt (London, 1870).

[7]A. N. McLaren, *Political Culture in the Reign of Elizabeth I* (Cambridge: Cambridge University Press, 1999), 23 n. 37; W. M. Lamont, *Godly Rule* (London: Macmillan, 1969), pp. 23-24.

[8]Jonathan Edwards, *History of Redemption* (published posthumously in 1774), 3.7.1.3. Edwards counts as one of America's greatest theologians. In his own time, however, he inhabited what were then the British colonies of North America, and his thought is a variation on ideas that were general in Britain.

[9]For evangelicals, the religious-national myth could cut both ways. On the one hand, it could provide a quasi-secular rationale for evangelism and allow believers to square their own faith with the social pressures to support nation and empire that would be felt by any person growing up and living in Britain. On the other hand, it led many, especially missionaries, to be highly critical of empire as they came to identify strongly with the natives among whom they worked and whose interests they came frequently to espouse. The universalist character of the gospel could lead evangelicals to reject imperialism in other ways. Hudson Taylor, for example, adopted Chinese culture, language and even dress in his desire to reach the Chinese people for Christ—and was repaid with a success that has won him acclaim ever since. Brian Stanley has argued brilliantly and persuasively (*The Bible and the Flag: Protestant Missions and British Imperialism in the Nineteenth and Twentieth Centuries* [Leicester: Inter-Varsity Press, 1990]) that it was the more theologically liberal missionaries who relied most strongly on the supposed civilizing mission of the empire while conservative evangelicals were motivated far more by soteriological considerations: by the universalist claims of Christian faith and the insistence that people outside of Christ were lost. In consequence, Stanley shows, the latter were far more willing, on average, to make cultural adaptations in favor of the people they were attempting to convert.

[10]Cited by Gregory S. Neal, "Imperial British-Israelism: Justification for an Empire," <http://www.revneal.org/Writings/british.htm>.

[11]Ibid.

[12]See Timothy Snyder, *The Reconstruction of Nations: Poland, Ukraine, Lithuania, Belarus, 1569-1999* (New Haven, Conn.: Yale University Press, 2003), pp. 1-7.

[13]Cited in Peter J. S. Duncan, *Russian Messianism: Third Rome, Holy Revolution, Communism and After* (London: Routledge, 2000), p. 10.

[14]Edmund S. Morgan, *The Puritan Dilemma: The Story of John Winthrop* (Boston: Little, Brown, 1958), p. 70.

[15]Sacvan Bercovitch, ed., *The American Puritan Imagination: Essays in Revaluation* (Cambridge: Cambridge University Press?, 1974), p. 9.

[16]Cited in Richard M. Gamble, *The War for Righteousness: Progressive Christianity, the Great War and the Rise of the Messianic Nation* (Wilmington, Del.: ISI Books, 2003), pp. 16-17.

[17]Mark A. Noll, *A History of Christianity in the United States and Canada* (Grand Rapids: Eerdmans, 1992), p. 317.

[18]Gamble, *The War for Righteousness*, p. 252.

[19]I mention this, as a non-American, with some trepidation. Yet, in the course of being interviewed on some twenty-five or thirty U.S. radio shows, including many in which I was required to answer questions from members of the public phoning in, this issue arose constantly. America was identified as Christian and its national interest as identical with the promotion of Christianity and Christian civilization. There is strong evidence that at least some individuals close to the heart of political life share the same outlook.

[20]This memorable phrase is used—and, so far as I am aware, coined—by Miroslav Volf, *Exclusion and Embrace: A Theological Exploration of Identity, Otherness, and Reconciliation* (Nashville: Abingdon, 1996), p. 104. In its immediate context, Volf is speaking of the uses of claimed or actual victimhood. His general argument, however, makes it clear that religion is frequently used in this fashion, that Jesus was overturning such uses by, for example, the Zealots, and that true Christian discipleship needs to challenge exactly this tendency in itself and in others. See pp. 111-19.

Chapter 7: So What Causes War?

[1]Gen 4:2, 12.

[2]Clearly, the more obvious points of the story include the need for humility before God and acceptance of his judgments; the idea that without the shedding of blood there is no covering for sin; a horror of fratricide and a condemnation of murder *tout court*. I am, however, focusing here on those aspects that particularly concern our present discussion.

[3]Roland H. Bainton, *Christian Attitudes Toward War and Peace: A Historical Survey and Critical Re-evaluation* (London: Hodder and Stoughton, 1960), p. 20.

[4]John Keegan, *War and Our World: The Reith Lectures 1998* (London: Pimlico, 1999), pp. xii, 28.

[5]Patricia Crone, *Pre-Industrial Societies: Anatomy of the Pre-Modern World* (Oxford: Oneworld Publications, 2003), pp. 3, 7-8.

[6]Ibid., pp. 7-8.

[7]John Keegan, *A History of Warfare* (New York: Vintage, 1993), p. 5.

[8]Keegan, *War and Our World,* pp. xi-xiii.

[9]Ibid., p. xiii.

[10]James Chambers, *The Devil's Horsemen: The Mongol Invasion of Europe* (Edison, N.J.: Castle Books, 2003), p. 6.

[11]Richard Fletcher, *The Cross and the Crescent* (London: Penguin, 2003), p. 21.

[12]Keegan, *War and Our World,* p. xiii.

[13]Immanuel Kant, *Perpetual Peace: A Philosophical Sketch,* sect. 2, in *Kant: Political Writings,* ed. H. S. Reiss (New York: Cambridge University Press, 1995), p. 100.

[14]Ibid.

[15]Francis Fukuyama, *The End of History and the Last Man* (New York: The Free Press/Macmillan, 1992).

[16]<http://www.whitehouse.gov/news/releases/2004/12/20041207-2.html>

[17]Samuel P. Huntington, *The Clash of Civilizations and the Remaking of World Order* (New York: Touchstone, 1998), pp. 113-14.

[18]Keegan, *War and Our World,* p. 39.

[19]Ibid., p. 40.

[20]Bernard Lewis, *The Crisis of Islam* (London: Weidenfeld and Nicolson, 2003), pp. 25-26, 30.

[21]Henri Daniel-Rops, *Cathedral and Crusade: Studies of the Medieval Church* (London: J. M. Dent, 1961), 3:275.

[22]James Bowman, *Honor: A History* (New York: Encounter Books, 2006), pp. 50-51.

[23]Ibid., p. 49.

[24]Niccolo Machiavelli, *The Art of War,* book 2, *The Prince and Other Political Writings,* ed. and trans. B. Penman (London: Everyman, 1981), p. 301.

[25]Niccolo Machiavelli, *Discourses,* 2.2, cited in Bowman, *Honor,* p. 58.

[26]Edward Gibbon, *The Decline and Fall of the Roman Empire,* ed. J. B. Bury, 8 vols. (London: Methuen, 1897), 4:162-63.

[27]Cited in Origen *Contra Celsum* 8.68.

[28]Anabaptists, Michael Servetus, Marian martyrs, Puritans, Elizabethan Catholics, Huguenots, Moravian Brethren: all are fascinating, heroic and full of importance for the future. But none of them were vox populi. They fascinate precisely because they represent the potentialities of the societies in which they lived that were not realized or not realized until later ages.

[29]It should be noted that, in that instance, Protestantism rode the tide of nationalism, not vice versa. A convergence of interests made Puritans the doughtiest supporters of an anti-Spanish policy and virtually forced Elizabeth to tolerate

them, despite her serious distaste for their religious program. The success of Protestantization during Elizabeth's reign (1558-1603), compared with the fragility of her predecessors' (Henry VIII and Edward VI) achievements, lay in the fact that the causes of nationalism and Protestantism came to seem synonymous from the 1570s to the 1590s.

[30]Chris Hedges, *War Is a Force That Gives Us Meaning* (New York: Anchor, 2002), p. 15.

[31]Samuel P. Huntington's recent book, *Who Are We: The Challenges to America's National Identity* (New York: Simon and Schuster, 2004) is a prolonged hand wringing over what he, along with many others, perceives as the latest threat to this precarious cultural balance, namely, the recent and continuing mass immigration by one, non-Anglophone and mostly non-Protestant group: the Hispanics.

[32]<http://www.whitehouse.gov/news/releases/2005/01/20050120-1.html>

[33]See Meic Pearse, *Why the Rest Hates the West* (Downers Grove, Ill.: InterVarsity Press, 2004).

[34]Hedges, *War Is a Force,* p. 3.

[35]Ibid., p. 7.

Chapter 8: Even Marx Was Right Sometimes

[1]By metanarrative we mean the overarching theory held by a person, group or, in this case, an entire society that explains, legitimizes, prescribes and justifies its actions, structure and behavior. It is the big story, usually a set of tolerably well interconnected ideas explaining the meaning of life, the origins of the universe, the destiny of the group. Christianity certainly counts as a metanarrative; so do most other religions.

[2]Karl Marx, *Towards the Critique of Hegel's Philosophy of Law* (1844).

[3]<http://www.gwu.edu/~e73afram/dw-ah-ek.html#trouble>. These examples, all composed by Henry T. Burleigh (1866-1949), postdate the experience of slavery but nevertheless come from a section of society that was segregated and suffered widespread legal and social discrimination, as well as material poverty.

[4]Eusebius of Caesarea *Life of Constantine* 2, 3.

[5]Ibid.

[6]Athenian democracy was not democratic in a sense that we should recognize. It subsisted with a large minority of the population, perhaps 40 percent being slaves, while the vote was restricted to adult freemen.

[7]Peter Heather, *The Fall of the Roman Empire* (New York: Oxford University Press, 2005), pp. 123-24.

[8]See Christopher Hill, *Puritanism and Revolution: Studies in Interpretation of the English Revolution of the 17th Century* (London: Secker and Warburg, 1958); *So-*

ciety and Puritanism (London: Secker and Warburg, 1964); *God's Englishman: Oliver Cromwell and the English Revolution* (London: Weidenfeld and Nicolson, 1970); *The World Turned Upside Down: Radical Ideas During the English Revolution* (London: Maurice Temple Smith, 1972). Hill's *A Turbulent, Seditious and Factious People: John Bunyan and His Church* (Oxford: Oxford University Press, 1988), published as Communism was visibly falling apart, is a partial reiteration of his long-held views while simultaneously qualifying them to an extent that amounts to a de facto retreat from ground that had become indefensible.

[9]Bernard Lewis, *From Babel to Dragomans: Interpreting the Middle East* (New York: Oxford University Press, 2004), p. 316.

Chapter 9: The Lord Mighty in Battle—and the Prince of Peace

[1]Jacques Ellul, *Anarchy and Christianity* (Grand Rapids: Eerdmans, 1991), pp. 25-26.

[2]Meic Pearse, *The Great Restoration* (Carlisle: Paternoster, 1998), p. 64.

[3]An article by Joel Elowsky in *Christianity Today* gives a good and accessible compendium of the chief quotations from church fathers that are generally used in this debate. <http://www.christianitytoday.com/ct/2003/143/21.0.html>.

[4]Basil of Caesarea *Letter* 106.

[5]Athanasius of Alexandria *Letter* 48.

[6]William Dalrymple, *From the Holy Mountain* (London: HarperCollins, 1998), pp. 388-89.

[7]F. H. Russell in Alan D. Fitzgerald, ed., *Augustine Through the Ages: An Encyclopedia* (Grand Rapids: Eerdmans, 1999), pp. 875-76. Russell takes a strongly sympathetic view of Augustine, yet he is clear that in his "exegetical revaluation," "the pacific precepts were transformed so that love of neighbors could legitimate their deaths, and not to resist evil became an inward attitude compatible with outward belligerence."

[8]See J. W. Rogerson, Christopher Rowland and Barnabas Lindars, *The Study and Use of the Bible* (Grand Rapids: Eerdmans, 1988), chap. 5.

[9]Augustine *Epistolae* 93.9.

[10]Augustine *Against Faustus* 22.74.

[11]<http://news.bbc.co.uk/2/hi/europe/5348436.stm> Although Sheikh Youssef al-Qardawi, Qatari Muslim cleric and head of the Islamic Scholars' Association, went on to a vaguely worded denial of the same basic facts of history, he nevertheless preceded this with a remark that gives some hope for the future: "Our hands are outstretched and our religion calls for peace, not for war, for love not for hatred, for tolerance, not for fanaticism, for knowing each other and not for disavowing each other." Ibid.

[12]P. Stephenson, "Imperial Christianity and Sacred War in Byzantium," in James K. Wellman Jr., ed., *Belief and Bloodshed: Religion and Violence Across Time and Tradition* (Lanham, Md.: Rowman and Littlefield, 2007), pp. 81, 82, 85. It should be noted that the account comes from Theophanes the Confessor, writing between 813 and 818, who relied on earlier manuscripts. As Stephenson points out, however, even if inaccuracy has crept in, Theophanes believes the report and approves its sentiments.

[13]Ibid., p. 86.

[14]Ibid., p. 91.

[15]Timothy Ware, *The Orthodox Church* (Harmondsworth: Penguin, 1963), p. 69.

[16]R. Guerdan, *Byzance* (Paris: Librairie Academique Perrin, 1973), p. 231.

[17]*Vita Lebuini*.

[18]*Diffundente Sole*, a chronicle from C13/14, reflecting C10 sources.

[19]*Chronicon Posoniense*, chap. 33.

[20]*Nestorian Chronicle*, pp. 52-53.

Chapter 10: Can a Christian Fight?

[1]Good places to explore this question include Robert G. Clouse, ed., *War: Four Christian Views* (Downers Grove, Ill.: InterVarsity Press, 1991); Ronald Sider, *Christ and Violence* (Scottdale, Penn.: Herald Press, 1979); John Stott, *Issues Facing Christians Today* (Grand Rapids: Zondervan, 2006).

[2]Actually, two. The other was San Marino.

[3]See, e.g., Henry Chadwick, *Augustine* (Oxford: Oxford University Press, 1986), 103-4; M. T. Clark, *Augustine* (London: Geoffrey Chapman, 1994), p. 100.

[4]Whether an enemy may be fought while simultaneously maintaining an attitude of love for that enemy may be doubted. C. S. Lewis, however, has argued, not entirely unpersuasively, that it is possible to square this rather awkward circle, even if his comments about pacifists, penned in the heated atmosphere of the Second World War, are more than a little unfair. C. S. Lewis, "Why I Am Not a Pacifist," in *Timeless at Heart* (London: Fount, 1987), pp. 48-65.

[5]Roland H. Bainton, *Christian Attitudes Toward War and Peace* (London: Hodder and Stoughton, 1960), p. 33.

[6]Augustine *Against Faustus* 22.75.

[7]Augustine *Commentary on Psalm 124.7*.

[8]Many recent conflicts have consisted of what military theorists now call asymmetric warfare, that is, where one side is far weaker, in conventional military terms, than the other. That side will frequently use tactics that dare the other to use its military might: taking hostages and keeping them at known military targets; hiding missile batteries and artillery in heavily populated areas; using hu-

man shields; threatening the use of poison gas; sponsoring terrorist cells in the enemy's home countries. The only effective response, in strictly military terms, to such tactics is for the stronger side to push the boundaries yet further: to bomb targets anyway; to threaten a nuclear first strike; to kill terrorist suspects before they can attack and so before they can (always) be proven to be plotting terror. Generally speaking, Israel proves willing to take further steps of this kind in confronting its enemies; the British and Americans are mostly, though not always, more restrained. But the degree of restraint tends to vary inversely with the level of threat. Israel is perpetually under grave threat; after 9/11, the Western powers, especially the Americans, showed signs of losing some of their inhibitions.

[9]Evelyn Underhill, "The Church and War" (London: Anglican Pacifist Fellowship, 1940).

[10]See, for example, articles 4 and 6 of the Schleitheim Confession of 1527, which swiftly became the most important Anabaptist confession of faith. John H. Yoder, ed., *The Legacy of Michael Sattler* (Scottdale, Pa.: Herald Press, 1973), pp. 38-41. For a narrative account of these movements, see Meic Pearse, *The Great Restoration* (Carlisle: Paternoster, 1998), chaps. 3, 6.

[11]This is a confusion into which Underhill, cited above, also seems to have fallen.

[12]John Keegan, *A History of Warfare* (New York: Vintage, 1993), p. 4.

[13]George Orwell, "Pacifism and the War," *Partisan Review* (August-September 1942) <www.orwell.ru/library/articles/pacifism/english/e_patw>.

[14]Stott, *Issues Facing Christians Today,* pp. 89-93.

[15]The government of China continues to reside with the Communist Party. Yet, dictatorship though it is, the social and economic system is no longer by any means Communist or socialist.

[16]Michael Ignatieff, *The Warrior's Honor: Ethnic War and the Modern Conscience* (New York: Henry Holt, 1998), pp. 126-28.

[17]Martin Luther King, *Strength to Love* (Glasgow: Collins, 1977), pp. 3, 54.

[18]Ibid., pp. 54-55.

[19]Eberhard Bethge, *Dietrich Bonhoeffer: A Biography* (London: Collins, 1970), pp. 575, 581-82.

[20]As Professor Corduan has been kind enough to point out to me, the German *Bundeswehr* does have a provision whereby its soldiers may disobey an order they deem to be morally impermissible, though he adds, "However, one wonders what would happen to this provision if Germany once again found itself in a true time of war."

[21]Interview in *Third Way* 28, no. 10 (December 2005), pp. 16-17.

[22]The agony of spending a lifetime revisiting such split-second decisions (to shoot

or not to shoot) and their consequences is poignantly expressed by a not very articulate Vietnam veteran: “The reality of war among civilians is worse than you could ever imagine even in a nightmare.” His reflections read as though they are the fruit of thirty years’ cogitation that has been dominated by little else—a fact that is worth as much as the tragedy recounted by the reflections themselves <http://www.amazon.com/Harrisons-Flowers-Sub-Dol-Dts/dp/B00006HAX6/sr=1-1/qid=1160061538/ref=sr_1_1/002-6304090-3756041?ie=UTF8&s=dvd>.

Chapter 11: The Relentless War Against Faith and Meaning

[1]David Martin, *Does Christianity Cause War?* (Oxford: Oxford University Press, 1997), p. 19.

[2]Samuel P. Huntington, in identifying the various civilizations that currently dominate geopolitics, does so in four cases by direct reference to religion: the West he defines as those societies stemming from historically Catholic/Protestant Europe; the Orthodox world; the Muslim world; and Hindu civilization. *The Clash of Civilizations and Remaking of World Order* (New York: Simon and Schuster, 1997), passim.

[3]Meic Pearse, *Why the Rest Hates the West* (Downers Grove, Ill.: InterVarsity Press, 2004), p. 169.

[4]Chris Hedges, *War Is a Force That Gives Us Meaning* (New York: Anchor, 2002), p. 9.

[5]Ibid.

[6]Emilio Gentile, *Politics as Religion* (Princeton, N.J.: Princeton University Press, 2006), p. xvii.

[7]Martin Wight, *Power Politics* (Harmondsworth: Penguin, 1979), cited in Lawrence Freedman, ed., *War* (Oxford: Oxford University Press, 1994), pp. 92-93.

[8]Robert Kuttner, “What Would Jefferson Do?” *The American Prospect* (November 2004), p. 31.

[9]A tolerable average of all estimates of deaths in the Crusades comes to one and a half million, but that includes the Crusaders themselves <http://users.erols.com/mwhite28/warstat0.htm#Crusades>. As for the Inquisition, Aletheia, *The Rationalist’s Manual,* gives a high-end estimate of 35,534 for the Spanish Inquisition over the course of four centuries; other estimates are lower <http://users.erols.com/mwhite28/warstat0.htm#SpanInq>.

[10]Mark A. Noll, “The Bible in American Public Life, 1860-2005,” *Books and Culture* (September/October 2005), p. 46.

[11]I am not here seeking to imply that entry of the United States into World War I in 1917 was monocausal, still less that that cause was mere propaganda. I point

merely at the rationale that was held to justify and sum up the various concerns that prompted the declaration of war.

[12]Ralph Peters, "The Roots of Today's Wars," *USA Today,* Wednesday, February 28, 2007, 11A.

[13]Buddhism has a reputation for pacifism, yet Buddhist Sinhalese fight to defend the ethnic and cultural identity of Sri Lanka against what they perceive as Hindu incursions. The Tibetan kingdom of the Dalai Lama was defended mostly by its extreme isolation, but it still possessed an army.

[14]It might perhaps be argued that the weaker the Jewish kings of Old Testament Israel were as kings, the more they found themselves forced to listen to the prophets and to destroy the baals. Was this perhaps the reason that God had wished for them to have no kings? Israelite religion worked by having a hold on a particular population occupying particular territory. But the consequence of that hold (entailing theological problems so large that we have had no space to enter into them here) was religiously inspired war.

[15]John Keegan, *War and Our World: The Reith Lectures 1998* (London: Pimlico, 1999), p. 55.

[16]<http://www.globalsecurity.org/security/library/report/2004/muslimext-uk.htm>

[17]Fraser Nelson, "Will Anyone Rise to Take al-Qaeda's Bait?" Scotland on Sunday, July 24, 2005 <scotlandonsunday.scotsman.com/opinion.cfm?id=1673742005>.

[18]Diego Gambetta, ed., *Making Sense of Suicide Missions* (Oxford: Oxford University Press, 2005), p. 293. Gambetta, based in Nuffield College, Oxford, provides impressive statistical and qualitative data to support this claim.

[19]Youssef Courbage and Philippe Fargues, *Christians and Jews Under Islam* (London: I. B. Tauris, 1997), pp. 123, 125, 129, 209.

[20]James Bowman, *Honor: A History,* pp. 47-48.

[21]Martin, *Does Christianity Cause War?* p. 19.

[22]Ibid., p. 17.

[23]Keegan, *A History of Warfare,* p. 4.

[24]Bowman, *Honor: A History* (New York: Encounter Books, 2006), p. 6.

[25]Martin, *Does Christianity Cause War?* p. 19.

[26]Ibid.

[27]Keegan, *A History of Warfare,* p. 15.

[28]Gentile, *Politics as Religion,* p. 11.

[29]A. Tilgher, "Numinosità del Dopoguerra," cited in ibid.

[30]Wright, *Power Politics,* p. 93.

[31]George W. Bush, second inaugural address, January 2005; Karl Marx and Friedrich Engels, *The Communist Manifesto* (Harmondsworth: Penguin, 1967), pp. 120-21.

[32]Edmund Burke, *Letters on a Regicide Peace,* in *Select Works of Edmund Burke,* ed. E. J. Payne, 3 vols. (Oxford: Clarendon, 1874-1878), 3.1.114-15.

[33]C. S. Lewis, *The Abolition of Man* (Glasgow: Collins, 1986), p. 47.

[34]Efraim Karsh "Section B: The Causes of War: Introduction," in Lawrence Freedman, ed., *War* (Oxford: Oxford University Press, 1994), p. 67.

[35]These points are the principal subject matter of Pearse, *Why the Rest Hates the West,* esp. chaps. 1 and 2.

[36]Martin, *Does Christianity Cause War?* p. 9.

[37]Madeline Albright, *The Mighty and the Almighty: Reflections on America, God and World Affairs* (New York: HarperCollins, 2006); N. Feldman, *Washington Post,* Sunday, May 14, 2006, BW04.

Index